MEXICO AND THE SPANISH CONQUEST

MEXICO AND THE SPANISH CONQUEST

Second Edition

Ross Hassig

UNIVERSITY OF OKLAHOMA PRESS : NORMAN

Also by Ross Hassig

*Trade, Tribute, and Transportation: The Sixteenth-Century Political
Economy of the Valley of Mexico* (Norman, 1985)
Aztec Warfare: Imperial Expansion and Political Control (Norman,
1988)
War and Society in Ancient Mesoamerica (Berkeley, 1992)
Time, History, and Belief in Aztec and Colonial Mexico (Austin, 2001)

Library of Congress Cataloging-in-Publication Data

Hassig, Ross, 1945–
    Mexico and the Spanish conquest / Ross Hassig. — 2nd ed.
    p. cm.
    Includes bibliographical references and index.
    ISBN 0-8061-3793-2 (pbk : alk. paper)
    1. Mexico — History — Conquest, 1519–1540. I. Title.

F1230.H37 2006
972'.02 — dc22

                                          2006042396

Copyright © 2006 by the University of Oklahoma Press, Norman,
Publishing Division of the University. All rights reserved.
Manufactured in the U.S.A.

            1   2   3   4   5   6   7   8   9   10

For my brother, Logan,
for his years of support.

CONTENTS

MAPS

ACKNOWLEDGMENTS

I owe thanks for help with this book to Professor J. Richard Andrews of Vanderbilt University, for his invaluable assistance, and to the Harry Frank Guggenheim Foundation, for a grant that supported the writing of the first version. I am grateful to colleagues with whom I have discussed many of the new ideas and interpretations that have emerged since the book was first published in 1994. Above all, I thank my wife, Susan, for tirelessly reading and commenting on new drafts, an invaluable aid as I rewrote the book.

NAHUATL PRONUNCIATION GUIDE

I have generally followed the standardized Nahuatl orthography published in J. Richard Andrews's *Introduction to Classical Nahuatl,* revised edition (2003), with the exception of not marking vowel length or showing glottal stops, which would have unduly burdened the general reader. I have minimized the number of Nahuatl personal names mentioned and have standardized all of them, but for the sake of clarity I have omitted the honorific *-tzin.* Typically, although not invariably, it would have been added to the names of kings and nobles, but it also obscures them.

Letter	Pronunciation
c + a or *o*	As in *can*
c + e or *i*	As in *cease*
ch	As in *church*
chu	Like *ckw* in *backward*
cu or *uc*	Like *qu* in *quick*
hu	Like *w* in *wake*
qu + e or *i*	Like *k* in *kit*
tl	Similar to *tl* in *settler,* but a single sound
tz	Like *ts* in *hats*
uh	Like *wh* in *wheel*
x	Like *sh* in *ship*
z + a or *o*	Like *s* in *sod*

All other letters are pronounced with standard Latin values. Except in the rare case of the vocative noun–final é, meaning "oh" (which does not occur in this book), Nahuatl words have no accent marks, because the penultimate syllable is always stressed. The names of gods are also standardized, as are those of towns, because the names of their inhabitants derive from them. For example, a person from Tlaxcallan is a Tlaxcaltecatl (singular), and more are Tlaxcalteca (plural), which I have Anglicized to Tlaxcaltec and Tlaxcaltecs. However, I have chosen to refer to Moteuczoma's subjects as Aztecs rather than Mexica, in keeping with common usage. Similarly, a person from Tetzcoco or Chalco is a Tetzcoca or a Chalca (from Tetzcocatl and Tetzcoca and from Chalcatl and Chalca, respectively), pluralized by adding an *s*. This approach also permits the singular form to serve as an adjective: "a Tetzcoca town," "a Chalca town." I use standardized names for towns, such as Ixtlapalapan, but the modern terms for geographical areas, such as the Ixtapalapa Peninsula, where the ancient town was located. Similarly, I use early spellings for places with Spanish names, such as Vera Cruz, reserving Veracruz for the modern state.

To make the book as accessible as possible, where English-language translations of the Spanish documents were available, I included parallel citations. Not all documents have English translations, or readily accessible ones, so some materials are necessarily cited only in the original Spanish. Moreover, because of the focus of my analysis, many recorded incidents of the conquest are omitted. Some are details, others are errors, and still others are contradicted in the sources themselves, but most are extraneous to the main thrust of this analysis. I invite readers to consult the original accounts for some fascinating details of this adventure, although I also warn against accepting any one source at face value.

SHORT CHRONOLOGY OF THE CONQUEST OF MEXICO

1492	Columbus reaches the New World
1502	King Ahuitzotl dies and Moteuczoma Xocoyotl becomes the ninth Aztec king
1515	King Nezahualpilli of Tetzcoco dies and is succeeded by Cacama
1517	
8 February	Córdoba sails from Cuba
Late February	Córdoba reaches Yucatan
29 March	Córdoba reaches Campeche
20 April	Córdoba returns to Cuba
1518	
3 May	Grijalva reaches Cozumel
31 May	Grijalva reaches Laguna de Términos
11 June	Grijalva reaches Coatzacoalco
15 November	Grijalva returns to Cuba
1519	
10 February	Cortés sails for Yucatan
21 April	Cortés reaches San Juan de Ulúa
12 May	Aztecs decamp, abandoning Cortés

3 June	Cortés reaches Cempohuallan
26 July	Cortés dispatches a ship to Spain
16 August	Cortés leaves Cempohuallan on his march inland
2 September	Cortés fights first battle with Tlaxcaltecs
23 September	Cortés enters city of Tlaxcallan
10 October	Cortés leaves Tlaxcallan for Cholollan
c. 25 October	Cortés leaves Cholollan for Tenochtitlan
8 November	Cortés enters Tenochtitlan
14 November	Cortés seizes Moteuczoma

1520

20 April	Narváez lands at San Juan de Ulúa
Feast of Toxcatl	Alvarado massacres the Aztec nobles
c. 27 May	Cortés reaches Narváez's camp at Cempohuallan
c. 28 May	Cortés attacks and defeats Narváez
24 June	Cortés reaches Tenochtitlan
29 June	Moteuczoma killed
30 June	Cortés and the Spaniards flee Tenochtitlan
11 July	Cortés and the Spaniards reach Tlaxcallan
1 August	Cortés marches against Tepeyacac
c. 15 September	Cuitlahua becomes the tenth Aztec king
Mid-October	Smallpox epidemic begins in Tenochtitlan
Early December	Smallpox epidemic ends in Tenochtitlan
4 December	King Cuitlahua dies of smallpox
28 December	Cortés begins his return to Tenochtitlan

1521

February	Cuauhtemoc becomes the eleventh Aztec king
3 February	Cortés marches on Xaltocan
18 February	Cortés returns to Tetzcoco
5 April	Cortés begins march against Yauhtepec
11 April	Cortés reaches Yauhtepec

13 April	Cortés conquers Cuauhnahuac
16 April	Cortés reaches Xochimilco
18 April	Cortés is forced to withdraw from Xochimilco
22 April	Cortés returns to Tetzcoco
28 April	Cortés launches his brigantines
22 May	Alvarado, Olid, and Sandoval are dispatched with three armies to begin the battle for Tenochtitlan
31 May	Sandoval and Olid link up at Coyohuacan
30 June	Sixty-eight Spaniards are captured in battle and sacrificed
Mid-July	Fresh munitions arrive from Vera Cruz
1 August	Spaniards reach the great market in Tlatelolco
13 August	Cuauhtemoc is captured and the Aztecs surrender

MEXICO AND THE SPANISH CONQUEST

INTRODUCTION

I doubt that a more heavily trodden trail exists than that of Hernán Cortés. The conquest of Mexico has captured historians' interest for centuries, and they have subjected the expedition to relentless investigation. Yet we have only a limited number of firsthand accounts by Spanish participants in the conquest — those by Cortés himself, Bernal Díaz del Castillo, Francisco de Aguilar, Andrés de Tapia, and the "Anonymous Conqueror" — supplemented by various shorter claims and legal testimonies. There are also some histories written by nonparticipants such as Pedro Martir de Angleria and Francisco López de Gómara, who had access to conquistadors. Indian accounts, although written decades after the conquest, throw light on events that are often otherwise unreflected in the Spanish histories.

Unfortunately, these accounts frequently conflict, even in such apparently objective facts as numbers, dates, and sequences of events. I have found no satisfactory way to reconcile them. Moreover, they were all written for political purposes — to justify actions, to gain political and religious legitimacy, and to seek favors — and all are patently self-serving. Nevertheless, I draw on all the firsthand accounts and many secondhand ones, though I emphasize the former. And at least for numbers and sequences of events, I put somewhat greater trust in Cortés's account, simply because he wrote it closer to the time of the events described, and so it is probably more trustworthy for these mechanical aspects.

Nevertheless, I see no convincing basis for choice in many cases, other than general preference for one author over another. Consequently, I do not focus on disputed events, at least where the specifics are not pivotal to my interpretation. For instance, in a major battle, an attack by two thousand Indians is as plausible as one by five thousand, and though the fact of the battle is important, the exact number of participants is less so. I have left the debate over such matters to others, focusing instead on what I consider to be the major elements of the conquest, about which there is considerable agreement among the sources.

The divergences between the various accounts offer enough latitude for scholars to reconstruct the conquest of Mexico in many different versions. Most histories of the conquest are taken largely at face value from the Spanish records.[1] Even those that give the Aztecs a voice depart little from the general script in terms of new analyses.[2] The reasons given for the defeat of the Aztec empire include the Aztec belief that the Spaniards were returning gods,[3] the psychological and ideological collapse of the Aztecs,[4] Cortés's and the Spaniards' personal characteristics,[5] the Spaniards' cultural, religious, or psychological superiority,[6] the Indians' poor or misguided war-making ability,[7] the Spaniards' superior weapons and tactics,[8] flaws in the Aztec political system,[9] the effects of smallpox,[10] and the Spaniards' superior grasp of the symbolic system.[11]

Often these explanations are posited because only by recourse to such ideological factors can the seemingly astonishing defeat of the Aztecs be explained. But believing in this seemingly miraculous feat depends on accepting the Spaniards' account of it. Once an Indian view of events is presented, the Spaniards' role is less impressive, and the campaign's outcome is more understandable. The relative importance of the factors suggested as pivotal depends on how the authors saw them. Many were less important than most writers made them out to be, as will be seen from the discussion of causal elements throughout this book. Most importantly, the psychological and ideological explanations offered by modern authors fare poorly when examined against the actual events of the conquest. The Aztecs of Tenochtitlan fought to the end—bitterly, effectively, and valiantly. Conquest accounts show no sign of the various forms of ideological or psychological undermining to which the Aztec defeat is often attributed. By focusing on the military and political aspects, including such mundane yet crucial issues as logistics and march rates, I hope to present a fuller and more accurate interpretation of these events.

Most past interpreters have explicitly or implicitly accepted Spanish accounts of the events of the conquest, largely as an artifact of the data available. But accepting a Spanish-centered interpretation assumes that Cortés must have fully understood native politics and manipulated them unerringly, which is highly unlikely. In fact, virtually everything that had to be "manipulated" was firmly under Indian control. The Indians already understood their political system and the personalities involved, and it is much likelier that they—not the Spaniards—were the primary manipulators of conquest events. Only Cortés's perfidy at the end undercut Indian goals, and this may well have been part of his plan, for he was doubtlessly seeing the endgame and going along with Indian manipulation. And it *was* Indian manipulation, because only they knew their political system so well and could act on it effectively. That is, it is much likelier that the Indians understood how the Spaniards could be exploited than that Cortés saw how he could use the Indians in a political system he clearly did not understand. An Indian-centered analysis does not support the notion that the Aztecs were defeated through a series of fortunate events for the Spaniards, as a Spanish-centered analysis demands. Rather, it makes the actions understandable in terms of both Spanish and Indian political interests, without recourse to chance as an explanation.

I attempt to present both sides of the conflict, even though the sources of information are a major obstacle to the endeavor. All firsthand accounts are by Spaniards, and the relatively few Indian accounts were written long after the events in question, often by nonparticipants, and in much sketchier fashion than the Spanish sources.[12] Thus, whatever flaws the Spanish accounts may conceal, they do treat matters ignored in the Indian accounts, which are heavily skewed toward events in the Valley of Mexico. Spanish records offer the best itinerary of Cortés's party and the best dates; although the Aztec calendar is largely understood, its correlation with the Christian calendar is still debated, and in any case, when Aztec dates are given in the written sources, they usually are only for months, not days. For these reasons alone, Spanish accounts remain the backbone of the conquest saga. I do not give them priority over Indian accounts, but using them allows me to present a fuller picture first and then weave in the less complete Indian accounts in a way that would be impossible if the procedure were reversed.

In many ways the conquest of Mexico is familiar: everyone knows what happened; the outcome is no surprise. The focus of analysis must be on the how and the why, and it is this that makes the story of the conquest so fascinating.

CHAPTER 1

THE SPANISH BACKGROUND TO THE CONQUEST OF MEXICO

Spanish colonial expansion into Mexico grew out of Spain's earlier success in expelling the Moors from the Iberian Peninsula, which in turn was part of a broader pattern of expansion by Christian Europe. The Moors had invaded from North Africa and conquered much of Spain in the early eighth century as part of a general expansion of Islam. There they remained for more than three centuries, with little effort by the Christian kingdoms to expel them. Even when the Reconquista (Reconquest) of Spain (al-Andalus) finally started, it did so gradually. By the beginning of the eleventh century, wider and more sustained ties had been established between Spain and the rest of Europe, largely through the emergence of the cult of relics centered on the pilgrimage church of Santiago (St. James) at Compostela and the gradual resettlement of much of Iberia by Christians. After the early, largely peaceful resettlement of Spain, the Reconquista became more militarized, with forced attempts to seize and hold territory, although this was a power struggle as much among Christian states as against the Moors. When Moroccan warriors began fighting for the Muslim states in Spain toward the end of the eleventh century, the Reconquista became more religiously and culturally defined, taking on the character of a crusade.[1]

The Reconquista was aided by internal disputes within the

Moorish states. What had been a united caliphate since A.D. 711 disintegrated into many small states after 1008 and no longer presented a unified front to Christian expansion. Those centuries also saw a major increase in commerce in Spain, as in the rest of Europe, and crusading knights and financial aid from other Christian countries and the papacy helped fuel the reconquest. In the early thirteenth century, King Alfonso IX received a pledge of fealty from the Moorish ruler of Valencia, who hoped to secure Christian help against royal contenders in Morocco. With Castilian support, this ruler conquered other Moorish states in Spain, including Córdoba, which Castile occupied after the Moorish ruler's assassination.

Events in North Africa also drew Moorish attention away from Iberia. Internal struggles over rule in Morocco led many Moorish leaders in Spain to raise armies and leave for battle across the Mediterranean, effectively ceding control of their Iberian territories to Christian rulers. Thus the Reconquista increased in momentum, fueled as much by Moorish distractions elsewhere as by Christian successes. Moorish populations increasingly became incorporated into Spanish kingdoms, and where Moorish rulers remained in power, they now did so as tributaries of Christian kings. Most of Spain was reconquered and in Christian hands by the end of the thirteenth century, with the major exception of Granada, which remained under Moorish rule. When Granada fell in 1492, the reconquest of the Iberian Peninsula was at last complete. But it by no means marked the end of Spanish political and economic expansion, which continued into Europe, the Mediterranean, and ultimately the Americas.[2]

Spain's expansion was part of a general European pattern that emerged in the wake of the economic and social dislocation following the massive depopulation caused by the Black Death in the fourteenth century. But Europe also felt threatened by Moors to the south and Ottoman Turks to the east, and much of its expansion — made possible by technological advances in seafaring — was dictated conceptually and guided geographically by these concerns. Along with other Europeans, Spaniards ventured into foreign lands, driven by the zealotry of the Church Militant but also encouraged by the lure of greater trade, new territory, and subject populations. Thus, when Spaniards moved into the Americas, they brought with them the powerful legacy of their expansionary experience, which was to color their relations with the Indians.[3]

The men who reached Mexico had already participated in the earliest Spanish exploration of what was to them the New World, and they built on their experiences of conquering and colonizing Arab Spain and the Canary Islands. Spanish expansion beyond Iberia was primarily economic in motivation, especially the push into the Canary Islands, which was undertaken in order to establish sugarcane plantations. Similar considerations undergirded the settlement of the Indies.[4]

Religious justifications, if not a crusadelike religious fervor, marked much of the expansion into Mexico, as it had the Reconquista. Such justifications are repeated throughout the accounts of the conquistadors, which describe, among other things, the appearance of Santiago on a white horse leading the Spaniards to victory—the same apparition credited with leading them during the Reconquista. The Spaniards used essentially the same ideology in their conquest of native populations as they had against the Moors during the Reconquista. The conquest of Mexico, however, was primarily a political and military affair.[5]

During the Reconquista, settlements throughout the Iberian Peninsula had organized town militias. These militias were used defensively, but they also took offensive actions against the Moors as needed and feasible. They produced a large pool of skilled and seasoned fighters, all free men and all required to bear arms, regardless of class. The subsequent success of Spanish forces against the Aztecs, however, was the result not simply of larger armies but of better organization.[6]

The Spaniards were the beneficiaries of a long tradition of

European military organizational development. Medieval warfare, at least up to A.D. 1200, largely reflected the politically fragmented condition of Europe after the fall of the Roman Empire in the West. Great emphasis was placed on the construction and defense of strongholds to control surrounding territories. Armies increasingly consisted of heavy (that is, armored) cavalry supported by archers and later crossbowmen, but these troops had to be constituted for specific campaigns; they were not part of a permanent, standing army. As a result, the armies seldom trained as units. They did emphasize quality over quantity, but at an individual level: armies rarely functioned as integrated wholes. Moreover, because the leadership came from the mounted knights, the use of infantry was largely discouraged except during sieges, and armies were small — rarely more than ten thousand men.[7]

This situation began to change in the thirteenth century. Greater wealth enabled kings to employ professional soldiers, and improved transportation significantly lessened logistical constraints. But most of the changes arose from new technological innovations. Heavier armor had kept the knights immune to most weapons, especially those of the commoner infantry, but by the mid-fourteenth century cannons had become widespread, followed by a variety of handguns, although they could not yet compete against the crossbow. All these weapons could pierce armor, and the role of mounted heavy cavalry diminished. Now, heavy infantry dominated European warfare. Wearing less armor and fighting in organized, trained units, infantry formations broke the domination of heavy cavalry. In the Spanish army in particular, pikemen often replaced fighters carrying swords and shields. The Spaniards would not face the same sorts of material and technological innovations in the New World, but their new organizational sophistication would serve them well there, in a way the earlier emphasis on heavy cavalry and little integrated-unit combat would not have done.[8]

By the beginning of the sixteenth century, the Spaniards had created the royal guards — heavy cavalry units of twenty-five hundred lances divided into twenty-five captaincies of a hundred men each, entirely under the control of the monarchs. Nevertheless, the Spaniards relied more heavily on infantry than did the French, who regarded commoner foot soldiers as incompetent. The Spaniards held them in high esteem and used them effectively. This reliance on infantry culminated in the famed *tercio* (corps) system, begun in 1536 and organized around a commander of ten 250-man companies, each divided into squads of twenty-five men, giving the reorganized Spanish forces enormous mobility and flexibility.[9]

Part of the emphasis on infantry was an adaptation to Spanish terrain. The hilly countryside was unfavorable to heavy cavalry, so infantrymen armed with pikes, swords, and shields dominated, at least during the late phases of the Reconquista. Combat was largely between opposing individuals rather than opposing organized forces. Spanish combat in Italy at the end of the fifteenth century and beginning of the sixteenth marked a change, with the partial adoption of the Swiss square of densely packed heavy infantrymen. Combining pikemen and harquebusiers (soldiers armed with harquebuses — smoothbore matchlock guns somewhat smaller than muskets, which replaced harquebuses in the mid-sixteenth century), the Spaniards decisively defeated the French. Thereafter the Spanish army was remodeled to emphasize pikes and harquebuses in large infantry formations.[10]

Some of these developments were irrelevant to the Spaniards who came to the New World, because much of the ongoing development of military strategy in Europe did not reach them before the conquest. But the conquistadors who reached Mexico did draw on general European trends, relying heavily on infantry armed with pikes and swords, wearing various quantities and types of armor, and augmenting the infantry with crossbowmen and harquebusiers. To the infantry was added a small cavalry unit, but the bulk of the combatants were foot soldiers trained in the Iberian tradition of individual combat.

The idea of national armies and national wars was still alien to

Europe, and although entire populations could be raised for battle, as in Spain's Reconquista, soldiers of many cities and countries fought for others on a financial basis. Nevertheless, these wars often entailed huge losses of life, and continual tactical, organizational, and technological advances combined to make them more deadly yet.

European formations, tactics, and arms were more than adequate defense against the first natives the Spaniards met in the New World—those in the Indies (now the West Indies, to distinguish them from what were subsequently known as the East Indies). Native political organization was relatively simple in the Indies—loosely centralized chiefdoms at best—and warfare was largely a matter of raiding and individual glory. It was not the organized clash of trained military formations. Spanish arms and tactics were decisive against the Caribbean Indians, so on the eve of the discovery of Mexico the Spaniards had no reason to believe that anyone they were likely to encounter elsewhere in the New World would pose a more serious military threat.

Aside from the martial disparity between the Spaniards and the native peoples of the New World, major differences existed in the ways wars were fought, the ways people were governed, and who the king was and what powers he could legitimately exercise. Warfare had a spiritual dimension; the conquest was also a conflict waged by Christians against non-Christians. But the religious imperative was not always present in European conflicts, and the Spaniards shared with the rest of Europe the idea that most war was a political exercise in the use of force. Religion provided a justification for war, but as we will see, the conquest found its cause in more pragmatic matters of wealth, power, and privilege.[11]

The Spaniards also brought to the New World broader European notions about what constituted legitimate and appropriate government—notions that were undergoing ferment. During the fifteenth and sixteenth centuries, strong European monarchs consolidated their power and increasingly claimed rule based on divine right. But who should rule depended on legitimate succession and was not simply a matter of power. The monarchs of Castile and Aragón ruled by divine right derived from their predecessors in a known and predictable fashion. Moreover, they ruled by law rather than by whim, at least in theory. They expanded into the inhabited lands of the New World under the color of law, although the legitimacy of the enterprise was the subject of long and acrimonious debate. Imperial expansion under such monarchs meant the domination — usually military — of other lands and the control of these territories under the laws of Spain. Thus, Spanish rulers exercised power by divine right, they could legally expand their holdings in the New World, and they held and dominated the territories they conquered, changing forever the lives of those they ruled.[12]

The Indies were the portion of the New World Christopher Columbus first reached in October 1492. Probably landing initially in the Bahamas, Columbus also sailed to Cuba and then to the island of Hispaniola (present-day Haiti and the Dominican Republic). He sought gold, which he believed must be plentiful, on the basis of the ancient idea that it was engendered by heat in these warm lands (whereas silver arose from cold), and he immediately began searching for it. Although he failed to find any on the first islands, he was spurred on by seeing a native ornament of silver and, in Hispaniola, a few natives wearing small gold ornaments and by hearing stories of large quantities of the metal. Ultimately, placer gold was discovered in the mountainous interior of Hispaniola.[13]

When Columbus arrived, the Indies were already densely populated, supporting almost six million people. These were largely divided between two distinct language families. The northern islands — the Greater Antilles: Cuba, Haiti, Puerto Rico, Jamaica, and the Bahamas — were occupied largely by Tainos (also called Arawaks). The southern islands — the Lesser Antilles — were mostly inhabited by Caribs.[14]

Filled with luxurious vegetation, the Indies had been colo-

nized as early as 5000 B.C. by groups from Central America—
Honduras and Nicaragua. A second wave of migration around
3000 B.C. brought the Tainos from lowland South America, who
pushed the earlier settlers into the more marginal areas. A third
wave of migrants, the Caribs, also from South America, entered
the Indies during the last few centuries B.C. They moved north-
ward, pushing the earlier inhabitants out, but by 1492 they had
reached no farther north than Puerto Rico.[15]

The Tainos were organized into ranked societies with rulers
(caciques) and other social statuses, which the Spaniards interpreted as classes, imposing the more rigid divisions of their homeland onto the flexible Indian societies. The Tainos were agricultur-
alists who lived in large villages sustained by the cultivation of
sweet potatoes, yams, and other tubers that they had originally
brought from South America. They also had a second, less important complex of seed crops, including maize, beans, and squash,
which had recently reached the islands from Mesoamerica. It was
in Taino fields that the Spaniards first saw the crops they were to
find and exploit on the mainland. Hunting and fishing supplemented this vegetable diet, but aside from ducks and dogs, the
Indies held no domesticated animals.[16]

Columbus embarked on a second voyage in 1493, intent on
settling the lands he had discovered. This effort was not aimed at
settling unoccupied areas but rather at settling where population
was densest, so that native labor could be readily exploited. Reaching Hispaniola in November, Columbus's expedition brought fifteen hundred men—no women—along with livestock, seeds, and
plants. With this, the colonization of the New World began.[17]

In the early years, Hispaniola, with its dense population, was
the primary focus of Spanish settlement. The inevitable clashes of
those years were eased by the tolerance of the Tainos, who did not
object to the Spaniards' presence, at least initially. In 1494, however, the first Indian rebellion broke out, in response to the capture
of a native ruler. Spanish retribution was harsh, and over the next

two years Columbus militarily subdued all the natives of the island and subjected them to Spanish control. Hispaniola offered little of direct material wealth for the Spaniards to seize, save the labor of the Indians themselves, and this they controlled through the institution of the *encomienda*. The encomienda was a political-economic system in which rights to the labor of the Indians residing in a granted area were allocated to designated Spanish *encomenderos*. Their labor was managed through the cooperation of the local caciques but enforced by the Spaniards.

Spanish subjugation of the indigenous population was a blow to native society, but it was disease that would prove the more devastating. New World populations had never been exposed to most of the major contagious diseases that had evolved in the Old World. As a consequence, the Indians lacked immunity to the diseases the Spaniards brought with them, leading to massive numbers of deaths and precipitous depopulation. In Hispaniola alone the population fell from perhaps one million in 1492 to fewer than sixteen thousand by 1518. Within thirty years of Columbus's landing, the native population of the island was virtually extinct. The same fate befell natives elsewhere in the Caribbean somewhat later, matching the slower rate of colonization in those areas.[18]

In 1499 a fleet of thirty ships brought an additional twenty-five hundred settlers from Spain, greatly increasing the Spanish presence on Hispaniola, which became the major settlement in the Indies. Because of war and disease, however, the Spaniards were left with a labor shortage, which encouraged them to make slave raids on other islands, especially the Bahamas, where the indigenous people also succumbed quickly to European disease, maltreatment, and war.[19]

Puerto Rico was first settled in 1508, and Jamaica in 1509, followed in 1511 by Cuba, where the town of Santiago became the main settlement until it was eclipsed by Havana as Caribbean trade changed. The 1514 attempt to settle what is now Florida was unsuccessful. Despite the flourish of activity in the Caribbean and the Gulf of Mexico, the Spanish population in the New World remained relatively small. Hispaniola was the most populous, followed by Cuba, Darién (in present-day Panama), and Puerto Rico, a distant fourth. An identified total of 5,481 people is known to have come to the Indies prior to 1520, which is probably some 20 percent of the actual total. Of these, only 308, or 5.6 percent, were women. Thus, by 1519, the entire European population of the Indies and Darién would have been some 27,000, minus the significant number of deaths the colonization entailed. The bulk of the Europeans settled on Hispaniola, from which all subsequent exploration of the Caribbean and surrounding areas was staged until Governor Diego Velásquez de Cuéllar launched his expeditions to Mexico from Cuba.[20]

Because this expansion into the Caribbean followed and grew out of the Reconquista and the occupation of the Canary Islands, it is unsurprising that many of the same political, economic, and religious institutions developed in those earlier enterprises were adopted for New World colonization. Spaniards settled the land, dominated local groups, and relied on the legalized expropriation of their labor to generate wealth. And perhaps most importantly, conquerors were not merely soldiers but also partners, earning shares in any land conquered. Thus, they were well poised for the next move, into Mesoamerica.

CHAPTER 2

MESOAMERICA AND THE AZTECS

When the Spaniards first reached the Yucatan peninsula in 1517, Mesoamerica had enjoyed almost three thousand years of high civilization, cultural achievements, and the successive rises and falls of many states and empires. Mesoamerica, the area of high indigenous civilization in Mexico and Central America, is enormously varied, bounded by the desert roughly 170 kilometers (100 miles) north of present-day Mexico City and encompassing Guatemala, El Salvador, Belize, and much of Mexico and Honduras. United by its sophisticated native cultures, the area featured everything from tropical lowlands to mountainous heights above 5,000 meters (18,000 feet), giving rise to many different societies.

Agriculture served as the economic basis for the rise of civilization in Mesoamerica. Emerging slowly over thousands of years, the basic complex of maize, beans, and squash provided a more reliable and bountiful food supply than hunting and gathering, permitting more people to live together for longer periods. Thus agriculture enabled the early Mesoamericans to shift from living in small, nomadic, hunting and gathering bands to settling in larger, sedentary, agricultural villages by 1500 B.C. Everywhere throughout Mesoamerica, societies were becoming more complex, but the first truly sophisticated culture was that of the Olmecs, who emerged on the Veracruz Gulf coast around 1200 B.C.[1]

Their rise was greatly aided by the movement of maize from the Mesoamerican highlands down into the tropical lowlands, where greater rainfall and more fertile soils permitted farmers to grow at least two crops a year. This agricultural surplus fueled the development of complex society, which included sophisticated gods and religious innovations, important ceremonial centers, a great art style, the emergence of classes, and the rise of kings.

By the sixteenth century Mesoamerica was a single culture area, united by its major shared, albeit varied, traditions. But at the beginning of the Olmec period, it was not. There was little interplay between various groups, and local traditions remained diverse. The emergence of the Olmecs, and their subsequent expansion, signaled the beginning of the regional connections that would ultimately mark Mesoamerica as an area of common traditions.

The Olmecs were the first Mesoamerican military power, with the first professional soldiers, the first weapons designed specifically for warfare (notably clubs, maces, and slings) — rather than hunting tools turned to military purposes — and the first kings, whose power depended on military success. But the Olmec expansion beyond the Gulf coast lowlands was not, in all likelihood, military. The Olmecs had too few soldiers to dominate vast areas by force of arms. Even more tellingly, they simply were unable to send and sustain enough troops over great enough distances to control faraway areas.

Except in toys, the wheel was never used in precolumbian Mesoamerica, perhaps because of the mountainous terrain and the lack of draft animals. Even by the time of the Spanish conquest, the only domesticated animals in Mexico were turkeys, dogs, and bees. Year-round navigable rivers were also notably lacking, which restricted the use of canoes and rafts primarily to coasts and lakes. Except for largely ceremonial palanquins and sedan chairs for the nobility, everyone traveled by foot, and all trade goods went by human porters (*tlamemes*). Each porter carried an average load of 23 kilograms (50 pounds) for 21 to 28 kilometers (13 to 18 miles) per day.[2] In comparison with the considerably more efficient wagons of the Old World, Mesoamerican transport was seriously constrained in distances and loads, so the cost of moving goods was significantly higher. This transport constraint had a pronounced effect on patterns of warfare in Mesoamerica. Every adult male soldier in Mesoamerica consumed, on average, 0.95 kilograms (2.1 pounds) of maize and half a gallon of water per day. Although this was not much individually, it created obvious logistical difficulties for an entire army. Either the soldiers themselves had to carry their food, which added to the burden of their arms and so could not have amounted to much, or else specialized porters had to accompany the army. At the most favorable ratio of one porter for every two soldiers (recorded much later for the Aztecs), an army could have traveled for only eight days on its own supplies, because each porter carried only twenty-four man-days of food.

The time limit that logistics placed on marches meant that armies could not go very far. Moreover, armies do not march as fast as individuals, because of the dynamics of mass movements. There is little reason to believe that any Mesoamerican army marched faster than its preindustrial peers elsewhere: 8 to 32 kilometers (5 to 20 miles) a day, a march rate that accords well with modern practice, or 4 kilometers (2.5 miles) per hour on roads and 2.4 kilometers (1.5 miles) per hour off. Mesoamerican societies, except for the Late Classic Mayas in Yucatan, did not build formal roads between cities. Instead, they used the dirt roads that sprang up between centers, so the march rate of their armies doubtless tended toward the lower figure — 19 kilometers (12 miles) per day. Coupled with logistical constraints, this march rate meant that an Olmec army was limited to a combat radius of no more than 58 kilometers (36 miles) — three days there, one day of combat, another for recuperation, and three days to return.

Despite the far-flung extent of Olmec influence, it is highly unlikely that their expansion was achieved militarily. Man-for-man, the Olmecs were doubtless the best soldiers of their day, but they could not have projected their force over such great distances.

Instead, the Olmecs tied much of Mesoamerica together in a trading network, spreading new religious ideas, new intellectual tri-
umphs such as writing, mathematics, and a calendar system, and
new forms of social organization that began linking the vast area
into a common cultural region.

By 400 B.C., however, their time had passed, and the Olmecs
withdrew back into the lowlands. As in the case of their expansion,
little evidence suggests that this withdrawal was militarily in-
spired. Rather, as irrigation agriculture developed in the highlands,
newly emergent local elites began to compete successfully with
the Olmecs for valuable trade goods. Because they were local,
they could do so without the tremendous burden of transporting
goods to the distant Gulf coast that hobbled the Olmecs. Without
their earlier competitive advantage, the Olmecs lost their dominance and reverted to being one among many emerging local state
systems.

After the Olmec decline, no single society dominated Mesoamerica for hundreds of years, but warfare increased among the
newly emergent states. New arms and armor were developed, including large, rectangular shields whose added protection hastened the decline of clubs and maces. The thrusting spear emerged
as Mesoamerica's dominant weapon. During this time of political
instability, warfare by professionally armed soldiers was rife, and
the earliest permanent Mesoamerican fortifications began to be
constructed everywhere.

Following this period of regional balkanization and conflict,
the city of Teotihuacan, in the northeastern Valley of Mexico,
gradually emerged in the first century A.D. as the capital of Mesoamerica's first major empire. Teotihuacan marshaled large numbers
of professional soldiers armed either with thrusting spears and
bucklers (small shields usually carried on the forearm) or with
spearthrowers (atlatls), darts, and rectangular shields, a standard-
ization that indicates state control of the armory. Thus equipped,
Teotihuacan's armies could pour dart fire into their enemies' ranks

and disrupt them before the two sides closed for hand-to-hand combat. This proved a devastating tactic when backed by the large body of soldiers Teotihuacan could muster from its huge population.

Teotihuacan was a cosmopolitan, multiethnic city, attracting and assimilating foreign people. This enabled it to become the largest city in Mesoamerica, with 60,000 inhabitants as early as A.D. 100 and a peak population of some 200,000 in A.D. 500. Teotihuacan was apparently a theocracy, its religious significance signaled by its enormous temple-pyramids. But the city owed much of its importance to its obsidian industry. Obsidian was the basic material for most tools and weapons in Mesoamerica, playing a role similar to that of iron in Europe. Teotihuacan controlled the main deposits in central Mexico and engaged in large-scale manufacturing of obsidian products. This industry underlay much of Teotihuacan's expansion as it sought foreign markets for its wares and exotic goods for its own consumption.

Within the first three centuries A.D., Teotihuacan had expanded over much of central Mexico, created mineral-producing settlements well beyond the boundaries of civilization to the north, penetrated the Maya lowlands of Guatemala, and established colonies as far south as the highland Maya city of Kaminaljuyu, on the site of modern-day Guatemala City. Elite Teotihuacan goods were in high demand in many places throughout Mesoamerica, but the creation of settlements and colonies, as well as the protection of incessant merchant expeditions, demanded an active military. This Teotihuacan could easily provide: its army was the largest in Mesoamerica; it was well trained and equipped; and by A.D. 400 its soldiers were armored as quilted cotton jerkins were adopted.

Teotihuacan's military-backed expansion was the second major wave integrating the various areas of Mesoamerica, and with it came the spread of many ideas, technologies, and patterns of organization. But the city's dominance was not to last. Teotihuacan could maintain its far-flung operations only with difficulty. Even as an urban giant, it could muster too few troops to man garrisons everywhere, and even if it could have marshaled enough soldiers, the logistical constraints on doing so were enormous. Moreover, while Teotihuacan grappled with the limits of its military power, the mere presence of its merchants, colonists, and other functionaries stimulated local social development. With sustained contact, colonized and contacted groups grew more sophisticated and eventually became competitors themselves. No city or group of cities actually rivaled Teotihuacan or directly confronted it. But at the great distances involved and the cost of dispatching and maintaining forces, even modest cities, their emergent elites increasingly seeking the very goods Teotihuacan itself sought, could compete with the great city.

With the increased competition born of its own expansion, Teotihuacan could no longer maintain its widespread holdings and began withdrawing from its most distant enclaves shortly after A.D. 500. This contraction alleviated its distant problems, but the city's internal development was predicated on the existence of colonial markets. Without them, Teotihuacan was now vastly overproducing. Workers were dislocated, and the wealth of the city declined. By A.D. 650 Teotihuacan's ritual center was burned, and the city's population shrank by 60 percent as it lost its empire.

Teotihuacan had not controlled and integrated all of Mesoamerica: many places were too undeveloped to merit attention, and others were too far away. Instead, it dominated many, though not all, major urban areas, largely ignoring relatively unimportant intervening territories. Teotihuacan's legacy was an increased regional interdependence and cultural homogenization of the areas in contact. With the city's demise, Mesoamerica again fragmented into a vast number of local cities and states. Some cities, such as El Tajín, Xochicalco, and Cacaxtla, rose to local prominence, but none exercised control over a significant area again until the rise of the Toltecs.

The end of the first millennium A.D. was a period of reintegration of Mesoamerica. The Toltecs emerged as the rulers of a mercantile empire, strongly supported by military innovation and might, that pushed out competing trader groups who had established themselves during the fragmentation of central Mexico after the demise of Teotihuacan. Yet the Toltecs did not dominate Mesoamerica in the same fashion or as extensively as had Teotihuacan, and regionally competing polities emerged elsewhere. The Toltec capital, Tollan, reached its height from A.D. 950 to 1150 with a resident population—many of whom were craftsmen—of sixty thousand, with an equal number of farmers in its immediate hinterland. An important obsidian source near Tollan, which Teotihuacan had exploited earlier, likely caused the Toltec capital to be situated where it was.

A sizable portion of Tollan's multiethnic population was composed of Mesoamericans imbued with the religious beliefs and cultural traditions of the region. But the majority were relative newcomers, migrants from the north who had recently moved south into the sphere of civilization, and it was the merging of these two traditions that gave rise to Tollan. Though Tollan was in many ways a continuation of Teotihuacan traditions—the Toltecs were not major cultural innovators—it nevertheless signaled a major political shift. Rather than being a theocracy, Tollan was ruled by more secular rulers. But like Teotihuacan, Tollan owed its dominance to its obsidian industry and commerce.

Still, there is ample evidence of warfare in Tollan, and conquest doubtless played a major role in the city's rise. Although less populous than its predecessor imperial capital, Tollan was larger than any other city of its day and enjoyed the advantages of new military technology and organization. Its primary innovation was a 50-centimeter (20-inch) curved sword with obsidian blades along each edge. This short sword provided a much larger cutting surface than previous weapons and did so with little extra weight. Most previous weapons were essentially crushers, using entire stones fashioned into points, but the short sword substituted small blades that could be glued into light wooden handles, relying on slashing for its effect.

Because of their lightness, short swords did not have to be chosen in lieu of other arms but could be carried with atlatls, allowing each soldier to function in a dual role. Arming Toltec soldiers with both projectiles and slashers doubled their effective strength in comparison with traditional Mesoamerican soldiers. Toltec soldiers could now provide their own covering fire with atlatls while advancing and still engage in hand-to-hand combat with short swords once they closed with the enemy. Toltec arms and armor, like those of Teotihuacan, included standardized weapons indicative of state ownership and control, a large army, and complementary weapons and units.

Both the nature and size of Tollan's empire is debated, but Toltec trade clearly extended throughout most of Mesoamerica and beyond, linking Tollan to Chiapas, Guatemala, and Central America, central Veracruz, the Huaxtec area, northern and western Mexico, and perhaps even the American Southwest. Yet this expansion was intermittent and apparently avoided strong competing sites. Instead of an area of uniform control, the Toltec empire was probably a series of ill-defined and rapidly changing relationships with other centers, some subordinate in varying degrees and others virtual partners.

The Toltecs established a trading empire that operated through merchant enclaves and settlements rather than by militarily colonizing outlying areas. Although military power was important for protecting merchants in hostile areas, the Toltecs lacked the manpower and logistical capacity to create and maintain a major empire. The general increase in population throughout Mesoamerica made distant logistical support increasingly feasible, but the Toltecs lacked a tributary network capable of providing support. Instead, they created colonial enclaves throughout much of Mesoamerica during a period when no large competitor existed. They linked the region through their own people sent abroad to trade, produce, and colonize. Like Teotihuacan, Tollan owed its economic position to a far-flung trade network that supplied the city's craftsmen with raw materials and sold the goods they produced. If control of this trade were left in the hands of others, Tollan would have been vulnerable, so it seized direct control of the trade. In spite of its military advantages, the Toltec empire ended around A.D. 1179 when Tollan met a violent end as the result of famine, rebellion, and barbarian invasions. Much of this can be attributed to long-term desiccation of the areas to the north, which forced many northern groups to abandon their homes and migrate southward into Mesoamerica, disrupting Tollan's control of its trade routes. A breakup into city-states and regional powers again overtook Mesoamerica in the wake of Tollan's abandonment, and new groups migrated in, taking over existing cities and establishing others of their own. A few city-states became the centers of larger polities, such as the Tepanec empire, which dominated the west side of the Valley of Mexico. But no city controlled vast areas until the emergence of the Aztecs following their overthrow of the Tepanecs in 1428.

The Aztecs entered the Valley of Mexico at the end of the twelfth century A.D. and settled at Tenochtitlan in 1345. As outsiders and relative barbarians, they needed allies to achieve political legitimacy among the other cities. They thus selected Acamapichtli, an Aztec married to a noblewoman from the city of Colhuacan, as their first king, and he exercised control over external matters, such as war. Internal matters, such as landownership and tribute collection, remained largely in the hands of the traditional Aztec leaders — the ward (*calpolli*) heads — who controlled the flow of tribute from the commoners and on whom the king depended. In traditional Mesoamerican fashion, Acamapichtli consolidated his position through marriage with the daughters of these leaders. The offspring united Acamapichtli's noble heritage with the de facto authority of the calpolli leaders and became the nucleus of an emergent Aztec nobility, paving the way for the eventual consolidation of both internal and external power in the hands of the king.

Being new and relatively few, the Aztecs became tributaries of the Tepanec empire in the western Valley of Mexico. The power of the Aztec kings grew slowly until the assassination of Chimalpopoca, Acamapichtli's grandson and the third Aztec king, which precipitated a major change in the Aztec system of selecting kings. Previously, sons had succeeded fathers, but because the king enjoyed little more than titular powers, exactly who ruled was not a crucial matter. Chimalpopoca, however, died without a suitable heir, so Itzcoatl, a skilled soldier, was elected king by the other nobles. With this election, political legitimacy within a larger pool of upper nobles no longer depended on strict hereditary succession but on ability, and having a skillful ruler became increasingly important as the kings' power grew.

Itzcoatl, the fourth Aztec ruler, became king during an especially turbulent time in the Valley of Mexico. King Tetzotzomoc, founder of the Tepanec empire, died, and the son he had chosen as successor was assassinated by one of his brothers, Maxtla, who then seized the throne. This undermined relations among the Tepanec cities, which were ruled by Tetzotzomoc's other sons — who had equal claims to the imperial throne — leaving Maxtla in control of little more than the capital city.

Seizing this opportunity, Itzcoatl allied with other rulers who were equally dissatisfied with the Tepanecs. Principal among them were the king of Tetzcoco, a long-time enemy of the Tepanecs, and the king of Tlacopan, one of Maxtla's disgruntled brothers and himself a pretender to the Tepanec throne. With their assistance, Itzcoatl struck, defeating the badly divided Tepanecs, and this Aztec-led Triple Alliance became the dominant power in the Valley of Mexico.

The overthrow of the Tepanec empire freed Tenochtitlan from external domination: Itzcoatl now received tributary goods and land from the defeated cities, income that did not depend on his own people. The king became notably less dependent on the commoners for either goods or political support, which significantly lessened the political importance of the ward leaders.

Some support for war in the emergent Aztec empire may have been ideological; religion played a role in it, as it did for many wars worldwide. But although Aztec religion supported war, it was not a missionizing religion and so did not directly compel war. Moreover, because religion in Mexico was widely shared by expansionistic and pacific societies alike, it does not explain warfare among the Aztecs. Rather, the commoners generally supported war because some of the tribute thus gained benefited them, and it provided one of the few available avenues for social advancement. Excelling in combat offered commoners the possibility of being elevated to noble status.

The Aztec rise gave the nobility more economic stability in the form of greater tributary wealth, but it also led to increased political instability, because of the way the Aztecs organized their empire. The Aztecs were faced with two alternative ways to structure their expanding realm. One was to conquer new areas and consolidate their hold by replacing local leaders and armies with Aztec governors and garrisons. This would allow the Aztecs to extract large quantities of goods in tribute, but at a high administrative cost in replacing local rulers and maintaining troops to enforce their mandates. The alternative was to leave the conquered government intact, reducing the empire's political and administrative costs. This approach would limit the amount the Aztecs could extract as tribute, because paying tribute would rely on some degree of voluntary compliance. The first approach—creating a territorial empire—provided greater political control and more tribute, but it limited expansion because exercising direct control quickly absorbed the available manpower in garrison duty. The second approach—creating a hegemonic empire—collected less tribute because it exerted less control, but it freed more men for further expansion. Faced with this choice, the Aztecs adopted the second alternative.

There are both advantages and disadvantages to the hegemonic system, which had ramifications for Aztec expansion. The more a hegemonic empire relies on power (the perception that one can enforce one's desired goals) rather than force (direct physical action to compel one's goals), the more efficient it is, because the subordinates police themselves. But the costs of compliance must not be perceived as outweighing the benefits: the more exploitative a political system is perceived to be, the more it must rely on force rather than on power, and the less efficient it becomes. The Aztecs' hegemonic system had a major weak point, however: it required a strong king. Because the Aztecs imposed few or no institutional changes in tributary areas, a weak or indecisive king left the empire vulnerable to collapse. The king's military prowess was not simply a matter of ideology or honor; it was essential in sustaining the empire. His death could disrupt the system if his successor did not guarantee continuity in policy or ability. Thus, for the Aztecs, military prowess was a major concern in selecting a king.

Longer term, the Aztecs imposed the seemingly benign practice of giving a royal daughter to be married to the newly subjugated king and often receiving one of his daughters to be married to the Aztec king. The effects of this exchange were extremely destabilizing to the conquered region. The king's successor was typically his son by his politically most important wife, which would now be his son by his Aztec wife. That helped bind the tributary kingdom to the Aztecs in the long term, but in the short term it caused considerable instability, both within and beyond the empire. It meant that the king's other sons now had little chance of succeeding to the throne, creating a potentially large, disaffected pool of royal pretenders. It reduced even more drastically the prospects of sons born of wives from cities outside the empire. It disrupted the entire power balance regarding succession in those independent cities as well, likely rendering them more vulnerable to subsequent Aztec expansion. In short, the "gift" of Aztec wives created zones of instability at the periphery of the empire and beyond.[3]

Much of the Aztecs' own support for the empire grew from their ability to amass ever more tribute, which demanded continued imperial expansion and a militarily successful king. Sustained military failure could incite rebellion, shrink the empire, and reduce tribute goods and land. Failure struck hardest at the interests of the nobles, and if the king lost their support, his safety could be imperiled. For example, Tizoc, the seventh Aztec king, was assassinated after five years of weak rule. Consequently, both wealth and self-preservation compelled kings to succeed militarily. Yet despite this impetus, the Aztecs were not continuously at war. Mustering troops, negotiating mass movements, and supplying logistical support were patterned by the May-to-September rainy season, which determined when troops could be successfully mobilized and where they could march.

The commoners who made up most of the army were also farmers and were occupied during the summer and early autumn. Even if they had been available year-round, food was not; supplies were most readily available just after harvest. Autumn also marked the beginning of the dry season, when troop movements were significantly easier: dirt roads dried out, permitting passage of large groups that would have turned wet roads into muddy quagmires, and swollen rivers shrank to fordable streams. As a result of all these factors, Aztec warfare was concentrated in a campaign season running from early December to late April.

Whatever the Aztecs' battle skills, combat effectiveness was only one aspect of warfare. The ability to project force against distant enemies meant that the Aztecs had to muster troops, gather supplies, and coordinate mass movements, all of which required considerable planning. In this, the king exercised overall authority, determining the army's route, the number of days it would march, and the battle plan once the target was reached.

The Aztecs suffered the same limits on marching that earlier empires had. But the rate of march was less important than the army's configuration. Because the Aztecs did not build roads for military purposes, they relied on those serving local trade. Wide enough only for two-way traffic, these restricted the army to double files, which stretched out the standard Aztec command of eight thousand men (a *xiquipilli*) over a distance of 12 kilometers (7.5 miles) — without considering the accordion effect that further lengthens the line. This meant that the last men would not begin marching until five hours after the first men had started. In order to complete its march by nightfall, each xiquipilli started its march one day after the previous xiquipilli — a necessary expedient, but one that greatly increased the time needed to assemble the entire force for the attack.

The Aztecs could have increased the number of files per column by going cross-country, but marching off roads is slower and, despite its directness, rarely offers significant time savings. Aztec armies, however, did frequently march along several alternative routes simultaneously, shortening the time required for everyone to reach the battle site and preventing the defenders from bottling up the Aztecs in a vulnerable pass.

Food was another limiting factor in warfare. Speeding the army was crucial to Aztec success because of the enormous logistical difficulties all armies experienced in Mesoamerica: any delay helped their opponents. Although individual soldiers carried some supplies, most food was brought by accompanying porters, although this still limited a self-sufficient army to a total of eight days in the field. With the great population growth in Mesoamerica since Teotihuacan times, the Aztecs were able to extend their range by adapting the tribute system to their imperial aims and demanding food supplies from subordinate towns en route. Messengers were sent along the designated route two days before the march to alert all major tributary towns, each of which then gathered food-stuffs from its surrounding dependencies to supply the passing

Aztecs. To do otherwise meant rebellion at a time when Aztec troops were already en route and when the tributary town was unprepared for war and had too little time to ready itself. The slow rate of march, the time needed to assemble the entire army in camp, and the clouds of dust kicked up by tens of thousands of feet on dirt roads stripped the Aztecs of tactical surprise, as did spies, foreign merchants, and even the advance warnings the Aztecs sent to their tributaries to gather supplies. But there was little a target city-state could do to take advantage of these warnings, because its occupants could not flee without leaving their city, homes, goods, and fields to the mercy of the Aztecs. Instead, most cities either surrendered or fought, but they were usually outnumbered by the Aztecs and were certainly outperformed.

Aztec battlefield assaults involved an orderly sequence of weapons use and tactics, as did the battles of earlier empires. The weapons had changed, however, notably with the addition of bows and arrows, which had been brought into Mesoamerica from the north around A.D. 1100. Signaled by the commander's drum or shell trumpet, the Aztec attack typically started at dawn. Fighting began with a projectile barrage after the armies closed to around 60 meters (198 feet). Wearing only breechcloths and sandals and perhaps carrying shields, archers and slingers could strike much farther, but the high rates of fire quickly exhausted the limited supply of arrows and slingstones, so they held their fire until they were close enough to guarantee the accuracy and effectiveness of their projectiles.

When the barrage began, soldiers advanced carrying stone-bladed wooden broadswords (*macuahuitl*) and thrusting spears (*tepoztopilli*). These were both relatively new innovations. The thrusting spear was an elaboration on earlier versions but now possessed an elongated wooden head inset with obsidian blades. The broadsword was a more radical departure that probably emerged in the mid-fourteenth century. Perhaps developing from the Toltec short sword, the broadsword was made of oak inset with obsidian blades. With its greater size (0.84 meter, or 2.75 feet), it displaced its predecessor. The most experienced and accomplished warriors were well protected, wearing quilted cotton armor under suits of woven feathers or skins and sometimes helmets, and carrying shields, which were as much badges of achievement as functional protection. Although the elite warriors were heavily armored, the novices wore no armor at all, a reflection of their respective accomplishments in battle.

Both sides opened with deadly barrages, particularly to the less protected, so the opposing armies closed quickly. As they advanced, the soldiers shot darts, or short spears, with their spear-throwers. These had a much shorter range than arrows or sling-stones but had greater striking force at close range, could penetrate cotton armor, and were used to disrupt the opposing formations. Soldiers carried only a few atlatl darts apiece, because each side advanced only about 30 meters (99 feet) before the armies met. At that point, they dropped their atlatls in favor of the greater effectiveness of swords or thrusting spears, and the combatants intermingled in combat, forcing a halt to the massed projectile fire.

The most experienced soldiers led the attack. First came the military orders (similar to those of medieval Europe), followed by veteran soldiers leading organized units. Last came novice warriors under the supervision of veterans who ensured that they were not unduly endangered. Slingers and archers were unarmored and required both hands to shoot, so they were extremely vulnerable if the enemy got close enough for hand-to-hand combat. They accordingly remained at the rear but continued to fire at isolated targets, harassing enemy reinforcements, covering withdrawals, and preventing encirclement by the enemy.

Aztec movements into and out of battle were orderly, maintaining coherent formations that allowed the soldiers to concentrate their fighting toward the front rather than on all sides. But once the army closed with the enemy, combat was inevitably an individual affair, although small skirmishing units remained cohesive. Otherwise, soldiers risked being separated and captured by the enemy. Oral commands could not be heard over the din of battle, so the soldiers followed the tall feather standards worn by their leaders. Strapped to the back, these standards towered above the combatants and allowed the soldiers to see where their comrades were going. If the standard bearer was killed, his unit was effectively blinded and could be thrown into disarray.

Battle was heaviest between the soldiers at the fronts of the armies, because only they could bring their weapons to bear effectively. The Aztecs usually extended their front as much as possible, taking advantage of their numerical superiority to envelop the enemy troops and cut them off from reinforcements and resupply. But they also used ambushes on occasion, typically at physically disabling times and places, such as narrow passes, where the advantage lay with the attacker. The most spectacular ambushes involved feigned retreats in battle. If executed convincingly, the enemy troops advanced to press their presumed advantage until they were drawn into a compromised position. Then the Aztecs turned on them while hidden troops attacked from behind, disrupting the enemy formations and cutting them off.

Defenders occasionally chose to wait behind city fortifications rather than meet the Aztecs in the open. Urban fortifications were atypical in late preconquest central Mexico, but some cities, such as Quetzaltepec, were completely encircled by high walls, often in concentric rings, although they were seldom free-standing. A more common type of fortification — as at Cuezcomaixtlahuacan — was the stronghold, detached from the city and usually atop an adjacent hill, where the advantage of height and a difficult ascent augmented walls and battlements. From there, simply throwing stones down on attackers provided an effective first line of defense. Strongholds, however, were most often used as refuges for dependents and political leaders and did not protect the city itself. Instead, they offered safety while the city's terms of surrender were negotiated.

Unless they gained entry by deceit or through treason or simply withdrew, the Aztecs had to breach or scale any fortifications they encountered, or they could lay siege to the city. Breaching fortifications was difficult and time consuming; scaling walls with ladders was a quicker alternative but was relatively uncommon, probably because the attackers needed so many more men than the defenders. The remaining option was to lay siege to the town. This was feasible in the Valley of Mexico, where the besiegers could be resupplied by canoe, but extended sieges were difficult to sustain elsewhere.

Fortified defenses could be very effective tactically, but they were seldom used, for several reasons. First, they were not fool-proof, whereas under favorable conditions the Aztecs' siege tactics were effective. Second, even if the defenders built effective fortifications, manning the entire perimeter required large numbers of troops, which sprawling agricultural towns had trouble raising. Third, and most important, the city could not be divorced from its wider social networks. Even if the city itself were safe behind fortifications, its fields and stores outside the walls remained vulnerable, as did its smaller, unfortified dependencies, and their loss meant economic catastrophe even if the city remained intact. Thus, only an active defense in which the enemy was met and vanquished would guarantee the city's continuation as the hub of a viable social network.

In any case, the Aztecs' primary objective was to induce the people to submit, not to destroy them, although conquered temples and associated buildings might be burned as the ultimate sign of Aztec victory. Beyond the symbolic significance of defeating the local gods, burning the temples was a devastating practical blow, because they were usually the most heavily fortified sites in the city and their destruction meant the strongest resistance had been overcome. Furthermore, the temple precincts contained the city's armories, so their destruction deprived the defenders of additional arms and war supplies. The entire town was burned only if the people continued to resist after their main temple was destroyed.

We have seen that climatic cycles dictated when campaigns were fought. Where they were fought depended on the earlier expansion of the empire, which established the availability of logistical support. But neither of these factors actually determined the strategic direction of the empire's expansion. Although there were doubtless strategic goals — probably related to economic and security concerns — Aztec imperial expansion had a course-of-least-resistance quality. The Aztecs launched all-out attacks primarily on towns they were sure they could defeat.

Much of Aztec expansion was determined by geography. Broken terrain channeled conquests through easily traveled territory, which gave the Aztec empire a patchwork-quilt appearance. Independent towns were often bypassed because they were unimportant to a particular campaign. Only towns posing a military threat to further Aztec expansion or needed to supply logistical support were conquered. Other towns could be bypassed in comparative safety, to be conquered later, either by force or by intimidation.

Most conquests took place along valley floors where major towns were located near their agricultural land. Only major towns had to be conquered, because their defeat meant the de facto submission of their surrounding dependencies as well. Comprehensive conquest was unnecessary: because the Aztecs exercised control through the existing political structure, unconquered dependencies also became part of the Aztec empire when their capitals were conquered. Thus, Aztec expansion depended less on a strategic vision than on the practicalities of logistical support, which dictated the immediate direction and sequence of conquests.

In other words, the Aztecs did not simply emerge from the Valley of Mexico in all directions, sweeping everyone before them. Rather, practical considerations fostered two general strategies for conquests — a relatively straightforward approach for easy targets and a more complicated approach for difficult ones. Because they were concerned with military success, the Aztecs concentrated on easier targets, maximizing their chance of victory and minimizing the risk of failure. The primary advantage of this strategy was that victories over weaker opponents exacted a smaller toll on Aztec manpower, so further expansion was unhindered. But this approach also eased three other goals of Aztec expansion. First, it enabled the Aztecs to build a far-flung logistical network to support their armies in transit. Second, success buttressed the reputation of the empire and discouraged rebellions by other tributaries. And third, it ensured the tribute the king needed to guarantee the support of the nobles. The Aztecs were excellent soldiers, and their emphasis on easy conquests and targets of opportunity reflected internal political considerations rather than military weakness.

An Aztec defeat at the hands of a city-state meant only the loss of a battle; an Aztec victory meant subjugation of the city-state and all its dependencies. The same was not true for battles against confederacies and other empires, such as the Tlaxcallan confederacy to the east and the Tarascan empire to the west. They controlled large hinterlands, so advance warning allowed them to marshal large armies and march to their borders to meet the Aztecs, profoundly altering the consequences of winning the battle. Under these circumstances, victory meant the conquest only of the area around the battlefield. Defeated confederated or imperial armies could withdraw into their territorial interiors, where the Aztecs, who depended on tributaries for logistical support, could not safely pursue them. For a city-state, losing a battle meant subjugation, but for a confederacy or an empire it meant the loss of only a limited area of its periphery. Mesoamerican logistical limitations offered large polities a protection their armies could not. A single, decisive blow to the heart of an empire was usually beyond the Aztecs' ability: conquering one of these was a long-term project achieved only by gradually chipping away at the edges of the polity. Even if the Aztecs had been able to conquer such large opponents, some were so strong that a victory would have left the Aztecs too weakened to maintain control elsewhere. The costs of such a conquest were too high for an empire that had to balance many strategic interests.

To deal with this situation, the Aztecs fought "flower wars" (*xochiyaoyotl*), designed to pin down major opponents while their own expansion continued elsewhere. Because of the prolonged nature of flower wars, early accounts claim that they were fought for military training, to take captives for sacrifice to the gods, and to display individual military skill. This was all true, but the flower wars were only part of a larger military strategy for dealing with major powers.

A flower war began as a show of strength in which relatively few combatants fought to demonstrate individual military prowess. An impressive display of capability could lead to the enemy's capitulation without further conflict. If the opponent remained unintimidated, additional flower wars would be fought — often over a period of years — gradually escalating in ferocity. In the initial flower war, injuries and deaths were not deliberate, and prisoners were not sacrificed afterward. As the war escalated, the number of combatants increased, captives were sacrificed rather than returned, and bows and arrows introduced indiscriminate death rather than individual demonstrations of skill and bravery, until eventually the flower war resembled a conventional war of conquest. Thus, a flower war began as a low-cost exercise in military intimidation, but both costs and consequences escalated until it became a war of attrition. And with that, the numerically superior Aztecs could not lose, because even equal losses by both sides took a greater toll on the smaller polity, gradually undermining its ability to resist.

It could take considerably longer to defeat an enemy through a flower war than through a war of conquest, but there were advantages. By engaging the enemy in limited but enervating warfare, the Aztecs could pin down strong opponents and reduce their offensive threat. They then conquered the surrounding groups and gradually encircled their opponents, cutting them off from external assistance and reducing their areas of logistical and manpower support. By escalating flower wars, the Aztecs slowly chipped away at their enemies' territory until they fell. Thus, the Aztecs' weak-opponent-first strategy generated tribute revenue and increased their logistical capability at low cost, while flower wars isolated and slowly reduced opponents too strong to be attacked directly.

But what exactly did it mean to be conquered by the Aztecs? The most obvious consequence was having to pay tribute to them, for the Aztecs were now inserted at the top of the existing tribute system. Although the crown, nobility, and temples frequently held their own land and laborers, most of their income came in the form of goods and labor paid as tribute by the commoner classes. In an independent city-state, the king was the highest level in the tribute system, but once the city-state was conquered, Aztec tributary demands were added, requiring the payment of additional goods and labor but operating through the local tribute system. The Aztecs merely tapped into the existing system, positioning themselves at the top. This tribute payment was a net loss to the subject towns, but conquest typically caused few other overt changes in the local society. Except in the case of recurrent rebellion, conquered rulers remained in place and exercised local control, which freed the Aztecs from local administration and allowed them to continue their military expansion.

Local economic relations were left largely intact, because the Aztecs sought to maintain healthy local economies that were able to pay their new tributary obligations. Imperial tribute siphoned off local wealth, but Aztec demands also stimulated local production and often expanded trade relationships to secure the goods required. Moreover, tributaries were now linked into an Aztec-dominated trade network that dispersed rare and elite goods throughout the empire. As long as local rulers complied with Aztec wishes, leaving them in power was more efficient than replacing them. Yet the system was constantly vulnerable to dissolution, because it did not shift the loyalty of tributary populations from their traditional rulers to the Aztec kings.

Aztec religious organizations solidly supported the Aztec state and its imperial aspirations, but religious conversion did not play a major role in Aztec imperial ideology. Wars were not primarily religiously motivated, although Aztec kings often manipulated religious mandates to further their aims. For example, they occasionally demanded labor and materials from both tributary and independent towns to help in the construction of temples to the gods; failure to comply meant war. The timing of these construction campaigns was decided by the king, not by priests or regular religious events, and the groups targeted tended to lie in the direct line of existing Aztec expansion, strongly indicating the primarily political use of religious mandates rather than the opposite. Moreover, conquered towns did not suffer forced religious conversion, and Aztec gods were exported beyond the Valley of Mexico only by the occasional migration of Aztecs themselves. Even then, the local gods and their ceremonies were left intact.

Not everything, however, continued as it was in conquered city-states. Aztec domination caused major, even if unintentional, changes in the local political system. In most central Mexican polities, rulership did not descend in a fixed fashion, such as from father to eldest son. Mexican kings typically had multiple wives, numerous children, and thus many potential successors. The selection of a royal successor was an issue internal to the kingdom, but who was chosen was greatly influenced by external ties. External as well as internal political support for a royal contender was crucial, and the single most important factor in terms of the formal requirements for eligibility was his mother.

Intermarriage among allied rulers was common, with rulers giving their daughters as wives to other rulers, which added an important political dimension to the selection of a successor. Consequently, the successor was likely to be the son of the king by his most important wife—the daughter of the king's most powerful ally. The pool of potential successors was determined by that kingdom's rules of succession, but which among the various eligible candidates was actually chosen depended on the larger political context, and this was massively altered by Aztec conquest.

To be without political alliances left a city-state vulnerable to aggression and breach of trade. The king of a conquered polity achieved and held his position in large part because of his alliances with other city-states. The Aztecs inevitably altered these alliances by inserting themselves as the most important ally. Moreover, not all of a given polity's original allies were likely to have been incorporated into the Aztec empire at the same time, and even if they were, their own political situation was also drastically altered. Whatever the effects of this on succession, Aztec conquest altered the local political environment and shattered the reigning king's political base. There were other political contenders who had different ties, and many of these nobles might well receive greater support under the altered circumstances. Thus, many reigning kings cleaved closely to their new dominant ally — the Aztecs — to avert overthrow from within. Nevertheless, the potential for dethroning kings remained, and any major shift in political power in the region could easily lead to a change in rulers.

Although the Aztecs reigned supreme in Mesoamerica, they did not rule everywhere, nor did they preside over a group of homogenized societies fully integrated into the empire. Many areas of Mesoamerica remained independent and often hostile. Nevertheless, most posed little military challenge to Tenochtitlan, despite their access to the same military technology as the Aztecs.

Most central Mexican armies shared common weapons and adopted others as they were disseminated by, or in advance of, the Aztecs. Commoner soldiers typically wore loincloths and primarily relied on weapons such as bows and slings, whereas the nobles and military leaders wore more elaborate armor, carried shock weapons (that is, crushers and slashers, such as maces and swords), and frequently used battle standards and war suits. These armies also shared similar forms of military organization, although their orders of battle varied widely. The military similarities between most Mexican city-states and the Aztecs were superficial, however. Although other armies had general access to Aztec tactics and weapons, how and whether these were incorporated depended on the size and composition of the army in question. This is illustrated particularly by the use of the atlatl. Among major conventional armies, such as the Aztecs', the atlatl was used to disrupt opposing army formations. But armies too small to train large numbers of specialists discontinued use of the atlatl, replacing it with the bow, which, for these forces, was essentially a lower-class tool turned to military use. As a result, atlatls remained important for large conventional armies but were discarded elsewhere. Groups who abandoned them included the petty Mixtec and Zapotec kingdoms of Oaxaca, the Totonacs of the Veracruz coast, the Huaxtecs of the northern Gulf coast, the Mazahuas in the Valley of Toluca, many Nahuatl-speaking city-states scattered throughout central Mexico, and the Maya city-states of Yucatan.

Although the Aztecs had not yet conquered all these groups, singly they posed no significant military obstacle. United, they could become formidable opponents. For most of Mesoamerica there is little evidence of the emergence of such larger political groupings at this time, but even regional powers could become powerful magnets for the disaffected and grow to threaten Aztec dominance.

Two such regional powers existed and confronted the Aztecs when the Spaniards arrived. One, the Tarascan empire, centered in the modern state of Michoacán in western Mexico, was probably the most powerful group facing the Aztecs. It was a multiethnic empire incorporating Tarascan, Otomi, and Nahuatl speakers, many of whom had fled Aztec expansion.

Much of the mechanics and underlying strategy of Tarascan warfare was similar to, though less sophisticated than, that of the

Aztecs, and the Tarascan empire, too, was organized as a hegemonic system. The Tarascans had the same weapons inventory as the Aztecs but used them in different proportions, relying heavily on bows and arrows.

The Tarascans had been victorious when the Aztec King Axayacatl (ruled 1468–81) invaded their territory, but they were nevertheless not a major military power. They had a relatively small population and made little provision for the specialized military training of commoners. Most Tarascan soldiers were unarmored and fought with bows and arrows; only the elites used armor and shock weapons. The Tarascan army's heavy reliance on archery gave it great defensive strength, but it was considerably less formidable offensively because it lacked large numbers of hand-to-hand combatants and consequently did not use the atlatl.

Although the Tarascans successfully expanded within the area around their capital, their early attempts to expand eastward against Nahuatl-speaking cities failed, and further efforts were thwarted by the Aztecs' preemptive conquest of the area. Nevertheless, their heavy reliance on archery gave the Tarascans a decisive defensive advantage in their own territory, where they had ample ammunition and a favorable logistical situation. These tactical advantages and the advantage of operating within a large hinterland that denied aggressors logistical support combined to thwart Aztec thrusts deep into Tarascan territory. The Aztecs, however, remained a significant threat, so the Tarascans built a series of fortifications along the major routes from Aztec-allied areas. Responding in kind, the Aztecs built counter fortifications, but their main expansionary thrust was around Tarascan territory. Bypassing the Tarascan fortifications, the Aztecs conquered and incorporated the surrounding groups as part of a long-term strategy to strangle the Tarascans, a process cut short by the Spanish conquest.

The second major power to confront the Aztecs was the Tlaxcallan confederacy, made up of Nahuatl-speaking city-states in central Mexico. Individually these city-states were too weak to resist the Aztecs, but they joined in shifting alliances, at various times including Tlaxcallan, Cholollan, Huexotzinco, Atlixco, and Tliliuhqui-Tepec. Thus united, they posed a significant threat. Unlike some of the Aztecs' other adversaries, these fought wars the same way the Aztecs did and used the full complement of Mesoamerican weapons, although their commoners received less formal training than did most Aztecs.

Even though the Aztecs could muster a larger and better-trained army, Tlaxcallan controlled a powerful confederacy, and even in victory over it the Aztecs would have been badly mauled. Thus, they dealt with the Tlaxcallan confederacy through a series of flower wars, attempting to pin it down until it was completely encircled, cut off, and crushed. This was a decades-long process, but by the time the Spaniards arrived, the Aztecs had completed their encirclement and escalated the ferocity of their battles. Tlaxcallan's final defeat was perhaps no more than a decade away. The Aztecs were dealing effectively with the Tarascans and the Tlaxcaltecs, but both remained threats, partly because of their military potential but primarily because of their political potential to lure and unite other disaffected Mesoamerican groups.

In brief, Tenochtitlan was the capital of the mightiest empire in Mesoamerica, yet it did not rule unchallenged over a unified region. Even within the empire, individual tributaries could revolt and did so almost at will if the Aztecs proved too weak to compel continued allegiance. This was because the various parts of the empire were not politically, economically, ideologically, or socially integrated into the whole. The Aztecs thus ruled over an empire with a remarkably varied social and political mosaic. Independent groups had little incentive to become part of the empire, but whether or not they resisted the Aztecs depended largely on the balance of power. The only large powers anywhere near Tenochtitlan — the Tlaxcallan confederacy and the Tarascan empire — remained free, but both were being slowly encircled, and their days were numbered. The Aztecs were undoubtedly the greatest power in Mesoamerica, and without external intervention, no one seriously threatened the internal security of Tenochtitlan.

CHAPTER 3

THE DISCOVERY OF YUCATAN

As we have seen, Spaniards' expectations about what they would find in Mexico were conditioned by the peoples they had already encountered in the New World. In comparison with the conquest of Mesoamerica, the Spanish conquests of the Indies, Central America, and Florida were relatively easy. The Indians in these places, although they were often fierce warriors, lacked the arms and organization to mount a sustained military challenge that would seriously threaten Spanish exploration or settlement. Guns, crossbows, steel swords, and armor had proved decisive against native forces, so when Governor Diego Velásquez of Cuba dispatched Francisco Hernández de Córdoba on yet another journey of exploration—this time to the as-yet-unknown Yucatan peninsula— there was every reason to think his force of three ships and 110 soldiers would be adequate.[1]

Córdoba left Cuba on 8 February 1517 and three weeks later, having been delayed by a storm, reached Cape Catoche, Yucatan (map 1). There, for the first time in the New World, the Spaniards encountered cities, states, and organized resistance. Nevertheless, they felt they had a right to enter Indian communities, trade freely with the inhabitants, and ultimately conquer them under Spanish laws, as they had in the Indies. The Mayas of Yucatan lived in organized cities and provinces under their own kings, and their laws, too, governed foreign contacts and trade, all of which precluded the Spaniards' plans. Because the two sides held conflicting attitudes about what actions were permissible, this first Spanish-Mesoamerican contact was almost guaranteed to provoke a clash. Moreover, both sides were confident of their superiority — the Mayas by virtue of their numbers, and the Spaniards by virtue of their military technology and culture.[2]

Spanish accounts claim that the natives' friendly overtures induced them to come ashore, where they were treacherously ambushed. The Indian version went unrecorded, but the Mayas may have had both advance knowledge of these bearded white men and reason to fear them. Christopher Columbus's ships had encountered seagoing Maya traders at the end of the fifteenth century, and in the following decades native societies must have been unsettled by ship sightings, shipwrecked foreigners washing up on their shores, and stories of the devastation overtaking the native societies of the Caribbean. Moreover, Córdoba and his men belied their peaceful intentions by disembarking heavily armed with crossbows and harquebuses.[3]

The Spaniards could not have known Maya political etiquette and most likely misconstrued events at their initial encounter. They were probably received in peace until they seized, or appeared to be seizing, Maya property without permission, initiating the eventual clash. The Spaniards were familiar with native weapons such as bows, lances, slings, and shields, which they had seen in the Indies. But this was certainly their first encounter with natives who fought in well-ordered, armored military units following an organized combat sequence, as in European warfare. The battle that met Córdoba's men began with an initial barrage of arrows and slingstones that wounded fifteen Spaniards (two subsequently died). This was quickly followed by the Mayas' closing for hand-to-hand combat.[4]

The Spaniards were immediately placed on the defensive, but their weaponry prevailed. Neither side was prepared for the other — not the Spaniards for Indian organization or the Mayas for Spanish weaponry. Spanish swords were no sharper than native

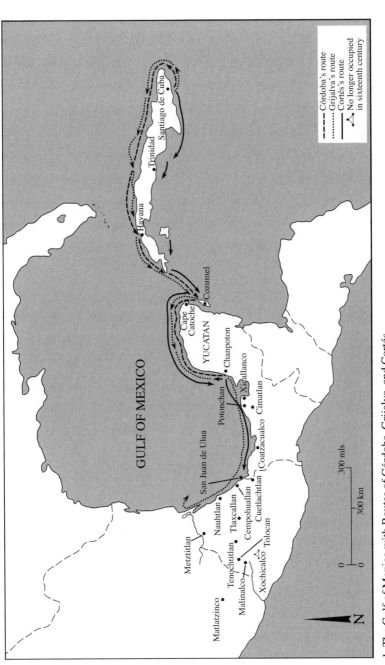

1. The Gulf of Mexico with Routes of Córdoba, Grijalva, and Cortés

ones but kept their edges longer and could be used for forward thrusts as well as for vertical and lateral slashes. The impact of the fifteen crossbows and ten harquebuses must have been devastating psychologically as well as physically.[5]

Clubs and swords had their effect, but Spanish steel armor was proof against most Indian projectiles, except perhaps darts cast from very close range. Indeed, Spaniards' wounds were typically limited to the limbs, face, neck, and other vulnerable areas unprotected by armor, which meant the Spanish soldiers faced considerably less risk than did their Indian adversaries, whose entire bodies were vulnerable. Spanish infantry arms were also superior. Pikes and meter-long swords had Indian equivalents, but the Spanish steel versions were stronger and retained their edges far longer.

The Spaniards' main advantage, however, lay with their crossbows and harquebuses. Military crossbows of that period weighed 5.5 to 6 kilograms (15–16 pounds) and fired 1.5- to 3-ounce wooden bolts with metal heads for distances of more than 320 meters (1,050 feet) in an arc, or 64 meters (210 feet) point blank, in comparison with a probable maximum range of 180 meters (600 feet) for Indian bows. Reloading was slow, however, limiting crossbow fire to one bolt per minute, in comparison with six to ten arrows by bow for the same time. Nevertheless, crossbows had the advantage of greater range and power while demanding far less skill than bows.[6]

Spanish harquebuses were between 1 and 1.5 meters (3.25 to 5 feet) long, weighed 8 to 9 kilograms (17.5 to 20 pounds), and fired a 47- to 140-gram (2–6 ounce) lead ball up to 137 meters (450 feet), although it was effective for only about half that distance. In addition, reloading was slow, limiting the harquebus's rate of fire to no more than one round each minute and a half.[7]

Despite these low rates of fire, the greater range and impact of crossbows and harquebuses gave the Spaniards unprecedented hitting power in Mesoamerica, allowing them to fire into armored opponents with deadly effect. Because of their weight, however, crossbows and harquebuses could not be used for long; the soldiers' arms became unsteady after a half hour's rapid fire. Also, because crossbows and harquebuses were most effective at point-blank range, they could be used only in two ranks, so their fire could not be as concentrated as arrow barrages. Archers in the back rows could lob volleys over the front ranks, so they could coordinate fire for up to six ranks and could fire at a much faster rate than crossbowmen and harquebusiers.[8]

Fifteen Indians were killed in this initial clash with Spaniards before the Maya forces broke off contact. The attackers probably numbered only in the hundreds — too few to force a decisive result against 110 well-armed Europeans. In the face of this defeat, the Mayas abandoned their town to the Spaniards, who then looted the houses and temples of whatever gold they could find. They also took two Maya prisoners, who were later baptized Julianillo and Melchorejo and eventually taught Spanish so they could serve as translators.[9]

The Spaniards returned to their ships and sailed west along the coast until they reached the town of Campeche on 29 March, renaming it San Lázaro. They sailed only during the day and thus traveled slowly. News of the earlier battle probably preceded them, so the Mayas knew the Spaniards were vulnerable to greatly superior numbers. They were unlikely to take any more Mayas by surprise. Consequently, Córdoba was cautious in initiating further contacts: he was neither authorized nor equipped to make forays inland, and much of his exploration was carried out from the safety of his ships. The Spaniards already knew what the area offered and that gold was scarce, yet they landed repeatedly — perhaps for trade and exploration, but certainly for food and water.[10]

Because the expedition lasted so long and the ships were small, the Spaniards could not carry all the supplies they needed. The soldiers hunted some additional food in the relative safety of rural and forested areas, but the main reason the Spaniards stopped at Maya cities was their persistent need for water. Each man required at least 1.9 liters (2 quarts) of drinking water per day — 208 liters (55 gallons) per day for the original complement of soldiers, in addition to the needs of the sailors. The Yucatan peninsula, however, is essentially a large limestone slab with scant surface water. Although rainfall is plentiful, the runoff does not flow into rivers and streams but instead drains into the rock and collects in natural cisterns, called *cenotes*. It was the presence of these natural reservoirs that permitted the growth of cities in Yucatan and dictated their locations. Such water sources were virtually impossible to see from shipboard, so the Spaniards could be assured they had found one only when they sighted a city. This meant that whatever other motivations they might have had, and despite the obvious dangers of doing so, the Spaniards were forced to stop at Maya cities.

Though fearful of attack, the Spaniards landed all their forces near Campeche to refill their water casks. They were led into the city by a party of Indians but left when ordered and sailed another ten days before reaching the political center of Chanpoton, where they once again landed for water. The well-armed Spaniards camped ashore, remaining anxiously on the defensive. They were surrounded by a force of Indians during the night and attacked at dawn. The Mayas wounded more than eighty Spaniards with a barrage of arrows, darts, and stones and then advanced for hand-to-hand combat. The Spaniards repulsed them, despite being greatly outnumbered — allegedly by two hundred to one — because their arms and armor were superior to those of the Indians and because once the Mayas had closed, only their first few ranks could actively engage the Spaniards, which diminished the significance of their numerical advantage. Once they pulled back to relative safety, the Indians again used their superior numbers to fire into the Spanish camp. When Maya reinforcements arrived, the Spaniards could no longer resist and, in close formation, broke through and fled toward their boats under constant assault. The battle had lasted only an hour, but the Spaniards were decisively defeated. Of the 110 Spanish soldiers, fifty were killed, two were carried off alive, and all but one survivor were wounded, some dying soon thereafter.[11]

Now shorthanded, the Spaniards were forced to abandon one of their ships, which they burned. They set sail and eventually reached Cuba on 20 April 1517, where Córdoba soon succumbed to his wounds. Word of these events spread throughout Cuba: in just two and a half months, a new land of great cities and gold had been discovered, but it was also a dangerous land of large armies that had defeated the Spaniards.

We can only speculate about the reaction among the Mayas, but surely they felt considerable apprehension. True, half of Córdoba's men had been killed at Chanpoton, but the Spaniards were formidable fighters, and the Mayas had won with great difficulty and loss of life. Moreover, the Spaniards possessed wonders never before seen, including large sailing ships, harquebuses, crossbows, and other steel arms and armor. They were of very different aspect, with their pale faces, pronounced facial hair, and blue as well as brown eyes. Still, their stay was brief and without lasting effect: they initiated no sustained trade, no political upheaval, no religious revolution. Córdoba's arrival left few traces, and had the Spaniards not come again, his arrival probably would have faded into legend.

Córdoba's visit had even less effect on the Aztecs. His landings were all in the Maya area, well beyond Aztec control. Nevertheless, merchants linked the two areas, and the Aztecs had outposts at Xicallanco and Cimatlan, so some word of these unusual events must have reached their capital, Tenochtitlan. There are no direct records of Córdoba's visit in native accounts, but there are stories of wondrous and troubling events — comets, temples burning, the lake boiling, a wailing woman at night, two-headed men, and a miraculous bird with a mirror on its head. These were later said to be omens foretelling the destruction of the Aztec world, but they might have reflected distorted accounts of strange invaders that went through many tellings before reaching Tenochtitlan.[12]

Encouraged by the discovery of gold and other wealth in Mesoamerica, Governor Velásquez dispatched a second expedition, led by Juan de Grijalva. Conscious of the danger, Grijalva left Cuba with a larger and better-armed second expedition. With four ships (three caravels and one brigantine that soon turned back), two hundred men, and a Maya interpreter, Grijalva reached Cozumel on 3 May 1518. Expecting to be attacked, he disembarked with a hundred armed men on 6 May and, finding the town abandoned, claimed it for the king. The Spaniards then reconnoitered the Yucatan coast but did not land before sailing on in search of Campeche. Grijalva's failure to land at any large settlement suggests a cautious approach. Like Córdoba, he needed water, but rather than stopping at cities where his reception was uncertain, he sailed on, straining his supplies, until he reached Campeche, the one city where Córdoba had resupplied without being attacked.[13]

By the time he arrived, Grijalva was sorely in need of water, and he landed with a hundred fully armed men, taking several cannons — weapons Córdoba had not possessed. Unopposed, he placed the cannons near a temple in the center of town and then landed another hundred men. When a Maya force approached, Grijalva said through his interpreter that the Spaniards only wanted food and water and would then leave. Disregarding Maya warnings, the Spaniards marched through the town in defensive formation until they reached a well, where they took water. The Mayas brought food and gifts and asked Grijalva to leave, which he declined to do, because he still needed more water. The next morning the Mayas attacked, but the Spaniards fired their cannons, killing three Indians and putting the rest to flight.[14]

The type of cannon Grijalva used is uncertain, but all were ships' guns, as would be expected for a coastal reconnaissance. Gun ports cut through the sides of men-of-war were a recent innovation in Europe and not yet employed in ships in the Indies.

Instead, guns were mounted on the rail topside, which favored light cannons called falconets.[15] Falconets of the day were 1 to 1.6 meters (3.25 to 5.25 feet) long and 6 to 7 centimeters (2.3 to 2.7 inches) in caliber. They typically weighed 225 kilograms (500 pounds) but could be as large as 500 kilograms (1,100 pounds). They fired a 1.7–5.5 kilogram (0.74–2.5 pound) ball for 140 meters (460 feet) point blank but could reach a maximum distance of 2,000 meters (6,600 feet). Falconets could be fired twice as rapidly as other cannons and harquebuses because they were breechloading: each gun was equipped with two or three removable chambers that were loaded and then placed in the breech, braced, and fired. Muzzleloaders, by comparison, were slower firing because they had to be swabbed out after each shot, then reloaded down the same barrel. The breechloading cannons' higher rate of fire, however, was achieved at a cost of significantly lower muzzle velocity. Chambers fit the barrel poorly, leaking gas and producing far greater windage than muzzleloading cannons. Still, this was a minor disadvantage against opponents who lacked comparable weapons, and the falconets played havoc with Indian formations. Their one significant drawback was their lack of mobility. They were not mounted on wheeled carriages and had to be carried into position, so a rapidly shifting tactical situation often meant they could not be moved with the battle, limiting their use.[16]

The cannons inflicted psychological as well as physical damage on the Indians, but the Spaniards' main advantage lay in their defensive formation, which, against steel arms and armor, the Mayas were unable to penetrate. The Spaniards continued to kill Mayas and burn their houses, but when they pursued the fleeing Indians, they became separated and their formation broke down. Some Spaniards followed Grijalva while others followed their standard, and once they were divided, the Mayas turned on the Spaniards in individual combat and forced them back, killing one and wounding forty. Only the covering fire of cannons, harquebuses, and crossbows staved off total defeat, and the Spaniards retreated to their camp. There they tended their wounded and were unmolested until, after securing enough water, they left.[17]

Grijalva then sailed to Chanpoton. Aware that Córdoba had lost half his men there, Grijalva scared off the canoes that approached his ship by firing two cannon shots and then left without attempting to land. On 31 May, the Spaniards reached Laguna de Términos, a large bay fed by rivers southwest of Yucatan's limestone shelf. At last, here was an area of abundant fresh water where the Spaniards could replenish their supplies without having to enter a city. Everyone went ashore, made camp, gathered food and water, and repaired their ships, remaining until 8 June before sailing on past the Grijalva River. There they were followed by more than two thousand Indians in canoes who shot arrows at them, which the Spaniards answered with a cannon shot that killed one Indian.[18]

The next day the Spaniards were approached by many canoes of Indians with whom they were able to trade for gold. The following day, with considerable ceremony, an Indian lord dressed Grijalva in an elaborate, gold-ornamented costume, and he was dressed in turn in Spanish attire. The exchange had little more significance for the Spaniards, but it was to give the Indians of central Mexico, and especially the Aztecs, their first lasting evidence of the arrival of these strangers.[19]

The Spaniards arrived at Coatzacualco on 11 June and then sailed to Isla de Sacrificios. There they also traded for gold, but despite his men's desire to establish a settlement, Grijalva sailed on. They passed the town of Nauhtlan (renamed Almería by the Spaniards) before reaching a much larger one where twelve canoes of Indians attacked the ships before being repulsed by artillery fire.[20]

The Spaniards then retraced their route, finally reaching Chanpoton, where Grijalva disembarked with a hundred men to secure badly needed food and water. They were again attacked by Indians in canoes, who were driven off by artillery fire, after which the Spaniards decided to take and burn the town. Finding it well defended and fortified with wooden palisades, however, the Spaniards left and sailed on to Campeche, where Grijalva landed with his men and four cannons. There he fended off an Indian attack and took food and water for the return trip to Cuba.[21]

As with Córdoba's expedition, Grijalva's landings had local effects on the groups contacted but caused little long-term or fundamental change. Whether or not stories of these contacts reached Tenochtitlan through merchants trading in the Maya area, Grijalva's expedition had sailed along the Gulf coast into areas dominated by the Aztecs. The noble who so ceremoniously dressed Grijalva in fine attire was an Aztec who wanted to find out about these strangers so he could send this information and the goods he received to Moteuczoma (Montezuma). Thus the Aztecs learned of the Spaniards' arrival in concrete terms, but who they were and the significance of their presence remained unclear.[22]

The Aztec king and his advisors discussed the situation, but they kept the foreigners' arrival secret from the people. They decided that the coast should be watched in case the strangers returned, and Moteuczoma dispatched men to do so. This did not resolve the matter of who or what the strangers were.[23]

It is a widely accepted interpretation that the Aztecs thought the Spanish leader was the returning god, Quetzalcoatl. This does not appear to have been the case, but the general interpretation may well have merit. To understand who and what these Spaniards were, the Aztecs drew on their own background in order to interpret them in a meaningful way. The Spaniards were unlike any people seen before, and they had technological capabilities that seemed godlike, so a supernatural origin had to be considered, especially in the Aztec worldview, in which gods could play direct roles in human affairs. After considerable thought and discussion, the notion that the strangers might be gods may have been accepted — not, apparently, as a fact, but as a disturbing possibility.[24]

Even if the Aztecs had decided that these strangers were only mortal men, there was little they could have done to prevent their return. The Aztecs had faced sustained threats elsewhere in Mesoamerica, but these were predictable, as we have seen. Any attack would have been limited to a specific time of year, the armies would have traveled through a limited number of mountain passes, and their advance would have been fairly open because of the slowness of the march. The Spaniards, by contrast, presented an unprecedented situation. Their sailing ships offered little warning of their approach, and they could land anywhere along hundreds of miles of coastline, easily thwarting any defensive forces posted to intercept them. Until the Spaniards fully landed, the Aztecs had no feasible defensive strategy.

Governor Velásquez began preparing for a third expedition to Mexico even before Grijalva returned to Cuba. He appointed a young man named Hernán Cortés as its leader. Cortés had learned much about Mesoamerica from the earlier expeditions, and some of his men had been on those voyages and gained firsthand experience with the groups they set out to contact and subdue. Nevertheless, support among his Spanish backers in Cuba was decidedly mixed. Political calculation and intrigue affected the staffing and equipping of the expedition, as well as the course of action subsequently adopted in Mexico.

Governor Velásquez provided the political authorization for this third expedition, as well as its primary financial backing, as he had with the two previous ones. Cortés, however, was a controversial choice for commander. More experienced men were available, but Velásquez distrusted them. Cortés's selection was also encouraged by the judicious lobbying of his allies — notably Andrés de Duero, the governor's secretary, and Amador de Lares, the king's accountant — who had formed a secret partnership with him. In addition to the ships, men, and provisions supplied by Velásquez, Cortés used his own money and borrowed other funds to outfit the expedition, so he, too, had a significant financial stake in its outcome.

More than 350 men were recruited for the expedition, but except for Cortés and a few of his more prominent followers, little is known about them. Most of those who settled the Indies during the early decades were from Andalusia and Castile, supplemented by men from a scattered sample of other Spanish provinces, Portugal, Italy, and a smattering of other countries. Many pretended to *hidalgo* (lesser noble or gentleman) status, but the accuracy of this claim is questionable, especially in light of the better-known social background of the conquistadors who went to Peru. About a fourth of those were hidalgos, but the rest were plebeians, and fewer than a third of the total could read and write. Successful men in the Indies generally remained where they were or returned to Spain. Those who went on exploratory expeditions were relatively new arrivals, had not fared well financially, and lacked high social positions. Most were single or had left their families in Spain. Thus the conquistadors were not triumphal noblemen of Spain but the relatively unsuccessful residue of the Caribbean experience.[25]

Although Cortés had already assembled his fleet and most of the men for the expedition, Velásquez began turning against him amid disquieting rumors about his trustworthiness and ambitions, as well as Cortés's own political maneuverings. Forewarned of Velásquez's doubts about him and alert to the possibility that he might remove him as leader, Cortés left Santiago de Cuba early and sailed to Port of Trinidad. He arrived a few days later and secured more arms, supplies, and horses, as well as additional men who proved to be among his staunchest supporters.[26]

On learning of Cortés's precipitous departure, Velásquez sent orders to the local authorities to have him imprisoned and the fleet detained. But Cortés had the support of his men, who were too formidable a force for local officials to challenge. Ten days later the fleet sailed for Havana, where still more men summoned by

Cortés had gathered. Velásquez sent orders for Cortés to be arrested there, too, but again without effect, and the fleet sailed for Yucatan on 10 February 1519.[27]

Spanish ships of the day did not sail well against the wind, so the timing of each expedition's departure depended primarily on the prevailing winds. The Gulf of Mexico and the Caribbean enjoyed winds from the east for only about three months of the year, so Spanish voyages of exploration were generally timed to take advantage of them and to avoid the hurricane season. The political situation forced Cortés to sail earlier in the year than the previous two expeditions, and weather conditions were still less than ideal.[28]

Cortés reached Yucatan with eleven ships and as many as 450 soldiers, including thirteen harquebusiers and thirty-two crossbowmen. His ships boasted four falconets and ten brass cannons. The exact nature of these cannons is unknown, but they were probably muzzleloading field guns of the day. Their size is also unknown, but they were doubtless larger than the falconets and would have had greater range and accuracy, though also less mobility. In addition, Cortés brought sixteen horses, a number limited by their scarcity and expense in the Indies as well as by the difficulty of carrying them on the open decks of the ships, where they had to be suspended from the rigging by belly slings lest they fall and injure themselves on the rolling deck.[29]

This expedition was significantly larger and stronger than earlier ones, but what is most striking is not the simple increase in soldiers but the far greater number of ships. Cortés had more than twice as many men as Grijalva but almost four times as many ships. Cortés did bring more equipment, but the primary reason for the greater number of ships was logistical.

Both of the previous expeditions had relied on local supplies, as was common for Spanish expeditions throughout the circum-Caribbean area. But the unique conditions of the Yucatan peninsula fostered unnecessary clashes, because the Spaniards had to enter cities in search of water and food. Moreover, they typically did so by force, and their timing was dictated by need rather than a favorable military situation. This led to casualties that could have been avoided had Spanish supplies been adequate. Cortés's response to this problem was to bring a much larger store of supplies. Although he still depended on local resupply, his needs were significantly less pressing, giving him greater freedom to consider social and military factors in deciding whether to make or avoid contact.[30]

Cortés's expedition followed the same general route as the first two and landed at Cozumel, where Grijalva's expedition had gone ashore. This was a friendly town, and Cortés enforced a policy of no looting, a practice designed to ensure friendlier relations and made feasible by Cortés's greater supplies.[31]

Members of both previous expeditions had seen native temples, idols, and direct evidence of human sacrifice but had made little attempt to convert the Indians to Christianity. The Spaniards had been militarily vulnerable and could ill afford to alienate the Indians further. Moreover, whereas the earlier expeditions had lacked priests, at least one accompanied Cortés. Cortés did break statues of native gods at Cozumel and replace them with a cross and an image of the Virgin, perhaps because conversion justified his conquest. But this was not a practice he followed everywhere.[32]

While on Cozumel, Cortés dispatched one of his ships to find Spaniards rumored to be held captive among the Mayas. One, Gerónimo de Aguilar, was found and returned to become a trustworthy translator of Maya. A second, Gonzalo Guerrero, had assimilated into Maya society, refused to return, and in fact had led the attack against Córdoba's forces at Cape Catoche two years before.[33]

Cortés then sailed along the coast of Yucatan until he reached Potonchan, bypassing Chanpoton because of adverse tides. The Spaniards landed near the city and camped on the beach that night, despite Maya protests and the arrival of a reported twelve thousand warriors. The next day Cortés decided to enter the town, even though it was strongly fortified with log barricades. He put the crossbowmen, harquebusiers, and cannons in the smaller boats and sent them up the Grijalva River toward the town while a force of two hundred men under Alonzo de Avila approached it by land. Their boats were met by canoes full of warriors, and Cortés ordered Aguilar to read the *requerimiento* (summons) in the Maya language. The requerimiento was a Spanish legal statement written just before 1514, during Spain's early years of overseas expansion. It demanded that the Indians recognize the authority of the church, pope, and king; refusal meant coercive subjugation, loss of property, and punishment befitting traitors. Its reading before each battle absolved the conquistadors of responsibility for their wars under Spanish law. Even if Aguilar's translation was adequate and he was close enough to be heard clearly, which is unlikely, the requerimiento would have been meaningless to the Mayas. In any case, the reading had no effect, and the Mayas allegedly fired first. The Spaniards responded with crossbow, harquebus, and cannon fire, pushing the Indians back to the town and destroying their barricades. At that point Avila's force arrived from the rear, the combined Spanish forces routed the Indians, and Cortés took possession of the town in the name of the king.[34]

Dividing forces in the face of superior numbers had led to disastrous consequences for the earlier expeditions, but there was a logic to Cortés's actions. His land force was large enough to fend off an attack and was not plunging into the unknown; it was marching along a known path to a fixed destination — the town. His sea force, although smaller, had the advantage of cannons and was more mobile, so even if it was repulsed, it could retreat to the ultimate refuge of the ships. Thus, neither Spanish contingent was dangerously vulnerable to the Mayas. Dividing his forces allowed Cortés to confront the Indians from the sea while his land forces surprised them from the rear, leading to a rout.

The next day two Indians brought Cortés a gift of gold ornaments and again asked him to leave. In response, Cortés demanded food, and the Indians promised to bring it. But the Spaniards' situation deteriorated when a captive named Melchorejo fled during the night. Melchorejo was one of the Mayas who had been taken during Córdoba's expedition and who was to serve as a translator on this one, and his flight caused the Spaniards to worry that he might divulge crucial intelligence to the Indians. Their anxiety increased when the Indians did not return with the promised food, so after two days Cortés sent out two foraging parties. Each numbered more than a hundred men, but both were attacked and forced back to their camp. Stretched out along trails, even forces as large as two hundred men were vulnerable to Maya attack if they were not supported by artillery or additional soldiers. Consequently, the next day Cortés landed the rest of his men and at least ten of his horses — the first to reach Mesoamerica.[35]

With horsemen and cannons, three hundred Spaniards marched on the Mayas, reaching a savanna near the town of Centla. From there the foot soldiers advanced without the horsemen, who had difficulty crossing a swamp. Again the requerimiento was read and a battle ensued. The Spaniards had little idea of the size of the opposing force when they set out, but neither did the Mayas, for only slightly more than two hundred Spaniards had engaged in the earlier clashes. Now they faced three hundred Spaniards, and just as the battle began, their rear guard arrived with another hundred men. Seventy of Cortés's men were wounded in the opening barrage, and one was killed after the Mayas closed for hand-to-hand combat. But the Spaniards fought in close formation and successfully defended themselves, even though the Mayas now completely surrounded them.[36]

Spanish arms and armor were superior to native arms, but the Mayas adapted to the situation by pulling back beyond sword range while sustaining their barrage of arrows, darts, and slingstones. This reduced their vulnerability to Spanish swords and pikes, but cannons played havoc with the tightly packed Indian formations. This tactic nevertheless favored the Mayas, so the Spaniards advanced to reestablish contact, regain the advantage of superior swords and armor, and avoid the murderous barrage.

After two hours of fighting, Cortés's horsemen arrived and charged from the rear. Dividing forces was a common tactic in Mesoamerica and would not have been totally unexpected, but the Mayas were surprised by the appearance and speed of the horses. Nevertheless, the horses afforded the Spaniards only a limited strategic advantage, because the terrain was broken, heavily wooded, boggy in places, and generally unknown. Indeed, the infantry were able to reach their objective faster than horsemen, because they could more easily traverse such barriers. But once the cavalry arrived, it could gallop across the open, flat battlefield so quickly that the Mayas had little time to react. Armed with 4-meter-long lances, the Spaniards held the weapons rigidly under their arms, hitting the enemy with the combined power and momentum of both rider and horse, penetrating native armor and riding through their formations. Mounted lancers thus gave the Spaniards the same ability to disrupt enemy formations as crossbows, harquebuses, and cannons, but also allowed them to pursue and even outpace the enemy, striking repeatedly with their lances.[37]

The battle lasted another hour before the Indians fled into the woods. It was the horses that had proved decisive. Aside from the psychological effect of these unknown but powerful creatures, mounted lancers provided the perfect counter to established Indian tactics. Until this point, the Mayas had been able to maintain a cohesive front, even when the foremost fighters fell, but the great force that could be channeled into the lances enabled the Spaniards to punch through their lines, disrupting their formations and allowing foot soldiers to pour through, now striking the Mayas from flanks and rear. Many Maya soldiers were killed, with very small immediate Spanish losses, although more than thirty-five Spaniards died later in Vera Cruz of wounds they received in this battle.[38]

Among the Maya prisoners were two captains whom Cortés sent back to their rulers with gifts and a peace entreaty. In response, thirty Maya nobles returned the next day, pledged fealty, and gave the Spaniards gifts of food, gold, cloth, and twenty women, including La Malinche, whose knowledge of both Maya and Nahuatl is credited with later permitting Cortés to speak to the Indians of central Mexico. Having subdued the Mayas, Cortés felt safe enough to begin their forced conversion to Christianity, so he had the statues of Maya gods removed from their temples and replaced with a cross. The Spaniards remained near Potonchan for five days, tending their wounded. Then, having been told that the Mayas got their gold and jewels from Mexico, they sailed away from the Maya area.[39]

The three Spanish expeditions to the Yucatan peninsula had met with a variety of responses from the groups they contacted, ranging from an apparent eagerness to trade to hostility, armed resistance, and flight. Much of this may be understood strictly in terms of military strength — smaller towns offered less resistance. But this masks a more important reality: Maya towns were part of larger political units, and the arrival of invading strangers put the dependent towns in a dilemma. Without direction from their political lords, who resided elsewhere, any attack was risky, not just militarily from the Spaniards but also politically from their own leaders. As a result, smaller towns typically did not resist the Spaniards, but larger cities that housed political leaders capable of making decisions of war and peace frequently did.

In their successive expeditions, the Spaniards learned which towns were likely to resist and acted accordingly. Moreover, the Spaniards could be more daring in their military actions because they could always fall back to the security of their ships if they miscalculated — whereas the Mayas, tied to their fields and towns, risked all. But whether successful or not, these clashes taught the Spaniards much about Indian warfare. Spanish tactics changed and adapted throughout the course of the three expeditions. They learned that combat units of at least two hundred men were necessary to resist massive Indian attacks, that harquebuses and crossbows were effective against Indian armor, that artillery was extremely disruptive, and that mounted lancers could disrupt formations and force the Indians to flee. This learning process was not one-sided: the Indians also adapted to Spanish warfare. Nevertheless, what the Mayas learned and how they adjusted to Spanish weapons and tactics had little effect on the course of Spanish expansion, because the Mayas were soon left behind. The Spaniards took their understanding of, and adaptation to, native warfare with them to central Mexico, where it gave them a significant advantage over the Indians they were soon to encounter.

CHAPTER 4

THE CONQUEST OF
CENTRAL MEXICO

On 21 April 1519, Cortés's fleet reached the natural harbor on the central Veracruz coast where Grijalva had stopped and traded previously and which was renamed San Juan de Ulúa (map 2). The ships were met by canoes full of Indians sent by Tentlil, the Aztec governor of the region, to collect information about the identity and motivations of these bearded strangers. The Indians were fed and given trade goods before they left. The next day Cortés landed his men, artillery, and horses, then built and fortified his camp.[1]

Although central Veracruz was the homeland of the Totonacs, it was under Aztec control, and the next day the Aztec governor and four thousand unarmed men arrived from Cuetlachtlan with loads of food for Cortés. They then gave Cortés more gifts, including many gold objects, and Cortés gave the Indians Spanish goods in return. Indeed, the Spaniards saw much more gold in Veracruz than in the Maya area, confirming what they had been told. It was Spanish greed for gold that sealed the Aztecs' fate.[2]

The Aztecs' primary purpose in meeting the Spaniards was to gather information for Moteuczoma. Reports of strange people had reached Tenochtitlan for years, coming not only from the Maya area but also from this very coast, where Grijalva had put ashore, and Aztec accounts of strange events allegedly foretold the Spanish arrival. The very nature of the intruders was in question.

65

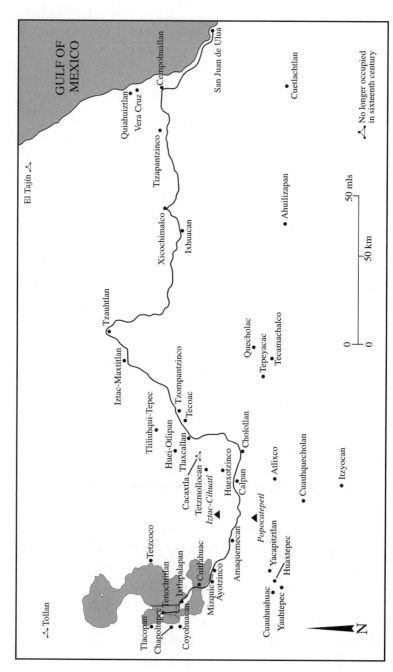

GULF OF MEXICO

El Tajín ⚲

Tollan ⚲

Tlacopan
Chapoltepec
Tenochtitlan
Ixtlapalapan
Cuitláhuac
Coyohuacan
Mizquic
Ayotzinco
Amaquemecan
Cuauhnahuac
Yauhtepec
Huaxtepec
Yacapitztlan

Tetzcoco

Iztac-Cihuatl ▲
Tetzmollocan ⚲
Cacaxtla
Tlaxcallan
Huexotzinco
Calpan
Popocatepetl ▲
Atlixco
Cuauhquecholan
Itzyocan

Tzompantzinco
Tecoac
Tiliuhqui-Tepec
Huei-Otlipan

Iztac-Maxtitlan

Tzauhtlan

Quecholac
Tepeyacac
Tecamachalco

Cholollan

Xicochimalco
Ixhuacan

Ahuilizapan

Tizapantzinco

Quiahuiztlan
Vera Cruz

Cempohuallan

San Juan de Ulua

Cuetlachtlan

0   50 km
0   50 mls

⚲ No longer occupied
in sixteenth century

N

2. Cortés's Route from Vera Cruz to Tenochtitlan

One conquistador, Bernal Díaz del Castillo, reported that the Aztec leaders asked for a Spanish metal helmet to see if it was like that worn by one of their gods. Accordingly, a helmet was sent to Moteuczoma.[3]

The Aztec nobles were accompanied by artists who faithfully drew and painted images of everything they saw — the Spaniards, their ships, horses, and dogs, and all their arms and armor. Noting this great interest, the Spaniards demonstrated their weapons for the Aztecs, charging their horses and firing their cannons. Tentlil ordered a camp built nearby for two thousand Indians who were to provide food for the Spaniards, and messengers were sent with the pictures to tell Moteuczoma all they had seen.[4]

A week later Tentlil returned with more than a hundred porters and gave Cortés still more lavish gifts. Among these, Moteuczoma reportedly sent Cortés gifts normally offered to the gods Quetzalcoatl, Tezcatlipoca, and Tlalocateuctli (though this interpretation only emerged decades after the conquest), which suggests that the Aztecs were still uncertain about the identity of the Spaniards. Cortés later dutifully forwarded these gold- and turquoise-inlaid objects to Spain. The Aztecs relayed Moteuczoma's message that the Spaniards should remain where they were and not come to Tenochtitlan.

Moteuczoma's presentation of gifts may be interpreted in two ways. He might have been acknowledging that the Spaniards were gods, or he might have been tacitly acknowledging Aztec subservience. The presentation of lavish gifts was not simply an honor but also, in the Mesoamerican political world, an admission of hegemonic vassalage. The subordination, however, was conditional rather than complete. Moteuczoma was offering Cortés recognition of his superior rights if he would stay away and not come to Tenochtitlan. The Aztecs were accustomed to enforcing conditions on vassal cities; this was a type of relationship they understood. Whatever apprehension they might have felt, they were trying to incorporate the Spaniards into their world.[5]

In response, Cortés said that he must see Moteuczoma, or his own king would be displeased. He also refused to move his camp to another village six or seven leagues away, as the Aztecs had requested. This request might have been an attempt to keep Cortés away from the Totonacs, but it was also a test of his relationship with Moteuczoma. Had Cortés moved, his compliance with the request would have helped clarify the relationship as negotiable rather than dominant. But without more information, Moteuczoma dared not directly challenge the Spaniards' apparent claim to dominance, and the parameters of the relationship remained unclear.[6]

After Cortés refused to move his camp, most of the Indians stopped trading and bringing food. In addition, the Aztecs decamped on 12 May, possibly in response to the beginning of the planting season, which demanded their return home. It could equally well have been a political move, which is how the Spaniards interpreted it, leaving them fearful of an attack that never came. Perhaps Moteuczoma thought withdrawing support would force these strangers to leave, but the Spaniards already knew of the great wealth of Tenochtitlan, and with the Aztecs gone, other groups began to play a supportive role.[7]

Three days after the Aztecs withdrew, the Spaniards were visited by five Totonac Indians who had not dared come while the Aztecs were there. Having heard of the Spanish successes among the Mayas, they came to offer their services. This was the Spaniards' first inkling that the Aztecs had enemies, and one of two major events that set Cortés's course irrevocably toward conquest—the other being Cortés's manipulation of his legal status, which freed him from Velásquez's restraints.[8]

Cortés's relations with the local Indians were important, but even more so was consolidating his support among his fellow Spaniards. Many of them, especially Governor Velásquez's supporters, wanted to return to Cuba. Because the expedition had been authorized by Velásquez, Cortés remained legally bound by the governor's restrictions, which forbade any campaign of conquest.

But in a clever bit of legal manipulation, Cortés founded the town of Villa Rica de la Vera Cruz and established its own legal structure, so that it now functioned as a political entity directly under the authority of King Charles V of Spain. The town council appointed by Cortés then decided that the expedition had fulfilled Velásquez's mandate and therefore the authority granted by the governor had lapsed. It elected Cortés captain, directly under the king's authority. This dubious legal maneuver neatly freed Cortés of the restraints placed on him by Velásquez and permitted him to act as he saw fit. However, the likelihood that the king would uphold this legal sleight of hand depended on Cortés's success: it was essentially a political rather than a legal matter. If Cortés failed in his efforts, he laid himself open to charges of treason and other criminal acts against one of the king's loyal governors. If he succeeded in bringing new lands and wealth into Spanish hands, the king's support would be assured, and Velásquez's objections would be pushed aside.[9]

The Spaniards in the New World were accustomed to making decisions without the immediate political approval they required in Spain, because of the vast distances separating them from their king. It took two to three months for a ship to reach Mexico from Spain, and four and a half to return. Moreover, to achieve this, ships had to sail at times of the year when the winds favored them. Departures from Spain usually took place between April and August, and return ships from Mexico sailed between May and June. Otherwise, the ships faced adverse winds, and the journeys were substantially longer. As a result, an inquiry to the king from the New World would leave in spring or early summer, regardless of when it arose during the year, and the earliest response would not be received until the following summer. Each further clarification of instructions required an equal length of time, with an additional year's lag if the instructions failed to arrive until after the New World fleets had sailed for the year. Consequently, New World functionaries were accustomed to making decisions that would have to be approved formally long after the fact. This relative autonomy played a large part in Velásquez's concern in trying — and failing — to select a reliable commander for his third expedition. The great time lag between the New World and the Old was also what allowed Cortés to take the seemingly desperate political chances he did. There was little that could be done to stop his attempt to conquer Mexico, and he would have either succeeded or failed by the time the king could act. By then his political situation would probably be significantly different.[10]

This legal maneuver was carried out without the knowledge of Velásquez's supporters, who protested when they found out. To quiet them, Cortés said anyone who wished could return to Cuba. But through judicious inducements, he eventually won them over, primarily by promising an increase in their share of the proceeds from the expedition. Moreover, by cutting out Velásquez, there would now be more booty to distribute among the men.[11]

With his legal status resolved and dissension among the members of his expedition quelled, Cortés marched to nearby Cempohuallan, home of the Totonacs who had visited the Spanish camp. He reached the town on 3 June and was greeted with gifts of food and lodging. Several Maya groups had pledged nominal fealty to Cortés and given him supplies, but none had turned against their own lords. The Totonacs were the first Mesoamerican group to indicate a willingness — even an eagerness — to end support not for their own political lords, who governed legitimately, but for the Aztecs, a different ethnic group who were the Totonacs' political masters through right of conquest. This was a watershed for Cortés. The Totonacs had acquiesced to Aztec demands and become tributaries to the Aztecs under the reign of Moteuczoma's father, Axayacatl (ruled 1468–82). The Totonac ruler complained of this to Cortés, indicating that he paid allegiance not out of loyalty but out of fear. This was the first indication to Cortés that significant grievances and potential political cleavages existed among the Aztec tributaries, and he moved quickly to exploit these to his own advantage.[12]

It is tempting to credit Cortés with a grand scheme for the conquest of Mexico that he consistently and successfully carried out. But such does not appear to have been the case. Faced with entering an unknown, populous country, Cortés could have enlisted the help of more Spanish troops from the Indies, though this would have been complicated by his political difficulties with the governor of Cuba. The alternative was to entice large numbers of disaffected Indians to his cause, and the entire conquest period was marked by efforts to split and factionalize the Aztecs and their tributaries. Cortés promised to relieve the Totonacs' burdens and secured the Cempohuallan ruler's agreement to become a Spanish subject. This agreement ensured material support in the form of food, lodging, and porters but added little to his military capability.[13]

Two months later, on 18 August, the Spaniards marched farther up the coast toward another town, Quiahuiztlan, with fifteen horsemen, three hundred Spanish foot soldiers, and more than four hundred Indian porters. The Spaniards anticipated difficulty in conquering the fortified town, but to their surprise they were welcomed. Quiahuiztlan's rulers. too, complained of Aztec treatment, and Cortés again promised to do all he could, a pledge he would soon fulfill. When five Aztec tribute collectors arrived, they summoned the Totonac rulers and chastised them for feeding and housing the Spaniards without Moteuczoma's permission. Cortés in turn ordered the Totonacs not to pay any more tribute or obey Moteuczoma and to take the Aztecs prisoner. The Totonacs obeyed and seized the tribute collectors, but Cortés later had them secretly brought before him, pleaded ignorance about why the Totonacs had imprisoned them, and released two of them so they could assure Moteuczoma that the Spaniards were friends. When the Totonacs discovered that two captives were missing, Cortés feigned outrage and ordered the other three put on board his ship and guarded, but he secretly freed them as well. Nevertheless, Cortés gained Totonac pledges of fealty by promising to defend them from Moteuczoma's wrath. Still unsure about who might best serve his interests, Cortés was playing the two sides against each other.[14]

The ruler of Cempohuallan knew far better than Cortés what his pledge of fealty to the Spaniards was worth. Such pledges were not unusual in Mexico and were only as good as the new allies' ability to keep their subjects safe from Aztec retribution. If Cortés proved unable to do so, the Totonacs would quickly resubmit to the Aztecs, so the king's pledge was little more than a promise of support provided the Spaniards proved capable of defending this new political claim. The Aztecs had dealt with such uprisings before, typically reconquering rebellious cities and demanding increased tribute. But changing allegiance was an act that guaranteed devastating reprisals and was not done lightly or without a strong partner. The Totonacs doubtless saw the Spaniards as powerful, but their shift in allegiance was also forced by Spanish actions. Whether or not the Cempohualtecs played an active role in seizing the tribute collectors, the Aztecs would have held them responsible for the men's imprisonment, in effect forcing the Totonacs to ally with the Spaniards. Cortés's duplicitous actions cemented this realignment in the minds of the Aztecs.

Such local alliances were crucial to the Spaniards' success, because Cortés was not equipped to march overland without Indian support. His expedition had been planned for coastal exploration, and although his men and horses could march inland, they were ill equipped to transport the many supplies such a trek demanded. The Totonacs had, indeed, offered the Spaniards an opportunity to gain allies while dividing their opponents, but Cortés overestimated what he had gained and underestimated what he still faced.

So far the Spaniards had defeated all the Indians they had met and had done so unaided. They had decisively defeated the Mayas, cowed the Totonacs, and seemingly faced down thousands of Aztecs who refused to engage them in mock combat. The Spaniards were thus lulled into a false sense of military superiority. The armies they had faced were provincial forces, not a mainline Mexican army, well trained and battle hardened. Moreover, the Totonacs appeared to be valuable allies, because they numbered in the tens of thousands, but the advantage of this alliance was more apparent than real. For one thing, the Totonacs could not mount very formidable armies. The lowlands produced cotton, and some Totonac towns manufactured quilted cotton armor, but this was exported commercially and did not reflect local military use. While the Totonacs could muster many soldiers, theirs was not a professional army like the Aztecs'. They had a core of elite warriors, but most of their soldiers were commoners performing tributary service. Moreover, the Totonacs, like most other small Mesoamerican states of the time, had abandoned the deadly atlatl. The Totonacs' organizational weakness was belied by their numbers, giving the Spaniards a distorted view of what imperial Mesoamerican armies were like, and this misperception was the basis for Cortés's subsequent decisions about how to proceed against the Aztecs. During the first half of the trek inland, Cortés would remain confident of his ability to overcome all obstacles and would march with a force in which his Indian allies comprised a minority. He would rely almost exclusively on his own Spanish soldiers.[15]

Secure in their Totonac alliance, the Spaniards began building the city of Villa Rica de la Vera Cruz, including a fort with wooden walls, loopholes, watchtowers, and barbicans. In his chronicle, Díaz del Castillo claimed that Moteuczoma learned of the Totonac rebellion and raised an army to march against the Totonacs and the Spaniards, but such a course of action is inconsistent with Moteuczoma's other known behavior and is highly unlikely. Moteuczoma did send a party of high nobles to Cortés with a message of thanks for having freed the two Aztecs, but they also relayed complaints that the Spaniards had instigated the rebellion. In response, Cortés complained of the withdrawal of the earlier Aztec party, although he assured Moteuczoma that he knew this discourtesy was not the result of his orders. He explained that the Totonacs were now vassals of the king of Spain, that he and his followers were coming to Tenochtitlan to place themselves at Moteuczoma's service, and that thereafter the Totonacs would follow Aztec commands. The respect these noble Aztecs showed Cortés impressed the Totonacs, further buttressing the Spaniards' reputation and cementing their Totonac allegiance.[16]

The Cempohualtecs then asked Cortés's help against Tizapantzinco, whose Aztec garrison was destroying their crops. This put Cortés in an awkward position: he did not want to alienate the Aztecs, but Totonac support was his more immediate concern. Without it, an inland expedition was impossible — Cortés needed Totonac manpower as well as logistical and intelligence support en route, and the Totonacs' continued friendship was vital for the security of the settlement at Vera Cruz. Thus, Cortés decided to assist them and set out with four hundred soldiers, fourteen horsemen, his crossbowmen and harquebusiers, a hundred porters to carry the cannons, and four thousand Indian warriors. But the Aztecs had already left by the time Cortés reached Tizapantzinco, so he disarmed the remaining Indians and forced an alliance between the two groups before returning to Cempohuallan. This overt action against the Aztecs cemented Cortés's alliance with the Cempohualtecs, who then presented the Spaniards with eight women, all daughters of kings and nobles.[17]

As we have seen, intermarriage between ruling families of allied towns was a common way of strengthening political ties in Mesoamerica. Although the presentation of women had little actual effect on the Spaniards, it had great political significance for the Cempohualtecs in cementing this new political alliance. They could now expect Aztec reprisals, and without Spanish aid, the

Cempohualtec position was hopeless. Cortés took advantage of their dependence on the Spaniards to increase the division between the Aztecs and the Totonacs and simultaneously to tie Cempohuallan's rulers to him, which he did through religious conversion. Conversion was a prominent feature of the conquest, at least in the way the Spaniards later wrote of the events.

But whatever the sincerity of the Spaniards' religious beliefs and obligation to convert nonbelievers—after all, at least one of the Spaniards held captive among the Mayas had abandoned his faith—this was as much a legal requirement for justifying war as it was a religious imperative. There was a priest among the Spaniards, but his presence was apparently incidental, and Cortés's expedition did not include members of any regular orders to whom the conversion of the natives was entrusted. In any case, Cortés's efforts at conversion were thoroughly political. The prominence of temples and the ongoing human sacrifices reflected a powerful role for religion in native society, and Cortés challenged native beliefs only when it was politically feasible.

When Cortés first reached Cempohuallan, he asked that slaves being held for sacrifice be released. When this request was rebuffed, he did not insist, for that would have threatened the fledgling alliance he sought. But after the Totonacs openly broke with the Aztecs and became dependent on the Spaniards, Cortés's position was greatly strengthened. He took advantage of his increased power to destroy the Totonac idols and erect a cross and an image of the Virgin, despite protests by the native rulers. The Spaniards kept the Totonacs from attacking them over this affront only by seizing and threatening to kill their leaders. The Totonacs' knowledge of Christianity was superficial at best, but this was common in many missionization efforts. The Church was content with the acceptance of the outward manifestations of Christianity, leaving fuller understanding for the future. Superficiality alone, therefore, throws no doubt on Cortés's sincerity in his missionizing role, but his timing does. Cortés's aim in forcing even superficial religious conversions was primarily political, both to justify his actions to the Spanish throne and to cement his alliances in Mexico. Though they protested, Cempohuallan's leaders were no longer in a position to resist Spanish demands: they had to accept the destruction of their old gods and the introduction of new ones or risk the loss of Spanish support, which would mean their sure destruction at the hands of the Aztecs. And by acquiescing to Cortés's actions, the Totonac leaders lost the religious support of their own priests and probably needed the Spaniards to retain their political positions. The destruction of the Totonac gods marked a change in political support more than it did a change in religious belief by the indigenous leadership.[18]

Thereafter, the Spaniards returned to Vera Cruz, where a ship from Cuba had landed, bringing eleven men and two horses. The ship also brought news that King Charles had granted Velásquez authority to trade and establish settlements—a direct threat to the new legal position Cortés was working to create. Cortés decided he had to act, and in an effort to present his claim, he sent the king not just the royal fifth of the goods collected, to which he was legally entitled, but all the gold collected so far. This he dispatched to Spain by ship on 26 July 1519, some two months after he landed on the Veracruz coast. Despite Cortés's explicit order that the ship sail directly to Spain, it stopped in Cuba, and word of its purpose reached Velásquez, who tried to capture it. Although he failed and the ship continued to Spain, this obvious perfidy prompted Velásquez to ready a large fleet under Pánfilo de Narváez to capture Cortés.[19]

Even as Cortés forged an alliance with the Totonacs, disaffection was brewing among the Spaniards. When some of Velásquez's supporters conspired to seize a ship to sail to Cuba, Cortés arrested them and ordered the two principal conspirators hanged, the pilot's feet cut off, and the sailors given two hundred lashes each. Apparently, not all these sentences were carried out, for one of the men sentenced to death is recorded later in the conquest. Cortés was probably also concerned about reducing his forces, which could affect the success of his incursions into the interior. At the same time, he feared the disaffected Spaniards could still escape to Cuba. Accordingly, he stripped the ten remaining ships of their equipment, including anchors, cables, and sails, declared them unfit, and grounded them. The destruction of the ships was carried out in secret and caused outrage among many of the Spaniards, especially those loyal to Velásquez, but it left them with little option except to follow Cortés. The now shipless sailors were added to his army, as were six men captured later from a ship sighted near Vera Cruz.[20]

With no hope of returning home, Cortés and his army forged ahead with their plans to overthrow the Aztecs. The Totonac alliance was critical to these plans: it profoundly altered the Spaniards' capabilities by ensuring them supplies and overland transport. They would now be accompanied by Indian allies to carry food, water, and arms, serve as guides, aid in the fighting, and ease their passage through towns en route. With an inland trek now possible, Cortés put Juan de Escalante in command of Vera Cruz with 60 to 150 soldiers and prepared for the march.[21]

Cortés asked the king of Cempohuallan for forty or fifty warriors and two hundred porters, which he received. On 16 August he left Cempohuallan with three hundred Spanish soldiers accompanied by Indians carrying the artillery. Cortés had four falconets and ten larger cannons, referred to as lombards. Large numbers of native porters meant the falconets could accompany the army, but the heavier lombards were not very mobile. Their weight was a minor hindrance on ships or in encampments near shore, but there were too few Spaniards to carry them inland for any appreciable distance. Therefore Cortés left some of the cannons in Vera Cruz — probably the lombards, which would have placed greater demands on the porters and presumably were considered inessential against Indians who lacked firearms. They would be useful in Vera Cruz, for they would be more effective against any forces sent by Velásquez.[22]

Moteuczoma could not have remained ignorant of events on the coast, no matter how imperfect his intelligence might have been. A major tributary had rebelled, another had been conquered, and the Spaniards were marching toward Tenochtitlan against his expressed wishes. Yet the Aztecs still took no offensive action. Why was Moteuczoma so passive?

Between the landings of Grijalva and Cortés, Moteuczoma had consulted with his priests and advisors: how the Spaniards should be treated was not his decision alone but was also the considered opinion of his counselors. Moteuczoma probably played a major, if not pivotal, role in deciding to take no action, but the decision was one in which all the advisors had a stake, and not even the king could disregard or change it without risking his political support. Thus, unmolested by the Aztecs, Cortés's force marched toward Tenochtitlan, passing through Xicochimalco and Ixhuacan before reaching a cold, uninhabited desert. Their food was exhausted, and several Indians Cortés had brought from Cuba died of privation and exposure. The Spaniards and their allies marched for three more days before reaching Tzauhtlan, where they were again given shelter and food.[23]

As elsewhere, Cortés had the town's ruler instructed about Christianity and asked him to stop human sacrifice and idol worship, but did not insist. The people of Tzauhtlan were Aztec tributaries, and destroying their temples and idols would have provoked a violent response, precisely the result the Spaniards could least afford. The issue could be forced only if the people were dependent on the Spaniards, as they would be if they rebelled against the Aztecs. Thus, leaving intact the religious practices of Aztec loyalists, the Spaniards enjoyed a relatively unmolested inland trek. As long as the Aztecs took no offensive action, neither would their tributaries.[24]

Despite the recommendation of Tzauhtlan's ruler that he march to Tenochtitlan by way of Cholollan, Cortés followed the advice of the Cempohualtecs, who warned that the Chololtecs were treacherous Aztec allies. He chose instead to go through Tlaxcallan, which was hostile to the Aztecs. Cortés demanded and received twenty noble warriors from Tzauhtlan to accompany him and marched onward to Iztac-Maxtitlan. There he learned that the Tlaxcaltecs were armed against the Spaniards, so he dispatched Cempohualtec messengers with an appeal for friendship. The Tlaxcaltecs did not respond.[25]

What the Tlaxcaltecs understood is uncertain. They must have been aware of the Spaniards' arrival on the coast and of their progress inland. But because many of the accompanying Indians were Aztec tributaries, and because Cortés had just spent a number of peaceful days in towns allied with the Aztecs, the Tlaxcaltecs naturally presumed the Spaniards to be hostile.

The Spaniards continued toward Tlaxcallan until they saw a small party of armed Indians. Their horsemen advanced to capture them, but the Indians fought back, wounding three horses and killing two, and wounding two riders. This was part of a standard Mesoamerican stratagem in which a small force attacked and then fell back, enticing the enemy forward into a compromising position. When the Spaniards pursued them, a concealed force of perhaps three thousand ambushed the Spaniards in what should have been a decisive blow. But the Spaniards were saved by their crossbows and harquebuses, weapons hitherto unknown in central Mexico.[26]

The battle took place on level ground where the Spaniards could use their rapid-firing artillery, harquebuses, and crossbows, and the Indians were gradually forced back. The cannons and harquebuses were effective but probably functioned at less than optimum: the Spaniards had been on the march and had time to do little more than assemble into formations. This haste had no effect on the use of lances, crossbows, and swords, but it did on firearms, because there was no time to prepare their gunpowder properly. Although often impure, gunpowder of the day was usually one-half saltpeter, one-third charcoal, and one-sixth sulfur. The jostling of transport caused these ingredients to stratify and required remixing for effective use, so when the Spaniards were attacked, they either had to delay combat to remix their powder or fire poorly mixed powder that was less effective.[27] Tlaxcaltec weapons proved effective, especially missiles directed against unarmored soldiers. Arrows depended on penetration, which was largely thwarted by Spanish armor, but slingstones drew their effect from the force of impact, against which steel armor offered only partial protection and provoked many Spanish complaints. Four Spaniards were wounded in this battle, and one later died, as did seventeen Tlaxcaltecs.[28]

The Indians were beaten back, but the Spaniards had suffered a serious shock and were in for more in the days to come. The Tlaxcaltecs were professional soldiers, skilled beyond any the Spaniards had yet encountered in Mesoamerica. They attacked in unison, used complementary shock and projectile weapons, and displayed a high degree of expertise. Cortés's decision to march inland with virtually no allies had been based on the groups he had seen so far, but these warriors were a much greater threat than he could reasonably have anticipated. Had the Spaniards made a more informed and realistic assessment of the risks they faced, dissension would doubtless have been greater, and the expedition would have been endangered if it was attempted at all.[29]

The Tlaxcaltec attack was even more threatening politically than militarily. Cortés had promised aid to his Indian allies, so if he retreated now he would be perceived as weak and his promises meaningless. At best his allies would stop all aid; at worst they would turn on him. Cortés had gambled that he could overcome all potential adversaries, but the situation he met was vastly different from what he had expected. Still, once he had staked all on succeeding, the threat to his alliances prevented him from following the most prudent military course — withdrawal.[30] The battle ended at dusk, but the next day, 2 September, six thousand Tlaxcaltec warriors marched toward the Spanish camp. Cortés then released three Tlaxcaltec prisoners with the message that he did not want war. Releasing captives with peace entreaties was a standard Spanish tactic throughout the conquest, the goal being to acquire allies at minimal cost. This was consistent with Cortés's overall strategy of dividing the enemy, but now it was also vital to Spanish survival. If a truce could not be negotiated, the battle would eventually be lost, despite the Spaniards' technological advantages. Yet Cortés's entreaties went unanswered.

When the Tlaxcaltecs next attacked, they were driven back by cannon, harquebus, and crossbow fire, and the Spaniards followed their retreating enemies — right into another ambush. Surrounded and assailed on all sides, the Spaniards were afraid to charge with their horses lest their formation fragment and be routed. Under assault, they could not attack, but Spanish firepower was effective against the tightly massed Tlaxcaltecs, who finally withdrew. This allowed the Spaniards to fall back to some more easily defended nearby temples, though at a cost of one Spaniard dead, fifteen wounded, and four or five horses killed.[31]

The Spaniards were in a precarious position: they did not dominate the battlefield, they were seriously threatened, and they could only adopt a defensive stance. If they stayed on the defensive, the battle would degenerate into a war of attrition that the Spaniards would inevitably lose, given the Tlaxcaltecs' great numerical superiority. But attacking the Tlaxcaltec main forces was infeasible, because any advance would inevitably open gaps in the Spanish formations, with disastrous consequences. Therefore, the Spaniards directed their offensive at nearby towns, where their speed and power could be demonstrated without revealing the weaknesses that would be evident in a conventional encounter.

Hoping also to restock their rations, they sent out a party of two hundred soldiers, seven horsemen, a few harquebusiers and crossbowmen, and their Indian allies, attacked some towns, and captured twenty Indians, but failed to find any food.

Cortés had experienced little difficulty in securing local supplies to this point, but the Tlaxcaltecs followed a scorched earth policy that left virtually nothing behind, so once within Tlaxcallan territory the Spaniards could no longer count on local towns to provide food. They could rely only on the food they carried with them, yet their few porters could supply a force of that size for only a few days, which left the Spaniards dangerously underprovisioned. Once again they released prisoners to plead for peace, but these entreaties, too, were rejected.[32]

The Tlaxcaltecs attacked again the next day, beginning the battle in conventional Mesoamerican fashion with a barrage of arrows, slingstones, and darts before advancing for hand-to-hand combat. The Spaniards avoided being overwhelmed only by using their superior firepower to disrupt the attackers' formations. To concentrate and increase their effectiveness, Cortés divided his men, ordering some to reload crossbows and harquebuses while others fired, and he directed the mounted lancers to make short forays to disrupt the Tlaxcaltecs' formations, frustrating their attack and rendering them vulnerable to counterattack. The Spaniards, by contrast, faced no weapons equally disruptive of their own formations, and the Tlaxcaltecs eventually withdrew. But the clash left all of the horses wounded, one Spaniard dead, and sixty more injured.[33]

Having fared poorly in a frontal daylight assault, the Tlaxcaltecs next tried a night attack, a type of offensive that in Mesoamerica was generally restricted to small-scale raids. The main difficulty in a night attack is maintaining communications in the dark to deploy forces properly. That the Tlaxcaltecs launched one suggests that Spanish firepower was taking a heavy toll, and the Tlaxcaltecs doubtless hoped this change in tactics would be more successful. Cannons, harquebuses, and crossbows all had greater effective ranges than Indian weapons, and this larger killing zone meant that if the Tlaxcaltecs tried to close for hand-to-hand combat, they had to do so through a lethal field of Spanish fire. The Tlaxcaltecs were vulnerable longer because they had to charge into the guns, whereas the outnumbered Spaniards generally did not advance. Furthermore, because the Tlaxcaltec archers and slingers remained behind the frontline troops, their fire was even less effective than that of the Spaniards. A night attack, however, reduced this Spanish advantage by concealing the targets in darkness.

A standard Spanish tactic was to watch enemy arrows in flight and dodge or deflect them, and the farther away the archers were, the easier this was to accomplish. A night attack neutralized this advantage, leaving the Spaniards vulnerable to now-unseen arrows. The Spaniards could still shoot back, but at only one-sixth the rate of fire of the Tlaxcaltecs. The Spaniards depended on accuracy that the night denied them, while the higher rate of bow, sling, and atlatl fire allowed the Indians to pour multiple volleys into the massed and immobile Spaniards.[34]

Ten thousand warriors, led by their commanding general, Xicotencatl, attacked the Spaniards' camp. But in an effort to limit their exposure to the devastating Spanish fire, the archers, slingers, and atlatlists held back in units so they did not have to maneuver. From the protective darkness, they assailed the hemmed-in Spaniards on three sides. Then the Tlaxcaltec swordsmen rushed across the killing zone and engaged them hand to hand, forcing the Spaniards to defend themselves with swords and pikes, a fairer match for the native weapons. These tactics minimized the Spanish advantage in firepower, but the mounted lancers managed to disrupt the Tlaxcaltec formations and expose their vulnerable flanks to Spanish steel. Unable to reassemble in the dark, the Tlaxcaltecs ultimately failed in their attack.[35]

Despite this success, the Spaniards' position was eroding

badly. More than forty-five men had been killed since leaving Vera Cruz, another dozen were ill, several horses had been slain, and food supplies were dwindling. How serious this last problem was is uncertain, but both food and arms were being consumed at prodigious rates. Most of the food was carried by two hundred Indian porters from Cempohuallan. On average, each porter carried 23 kilograms (50 pounds, or roughly 23 man-days of food), although this was replenished en route through Spanish demands on local towns. But because there were two Spanish or Indian soldiers for every porter, Cortés's forces carried only eight days' supply, and once in hostile territory, this was rapidly exhausted.[36]

Equally seriously, Spanish arms were dwindling, too. Unlike swords, lances, and pikes, projectiles are exhausted in use, and the Spaniards had a limited supply. Most crossbow bolts probably were not recovered after battle, and at one shot per minute, each hour of combat cost sixty bolts — weighing 2.2–4.1 kilograms (6–11 pounds) — per crossbow, or 72–131 kilograms (200–350 pounds) for all thirty-two crossbows. Each harquebus could fire as fast as once every minute and a half, expending forty 47-gram (2-ounce) balls per hour, plus an equal weight of powder, for a combined total of 3.7 kilograms (10 pounds) per harquebus — 49 kilograms (130 pounds) for all thirteen harquebusiers — per hour. In addition, the four falconets each fired shot weighing 0.28–0.93 kilograms (0.75–2.5 pounds), with a like weight of powder, at least as rapidly as the harquebuses, for a total hourly cost of 22–75 kilograms (60–200 pounds). Thus, an hour of vigorous combat with all crossbows, harquebuses, and falconets consumed 150–260 kilograms (400–700 pounds) of largely unretrievable armaments — a total of eight to fourteen porter loads.

Each porter diverted to the task of carrying powder, shot, and bolts reduced Cortés's ability to march by twenty-three man-days, or one day's supply for the entire company for every twenty-nine porters so diverted. And each hour of vigorous combat cost the army from one-third to one-half a day's food supply. At these rates, even if half the porters carried powder and shot, the Spaniards could fight actively for only seven to twelve and a half hours, and they could subsist on their own food supplies for just four days. How many porters were engaged in transporting arms versus food is unknown, but because all the armaments had to be transported from Vera Cruz, Cortés had to have made this decision from the outset, and he underestimated the magnitude of the opposition he would meet. Considering the food required to support his men on some of the long stretches between sizable towns, Cortés must have used at least a hundred porters for carrying food. After having repulsed the Tlaxcaltecs, his supply situation must have been precarious.

The Spaniards would have been lost if the Tlaxcaltecs had encircled and contained them. Besieged, they would have been completely cut off from further supplies and unable to threaten nearby towns. As it was, the Spaniards successfully attacked undefended towns, and although they were too few to be a significant military threat, their perceived menace was doubtless much greater in Tlaxcaltec eyes. The Tlaxcaltecs did not try sustained encirclement, probably because this ran counter to Mesoamerican military practices, which were shaped by logistical constraints. Offensive armies typically lacked the logistical support to remain in the field for long, and if defeated, they usually withdrew. A major defeat or even a draw generally sent the invaders away, so encirclement and wars of annihilation were unusual and unnecessary. That the Spaniards did not withdraw, as the Tlaxcaltecs could justifiably expect, was less a tribute to their skills than to their lack of alternatives.

Once again Cortés sent messages of peace, coupled with threats to kill all the Tlaxcaltecs and destroy their country if a peace was not reached within two days. It was beyond Cortés's ability to carry out this threat, but the Tlaxcaltecs could not have known this with certainty. The Spaniards' limited success in battle and their precarious position further eroded support in Cortés's own camp. His men were near mutiny, demanding that they return to the coast, but doing so would have unraveled Cortés's fragile Indian alliance and signaled the end of his aspirations in Mexico. Once more, through cajoling and promises, he persuaded the men to stay.

Returning to the offensive, perhaps as much to forage for food and encourage his men as to bolster his threat to the Tlaxcaltecs, Cortés attacked the Otomi town of Tecoac, routed the defenders, and sacked it. The Spaniards next marched on Tzompantzinco, one league away, but its inhabitants fled. When the Spaniards did not harm the town, the lords of Tzompantzinco approached with food and apologized for not bringing it to their camp when first asked.[37]

Although mounted lancers played an important role in these offensive thrusts, they were not decisive alone. Horsemen had speed and mobility and could disrupt the enemy, but they could not hold what they had taken. Foot soldiers were needed to hold an objective, so except for scouting and short forays, the horsemen accompanied the foot soldiers, which reduced the horses' speed and mobility to that of the party as a whole.

By this time Cortés's forces were reduced to approximately 250 Spaniards (and not all were fit), about ten horses (all wounded), about two hundred noncombatant porters, and fewer than a hundred Indian warriors who, judging by their small losses, played a minimal role in combat. Facing thousands of enemy soldiers, Cortés's ultimate defeat was inevitable. The Spanish forces were battered and badly divided, though this remained unknown to the Tlaxcaltecs. Because Cortés continued to make forays against nearby villages and small towns, he was able to maintain a facade of success.[38]

The Tlaxcaltecs were now reconsidering their own position. They had received a series of messengers — Cempohualtecs as well as released Tlaxcaltecs — asking for peace and bringing information about Spanish actions elsewhere. Moreover, the Spaniards appeared to be successful: even though some Spaniards and horses had been killed, Tlaxcaltec losses were higher. Indeed, the disparity between their respective casualties probably seemed much greater, because the Tlaxcaltecs had an accurate view of their own losses but not of Spanish casualties, which Cortés tried to conceal. Just as the Spaniards were divided over what to do, so were the Tlaxcaltecs — perhaps even more so.

Tlaxcallan was a confederacy of four provinces — Quiyahuiztlan, Tepeticpac, Tizatlan, and Ocotelolco — each with its own king. When Cortés arrived, Tizatlan's ruler, Xicotencatl the Elder, and Ocotelolco's ruler, Maxixcatl, were vying for dominance of the confederation, with the allied city of Huexotzinco playing a secondary role.[39]

Maxixcatl's power was economic, because Ocotelolco was the site of the main market, whereas Xicotencatl the Elder's power lay with the military. Tizatlan controlled the army, whose leading commander was the king's thirty-five-year-old son and heir apparent, Xicotencatl the Younger. Xicotencatl's decision to attack the Spaniards was guaranteed to put Maxixcatl in the opposition camp.[40]

Many Spaniards had been killed, and almost all the rest were wounded. Tlaxcallan was winning, but the battles were dragging on, and the Tlaxcaltecs own losses were high, which must have weighed against the pro-war faction. Eventually the Spaniards and the Indians reached an alliance. Although Cortés took credit for it, the alliance was actually initiated by the Tlaxcaltecs, in view of their geopolitical situation. They had fought the Aztecs for decades, but they were now in an eroding situation, completely encircled by Aztec tributaries and largely cut off from external trade. Without a profound alteration of the political situation, Tlaxcallan's defeat by the Aztecs was only a matter of time. What impelled them to ally with the Spaniards was recognition of the superiority of their arms, which could mean a shift in the balance of power.[41]

Spanish cannons, harquebuses, crossbows, and horsemen

could all disrupt enemy lines at a distance and in a way Indian arms could not match. Once a breach was opened, Indian formations were extremely vulnerable. Even when combat was hand to hand, the Spaniards greatly benefited from their armor. Although many of the Spaniards did not have steel armor, they did have some, and all had cotton armor, so the most vulnerable parts of their bodies were protected, in contrast to most of their attackers.

Thus, while the Spaniards enjoyed greater firepower, which prevented their enemies from engaging them in organized formations, and although they could disrupt the enemy front much more easily than could Mesoamerican armies, they were too few to exploit these breaches fully. If they joined forces with large Indian armies, however, these allies could exploit the breaches created by the Spaniards while maintaining the integrity of their own units, because other Indian armies lacked the Spanish edge in arms and armor. Together they could wreak havoc on the enemy.

Both sides may have recognized that an alliance could produce an exceptional fighting force in which the Spaniards would serve as shock troops for the vastly larger Indian support forces. But the decision to seek an alliance did not lie with the Spaniards, who were being battered and were in danger of annihilation. It lay with the Tlaxcaltecs, for only they could halt the attack and initiate an alliance.

A Tlaxcaltec victory over the Spaniards would have been Pyrrhic at best. It would have cost so many dead and wounded that continued resistance to the Aztecs would have been greatly undermined and the Tlaxcaltecs' own conquest hastened. If, however, the Tlaxcaltecs allied with the Spaniards, the regional balance of power might shift to their advantage. They would suffer no more casualties against the Spaniards, they would gain a numerically small but powerful ally, and even more importantly, they would deprive the Aztecs of one. The Tlaxcaltecs could have defeated the Spaniards or simply withdrawn: their decision to seek an alliance was a deliberate choice and theirs alone.

This decision was not without opposition. The Tlaxcaltec council ordered the army's commander, Xicotencatl the Younger, to break off his attacks. When he ignored them, Chichimecateuctli, the commander of Ocotelolco's forces, withdrew his men and Huexotzinco's, leaving Xicotencatl with too few men to guarantee success. Even then, he sent spies into the Spaniards' camp on the pretext of delivering food, but Cortés seized and interrogated them, cut the thumbs off some and the hands off others, and sent them back.[42]

Such harsh dealings stood in stark contrast to his treatment of earlier captives. Previously, Cortés had desperately needed a cease-fire and gradually released his prisoners unharmed with requests for peace. But now, facing fewer attackers, he found the situation shifting to his advantage. He traded the olive branch for the sword and mutilated the Tlaxcaltecs as an exercise in political terrorism.

The Tlaxcaltecs had not been defeated: their decision to make peace was a political rather than a military one. Four nobles approached the Spanish camp and said they had fought because they believed the Spaniards were Aztec allies. They claimed that the first attacks had been carried out by the Otomis without orders from the Tlaxcaltecs. Both claims were probably true, at least in part. Because Aztecs accompanied the Spaniards, who had just come from an Aztec tributary town, Cortés did indeed appear to be their ally. And the Tlaxcaltecs had allowed Otomis fleeing the Aztecs to settle in villages on their borders to serve as buffers and guard against encroachment, so the earliest attacks probably were initiated by Otomis, although doubtless with the full knowledge of Tlaxcallan's rulers.[43]

In any case, these disclaimers enabled the Tlaxcaltecs to offer, and Cortés to accept, a peace at the status quo without requiring either retaliation or retribution. Accordingly, Cortés promised the Tlaxcaltecs assistance against the Aztecs, gave them gifts, and asked that a delegation be sent with fuller powers to make peace.

Although these and subsequent events make it clear that the Tlaxcaltecs were the dominant party in this alliance, again Cortés char-
acteristically claimed that they pledged fealty as his vassals, and
he soon traveled to Tlaxcallan.[44]

Aztec emissaries accompanied Cortés throughout his trek, so
Moteuczoma learned of these events shortly after they occurred.
Cortés's negotiations with their Tlaxcaltec enemies was disturbing
to the Aztec emissaries, and they asked him to defer any decision
for six days while they sent this news to Moteuczoma and awaited
a reply. Cortés agreed. Nobles soon arrived from Tenochtitlan with
gifts and a message from Moteuczoma, asking Cortés not to go to
Tlaxcallan because the people were treacherous. Spanish accounts
claim that Moteuczoma also offered to become Cortés's vassal and
pay him tribute, though this is at odds with both his subsequent
actions and his refusal to invite the Spaniards to Tenochtitlan.
Nevertheless, while the Tlaxcaltecs offered peace and an alliance,
Tenochtitlan was Cortés's primary goal, and he was still negotiating with the Aztecs.[45]

The Aztecs were clearly the more powerful group, but faced
with Moteuczoma's courteous intransigence, not to mention the
Spaniards certain annihilation if the Tlaxcaltecs continued to fight
them, their offer of an alliance from the latter could not be refused.
Cortés tacitly accepted the Tlaxcaltecs' offer and requested porters
to carry his cannons, which were quickly supplied. The next day,
23 September 1519, the Spaniards marched into Tlaxcallan, just
five months after landing in Veracruz.[46]

Despite allying with the Tlaxcaltecs, Cortés was intent on
preserving his relationship with Moteuczoma and asked that the
accompanying Aztec nobles be admitted to Tlaxcallan and lodged
with him, and this was permitted. Once Cortés was in Tlaxcallan,
its rulers presented him with gifts and with their daughters, a
common means of cementing alliances in Mesoamerica.[47]

Cortés claimed to have erected an altar where a mass was said,
and the next day he instructed the Tlaxcaltecs about Christianity

and asked, but did not insist, that they adopt it. The rulers said their priests and people would rebel if they were forced to adopt the new religion. They did permit one of the temples to be cleaned, however, so that a cross and an image of the Virgin could be erected, and the daughters of the rulers were baptized. But as with both previous and subsequent groups, the religious conversion of the Tlaxcaltecs was not immediate. They allowed Christian images to be erected because, as polytheists, they found the addition of foreign gods acceptable. But rejecting their own gods, as messianic, monotheistic Christianity demanded, was unacceptable, and forcing the issue could undermine the kings' support among both priests and commoners. The Spaniards sought conversions to secure their political alliances, and native rulers declared public conversion only after their political fates were inextricably tied to the Spaniards. This guaranteed continued Spanish support, without which the rulers were vulnerable, not just to the Aztecs but also to the internal unrest that such conversions would engender.[48]

Once in Tlaxcallan, Cortés sought information about the Aztecs. He was told about their large army and given a description of Tenochtitlan and its defenses, but still he underestimated the Aztec threat. He knew Moteuczoma had been unable to conquer Tlaxcallan despite many attempts, which led him to believe that this newfound ally was at least roughly comparable in power to the Aztecs. True, the Tlaxcaltecs had prevailed defensively where the advantage should have been theirs, and this did indicate a significant military capability, much of which Cortés had already witnessed. But what Cortés could not have appreciated was that the Tlaxcaltecs had not enjoyed this success in a conventional war but were locked in a flower war with the Aztecs.[49]

As I mentioned earlier, the goal of a flower war was to pin down strong opponents, encircle them, and slowly strangle them. This had been under way in Tlaxcallan for decades. Once it was isolated and without allies, it would be finally defeated, as other city-states and confederacies had been. Thus, Cortés's assessment of the relative strength of his allies was based on a misunderstanding. The Tlaxcaltecs had not enjoyed their success against the Aztecs in a series of conventional clashes — such victories would have supported his assessment. But Cortés's estimate of his allies' strength was seemingly supported by two other observations: Moteuczoma's continued gift giving and his failure to attack.[50]

Whenever an Indian group offered vassalage to the Spaniards, whether freely or following conquest, it gave them gifts in acknowledgment of this new status. But the Aztecs had brought the Spaniards gifts from the outset, leading them to believe that Moteuczoma, too, was offering vassalage. Offering gifts, however, did not necessarily mean political subordination, something the Spaniards either did not or chose not to recognize. The Aztecs' gifts were offered in homage to possible gods, not in vassalage to men, so the two sides viewed the significance of gift-giving very differently. Even had the Aztecs offered gifts in political homage, they would have done so within the Mesoamerican tradition of hegemonic rule, in which the goal was to acknowledge tacit vassalage and pay tribute in order to be left in peace. Cortés functioned with a European notion of political domination. Unsatisfied with moderate exaction and indirect control through the existing political regime, he sought the ouster of that regime, direct rule, and the undivided wealth this would offer.

That the Aztecs were acknowledging vassalage was further supported in the eyes of the Spaniards by Moteuczoma's failure to attack so far, which indeed seems strange. It can be attributed to three factors. First, Moteuczoma was still uncertain about the identity and intentions of these strangers and was reluctant to attack them until he had more information. Second, to reduce his vulnerability to overthrow by domestic challengers, Moteuczoma had reorganized Aztec imperial society to broaden his political support by incorporating nobles from tributary towns. This was an admirable strategy as long as Tenochtitlan remained the dominant power, but the arrival of the Spaniards and their alliances with city-states to the east significantly changed this, undermining Moteuczoma's external political support and weakening him at home. This made changing his original position on the Spaniards dangerous if it now supported the position of any potential challenger. And third, even if he had wanted war, Moteuczoma could not have marshaled a large army at that time. Only during the dry period following the harvest were large numbers of men available for such service, adequate food supplies available to sustain them en route, and roads passable and streams fordable by large armies. This is why Aztec wars took place primarily between December and April. During the summer rainy season, most commoners were engaged in agricultural and related pursuits and could not be diverted without damage to the economy. Moteuczoma did have a corps of elite soldiers — perhaps a few thousand — but they were too few for an assault against the Spaniards and their allies in distant Tlaxcallan.

Thus, Moteuczoma's failure to attack was soundly based, but the Spaniards probably misinterpreted it as weakness. Nevertheless, Cortés's experiences in battle against the confronting Tlaxcaltecs resulted in a significant shift in his own strategy. Although he had confidently begun his campaign with only a minority of allied support, after his beating at Tlaxcaltec hands he was always accompanied by far larger allied forces, such that his own Spaniards constituted no more than 10 percent of the army's force.[51]

CHAPTER 5

THE MARCH TO TENOCHTITLAN

Cortés stayed in Tlaxcallan for seventeen days before resuming his march to Tenochtitlan. When he did, he went by way of Cholollan, where, according to conventional accounts, one of the least explicable events of the trek took place. Cholollan was an Aztec ally, and the Tlaxcaltecs reportedly tried to dissuade Cortés from going there. Cortés's own stated purpose in going to Cholollan was to gather supplies, because it was a large city, but this claim does not ring true. Cholollan was no closer to Tenochtitlan than was Tlaxcallan (see map 2), where supplies were already available, so a logistical purpose for the trip is unlikely. If supplies actually were a concern, Cortés would have been significantly better off obtaining them from allied Huexotzinco, which was a full day's march closer to Tenochtitlan. His real purpose in going was political.[1]

Cortés and an accompanying five thousand to six thousand Tlaxcaltec warriors marched toward Cholollan, completing most of the trek before making camp for the night. He was welcomed by Chololtec nobles who brought food and requested that the Tlaxcaltec warriors remain there, which they did. Only the Spaniards entered Cholollan the next morning, accompanied by the Cempohualtecs and Tlaxcaltecs who carried the cannons. They were well housed and fed for two days before the food inexplicably stopped arriving. This was only one of several acts the Spaniards recorded as hostile or suspicious. Others were that concealed pits with sharpened stakes had been constructed around the city; that the city itself was filled with barricades and that stones were piled on the rooftops, waiting to be thrown; and that an Aztec army of twenty thousand to thirty thousand men was hidden nearby, waiting to attack. These observations or rumors foreshadowed the Cempohualtecs' report that the Chololtecs planned to attack the Spaniards. In a preemptive move, Cortés assembled Chololtecs in the main courtyard, placed armed Spaniards at every entrance, and then massacred the unarmed Indians.[2]

Despite nearly unanimous Spanish support for this account of the Cholollan massacre, it, too, rings false. As for the Aztec army, it is unlikely that Aztec messengers could have run from Tlaxcallan to Tenochtitlan (at least one day's run), raised an army (normally requiring five to eight days), especially in the agricultural season when few men could be spared from the fields, and marched to Cholollan (at least three days) in the short time required for the Spaniards to reach and enter Cholollan. Moreover, this army apparently evaporated after the massacre; none of the Spaniards mentioned it again.[3]

As for the other ominous portents Cortés claimed, camouflaged pits with sharpened wooden stakes in the bottom were developed in Europe as an anticavalry defense but were not used against slow-moving infantry, who could more easily detect and avoid them. It seems far likelier that these pits were a Spanish fabrication based on what they might have encountered in Europe than that the Chololtecs invented an ideal anticavalry defense, unprecedented in Mexican warfare, despite having never before seen horses.[4]

The last two items of evidence of Chololtec hostility — the stoppage of provisions after two days and the barricaded streets and stones on rooftops — cannot be verified either way. If true, the barricades and stones were openly apparent and probably not directed against the Spaniards. And if food was stopped, it might have been aimed at encouraging the Spaniards to leave, or perhaps it had to do with the four-day fast accompanying the festival of Tlalocan, which took place around this time.[5]

When the claimed provocations are more fully examined, it appears that Cortés did not take desperate measures against a duplicitous enemy but rather created a pretext for the massacre. Why did he do it? The answer lies in his subsequent actions.

After the massacre, Cortés claimed that he placed another noble on the throne before departing Cholollan. It is true that a massacre happened there and that a new ruler took the throne. Cortés's hand may have struck the blow, but the mastermind was Tlaxcaltec.[6]

Though Cortés was now nominally an ally of the Tlaxcaltecs, they could not have trusted him. When he first entered their territory, he was accompanied by Aztecs and by Totonacs who were apparently still Aztec tributaries, and he had initiated the attack on the Tlaxcaltecs. Proof of his trustworthiness was needed, and Cholollan offered the perfect test.

Cholollan had been a Tlaxcallan ally until the previous year or two, when it shifted to the Aztecs. Losing Cholollan as an ally politically diminished Tlaxcallan and posed a military threat. The shift struck particularly hard at Maxixcatl, ruler of the Tlaxcallan province of Ocotelolco, because he was tied by kinship to Cholollan's previous ruling lineage. The new ruler of Cholollan had not yet had time to consolidate his position, and the city remained divided, with half the nobles supporting Tlaxcallan and half the Aztecs. Toppling the new ruler and reinstating the previous ruling lineage would change all that. The events at Cholollan, therefore, transformed Tlaxcallan from an embattled confederacy surrounded by enemy states to a significant power with a renewed alliance with Cholollan and a new ally who possessed pivotally effective arms. And within the Tlaxcallan confederacy, Maxixcatl's eroding position vis-à-vis Xicotencatl the Elder had been greatly enhanced.[7]

Cortés did benefit from the conquest of Cholollan by removing an Aztec ally that straddled the main route between Tenochtitlan and Vera Cruz, posed a danger to communications between the two, and would have threatened Cortés's rear once he marched on to Tenochtitlan. But were these remarkable political transformations the fruits of Cortés's military and political genius? It appears extremely unlikely.

It is unclear how much Cortés understood about the nature of rulership and alliances in Mexico. Even if he had grasped how the local political system worked, he would not have known which nobles supported which side, and in any case his troops were militarily subordinate to the more numerous Tlaxcaltecs. Yet all the pieces fell unerringly into place, resulting in a major political reconfiguration of the region. And the primary beneficiaries were the Tlaxcaltecs — the same people who needed to test the Spaniards' loyalty, who knew how Mexican royal succession systems worked, and who knew which of the Chololtec nobles supported them and which supported the Aztecs. In short, although Cortés chronicled the massacre as having been provoked by Chololtec duplicity in order to justify it under Spanish law, it far likelier was an unprovoked massacre carried out at the behest and with the assistance of the Tlaxcaltecs. The attack was a litmus test of Spanish loyalty; it would undermine a now despised enemy and place the Spaniards in opposition to Moteuczoma. Moreover, it forced the Spaniards to demonstrate their loyalty while the Tlaxcaltecs risked nothing. A Spanish hand was on the sword, but Indian minds guided it.

Some of the Spaniards later justified the massacre by claiming that one of the Indian women accompanying them, La Malinche, learned of a Chololtec plot from a local woman and warned Cortés, who then turned the tables on the Chololtecs. But La Malinche's part went virtually unreported in the earliest account, Cortés's; it emerged and was elaborated only decades later, most likely to justify Cortés's actions under Spanish law. And although the massacre was widely known, La Malinche's "discovery" of the plot was not. Moreover, whatever she might have learned (she spoke only Maya and Nahuatl), she could have told only to Gerónimo de

Aguilar, the former Maya captive (who spoke Maya and Spanish), who would have told Cortés in turn.[8] At most, only La Malinche, Aguilar, and Cortés knew about the justification—or probably only Cortés, because the tale was most likely a fabrication, and all the reports of a Chololtec plot trace back to him. The rest of the Spaniards received their information about the plot from him, and he had a compelling interest in justifying his actions for the crown. If, as the circumstances strongly suggest, the Chololllan massacre was an unjustified, preemptive assault, it leaves little room for a heroic Malinche.

When he learned of the wanton destruction of his allies, who had peacefully received the Spaniards, Moteuczoma must have been thoroughly dismayed. This can only have reinforced his reluctance to have Cortés come to Tenochtitlan. Moteuczoma dispatched a delegation of nobles to greet Cortés and learn his true intentions, but he also sent soothsayers and magicians to stop him supernaturally. These had no effect, and having exhausted both diplomacy and magic, Moteuczoma ordered the main road from Chololllan to Tenochtitlan planted with magueys (century plants). This traditional means of sealing off roads and signaling a breach in relations was a last-ditch effort to deter the Spaniards.[9]

Cortés, too, had learned from his experiences so far. He had gained confidence from defeating the Mayas, intimidating the Cempohualtecs, and seemingly having done the same to the Aztecs. He had learned the wrong lessons, but the Tlaxcaltecs had been excellent teachers. From the inability of his Spanish forces to defeat the Tlaxcaltecs, coupled with the effectiveness of his troops in Chololllan when supported by thousands of Tlaxcaltecs, he finally recognized that his own force could not prevail alone. From Tlaxcallan onward, he was always accompanied by thousands of Indian troops.

After two weeks in Chololllan, Cortés marched to Calpan, a dependency of Huexotzinco. There, according to Spanish accounts, he was told that two roads led to Tenochtitlan but that one was blocked and the Aztecs had set up ambushes along it. There is no evidence to support the latter contention, but in any case Cortés took the other path and reached Amaquemecan after two days. There, people from Amaquemecan and neighboring towns and cities, including Chalco, Chimalhuacan, and Ayotzinco, brought presents to the Spaniards and complained about the Aztecs. Cortés promised them they would soon be free.[10]

In addition to the influence the Tlaxcaltecs wielded over Cortés, which probably affected his decision, there are other reasons for doubting the Spanish version of why Cortés chose the route he did. Calpan was on the east side of the mountains ringing the Valley of Mexico, and there were indeed two major routes to Tenochtitlan, both skirting the 5,230-meter-high (17,159-foot) mountain Iztac-Cihuatl. The main route went through a 3,000-meter-high (9,843-foot) pass to the north. The other road was narrower and offered a more difficult trek through a 3,500-meter-high (11,483-foot) pass to the south.

Part of Cortés's claimed rationale for choosing the southern route was to avoid an Aztec ambush, but this threat was unlikely; the Aztecs had laid no ambushes before. Moreover, they were following Cortés's progress and could have ambushed him by dispatching a force to the south pass as easily as to the north. They could have intercepted him well before he ended his two-day march, for they did send emissaries to meet him at Amaquemecan. Indeed, because the south pass was narrower and more rugged, an ambush there would have been far easier.[11]

Cortés was most likely guided in selecting the southern route by Tlaxcaltec knowledge of the political configuration of the Valley of Mexico. The north pass emptied out into the Tetzcoco area, which strongly supported Moteuczoma, whereas the south pass led to the Chalca city-states. These cities had been conquered by the Aztecs in 1464 after fighting a bitter flower war for eighty years. Their kings were removed, the cities were ruled by Aztec governors until 1486, and the area became the main breadbasket for the

Aztecs. The Chalca cities deeply resented their subordination to Tenochtitlan (they had earlier been tied to Huexotzinco), and of all the cities in the Valley of Mexico they were the most promising for Cortés's — and the Tlaxcaltecs' — purposes.

From Amaquemecan the Spaniards marched to Ayotzinco, where Moteuczoma's nephew, King Cacama of Tetzcoco, met and accompanied them into Tenochtitlan. The next day they crossed the Cuitlahuac causeway and reached Ixtlapalapan, to be greeted by the rulers of the surrounding cities. And the following day, 8 November 1519, escorted by these rulers, the Spaniards traveled along the causeway into Tenochtitlan, where they were greeted by Moteuczoma.[12]

Perhaps the best conquest-era description of Tenochtitlan was penned by the Anonymous Conquistador, who wrote that Tenochtitlan, built in the lake, was two and a half to three leagues in circumference and tied to the shore by three high causeways. The city had wide, beautiful streets and canals, many large plazas, numerous temples, and houses and gardens as beautiful as any in Spain.[13]

Here, deep within enemy territory, Cortés, with fewer than three hundred Spaniards and a few thousand Indian allies, walked into the capital of the most powerful empire in Mesoamerica. Why did he take this seemingly foolhardy step? Was it a sense of cultural or military superiority? Perhaps. Certainly these factors cannot be discounted. But his action might be better explained by examining the way Moteuczoma and Cortés understood their respective positions.

Moteuczoma might have had several reasons for permitting the Spaniards to enter Tenochtitlan without overt opposition. He might still have been uncertain about the Spaniards' status as men or gods, and his army was still limited by the preharvest shortage of manpower. Even had he wanted to oppose Cortés's entry, Moteuczoma lacked the forces at that time to take decisive offensive action, although he could have had Cortés himself seized

and killed once he entered Tenochtitlan. But a major reason Moteuczoma did not oppose Cortés's entry was political. He knew
about the massacre at Cholollan and that the new king there had
assumed power with Spanish and Tlaxcaltec help. He knew that
his own politically divided city and region also harbored dissident
factions. Any opposition to Cortés could embolden these groups
and threaten his position. Moteuczoma's ostensibly conciliatory
actions offered Cortés a strong ally and effectively blocked the
option of alliance for any emergent dissident faction. In light of
the reception the Spaniards had received in the Chalca cities,
Moteuczoma did not move against them lest this splinter the political coherence of the Valley of Mexico — but it left him to face
Cortés in a weakened position. Thus, Moteuczoma's acquiescence
to Cortés's arrival, which appears inept from a Spanish-centered
perspective, was considered and logical in terms of the political
dynamics of Mesoamerican society.

This might explain why Moteuczoma permitted the Spaniards
to enter Tenochtitlan, but not why Cortés voluntarily placed his
vastly smaller force in such a dangerous position. Part of his as-
surance doubtless arose from his having successfully subdued or
allied with all his opponents so far. Most of the towns he had
encountered were small, holding only thousands of inhabitants —
the largest cities a few tens of thousands — and he had successfully
allied with Tlaxcallan, multiplying his strength many fold. Cortés
was doubtless buoyed by his initial successes and his greatly
bolstered position following his alliance with Tlaxcallan and the
defeat of Cholollan.

At the same time, Cortés's experiences in Spain probably led
him to believe he could subdue any potential force in Mexico,
especially now that he had Tlaxcaltec allies. The largest city
Cortés was likely to have seen was Seville, with 60,000 to 100,000
inhabitants. The largest city in Europe was Paris, housing 100,000
to 150,000 people at a time when London held fewer than 60,000.
Cortés probably based his assessment of the Aztec threat on the

military forces he had met so far, the sizes of cities in Europe, and
the sizes of the Mesoamerican towns he had seen to that point.[14]

Tenochtitlan was another story altogether. In 1519 it held at
least 200,000 people — far more than any city Cortés had ever seen
before. The entire Valley of Mexico, which formed the capital's
metropolitan area, held from 1 million to 2.65 million people.[15]
Cortés had doubtless been told of the size and splendor of Tenochtitlan, but given the general inaccuracy of his sources' descrip-
tions and the tendency to exaggerate by Indians and Spaniards
alike, he had probably discounted these stories and assessed the
potential threat in terms of the sizes of cities he knew. When
Tenochtitlan proved vastly larger than anticipated, he was no
longer in a position to retreat.

Cortés's strength did not lie primarily in his own men. He was
almost entirely dependent on Indian supplies, labor, and now aux-
iliary troops. These were ensured as long as his alliance with them
lasted, but that depended on their perception of him as powerful
and able to defend them against Aztec retaliation. A retreat in the
face of the obvious power of the Aztec empire would have undermined Cortés's position. The Aztecs would have been embold-
ened, and even more disastrous for the Spaniards, their allies
would have abandoned them — the Tlaxcaltecs retreating to their
home province, allied Indians seeking Aztec forgiveness for their
transgressions, and wavering towns reaffirming their allegiance to
the Aztecs. In short, having decided to go to Tenochtitlan, Cortés
was now confronted with the immensity and power of his opponents but had no way out. He had to continue fearlessly into the
city or risk abandonment by his allies. He could not retreat to Cuba
without facing charges of treason, and any misstep now would
leave him at the mercy of the Aztecs.

CHAPTER 6

MOTEUCZOMA'S TENOCHTITLAN

By whatever plan or miscalculation, the Spaniards found themselves in Tenochtitlan, the largest city in the New World and capital of Mexico's greatest empire. Moteuczoma presented the Spaniards with gifts, fed them, and housed them in the palace of
Axayacatl, the sixth Aztec king and his father. Whatever his private thoughts, Moteuczoma publicly befriended Cortés.[1]

If Moteuczoma still felt the Spaniards might have been gods,
this idea surely faded quickly with firsthand contact. Perhaps
Moteuczoma wanted Cortés inside Tenochtitlan where he could be
seized and killed, or perhaps he was biding his time until the war
season, when he could again raise a large army and deal with the
Spaniards as well as the Tlaxcaltecs and all the rebellious provinces to the east. But whatever the king's motivations, Cortés entered Tenochtitlan and Moteuczoma embraced him, which would
have stilled any public rift among the Aztec rulers and nobles.[2]

The Valley of Mexico over which the Aztecs presided was cut
by political and ethnic divisions. Nine major ethnic groups lived in
the valley, including the dispersed Otomis. The others, centered in
city-states or larger polities, were the Mizquicas and Cuitlahuacas
in their respective towns, the Aztecs (or Mexica) in Tenochtitlan,
the Colhuas on the Ixtapalapa peninsula, the Chalcas in the south-
eastern corner of the valley, the Xochimilcas to the south, the
Tepanecs on the west side, and the Acolhuas on the east. By the
time Cortés arrived, these groups had all been incorporated into

the Aztec empire, through acquiescence, conquest, or co-option, though dissident factions existed everywhere.[3]

Tenochtitlan was a formidable city commanding great resources and home to an enormous population. Moreover, it was situated on an island connected to the mainland by only three major causeways. The Spaniards recognized that these could easily be severed, trapping them inside the city. The causeway over which they had entered Tenochtitlan was wide enough to accommodate eight horsemen abreast, but it could be cut by removing its wooden bridges, and it was defended by merloned fortifications. The city also held large, well-stocked armories.[4]

The danger of their position quickly became apparent, and the Spaniards later wrote that they believed Moteuczoma had enticed them into Tenochtitlan in order to kill them. Regardless of what they believed at the time or what Moteuczoma actually intended, once inside the capital, the Spaniards were in a precarious position. Most of the Tlaxcaltecs remained outside the city and, separated by causeways, could be of little assistance. Even with their technological advantages, the few hundred Spaniards could easily be overwhelmed and destroyed. Despite the shift of Aztec opinion against the Spaniards, Cortés could not withdraw without undermining the support of his allies. His only hope lay in Aztec restraint.[5]

Word soon reached Cortés that the Aztecs had attacked the Totonacs at Nauhtlan for refusing to pay tribute. The Totonacs had asked the Spaniards at Vera Cruz for help, and Juan de Escalante had led a force of forty to fifty Spanish soldiers, with two horsemen, two cannons, three crossbows, two harquebuses, and eight thousand to ten thousand Totonacs, against the Aztecs. During the attack, the Totonacs scattered and seven Spaniards were killed before the rest also fled, leaving the Aztecs victorious and the region in turmoil. The Spaniards were obviously neither immortal nor invincible. If they could not defeat the Aztecs, then other towns loyal to the Spaniards would defect, endangering the garrison at Vera Cruz, cutting Cortés's line of communication to the gulf, and precipitating even more defections.[6]

Cortés could not risk leaving Tenochtitlan, but neither could he ignore this reversal, so he exercised the only available option. He went before Moteuczoma and seized him. With Moteuczoma in Spanish hands, the rest of the Aztecs could be controlled, and Cortés would not have to fear an armed attack or face the cutoff of his food and water. The king went without resisting, and Cortés held him captive for the entire eight months he stayed in Tenochtitlan, indirectly ruling the city.

Why Moteuczoma cooperated with Cortés so freely is uncertain. Perhaps he was weak or simply too concerned for his own safety to take decisive action against the Spaniards. Perhaps it was a calculated political decision: if he continued to rule, even under the influence of Cortés, he retained power. Refusal would have paralyzed the Aztec government, strengthened the position of other power contenders who had opposed allowing the Spaniards into Tenochtitlan in the first place, and ultimately led to Moteuczoma's ouster or assassination as others struggled for the throne. He might also have been passive initially in order to find out more about the Spaniards or to wait until the war season, when his armies would reassemble — but if the latter, he did not act after he had been taken prisoner. Why Moteuczoma cooperated is puzzling, but he did so. Fear for his personal safety is a less likely explanation than fear for his political future.[7]

From captivity, Moteuczoma ordered the leader of the Aztec army that had attacked Nauhtlan to be seized and brought to Tenochtitlan. There, truthfully or not, he denied that Moteuczoma had ordered the attack, and at Cortés's insistence the king had him burned to death — a European rather than a Mesoamerican form of capital punishment and one that horrified the Aztecs. This act generated considerable resentment in Tenochtitlan but reaffirmed Cortés's authority among his allies. On learning what had happened, the Totonacs resumed supplying Vera Cruz.[8]

Although Cortés ruled through Moteuczoma, the imprisoned
king did not provide the secure control he had expected. Selection
for, and retention of, the Aztec throne depended on ability and
performance, but held hostage by the Spaniards, Moteuczoma now
appeared weak. Aztec tributaries were not organizationally integrated into the Aztec state; control depended on their cooperation,
reinforced by the perception of the Aztec king's ability to act
decisively. Weakness also struck at the interests of the nobles, for
both they and the empire depended on tributary revenues whose
flow would quickly dry up if not enforced. The single previous
weak king to rule the Aztec empire, Tizoc, had been assassinated
after a prolonged period of inaction. Moreover, there was never a
shortage of able and eligible nobles qualified to become king, as
Moteuczoma warned Cortés.[9]

Reaction to Moteuczoma's weakness did not emerge first
among the nobles of Tenochtitlan, where his power was most obvious, but in allied Tetzcoco, whose king, Cacama, plotted with the
kings of Coyohuacan, Tlacopan, Ixtlapalapan, and Matlatzinco to
attack the Spaniards. Even though Moteuczoma's authority was
eroding, directly challenging his commands remained dangerous.
With too many conspirators and divided loyalties, word leaked
out. Moteuczoma learned of Cacama's plot and told Cortés.[10]

Although he lacked unanimous support for his planned overthrow at this point, Cacama was determined to continue. His own
domestic support was weak, however, because Tetzcoco's nobles
had been divided ever since his own succession to the throne.
When his father, Tetzcoco's King Nezahualpilli, died in 1515,
Cacama had been placed on the throne largely at Moteuczoma's
insistence. It was this very support that he had now defied.[11]

At Cortés's insistence, Moteuczoma dispatched six loyal nobles to Tetzcoco, captured Cacama with the help of Tetzcoca dissidents, and sent him to Tenochtitlan. He also seized and imprisoned
the rulers of Coyohuacan, Ixtlapalapan, and Tlacopan. On the
king's advice, Cortés made one of Moteuczoma's sons, Cocozca,

king of Tetzcoco. Doing so left bitter divisions that would later prove fatal.[12]

Moteuczoma assembled his nobles and ordered them to pledge fealty to Cortés, which they did, but resentment was growing against both the king and the Spaniards. Then, at Cortés's insistence, Moteuczoma ordered tribute gathered and delivered to the Spaniards. Despite holding Moteuczoma prisoner, Cortés lacked a full understanding of the nature and limits of the king's power. Moteuczoma's tenure in office depended on proper actions, yet most of what he ordered at Cortés's insistence undermined Aztec interests, and his support among both the people and the nobility eroded. The first major threat to Cortés's control, however, came not from the Aztecs but from other Spaniards.[13]

While the Spaniards were seizing control of Tenochtitlan, Governor Velásquez in Cuba had assembled a powerful fleet under the command of Pánfilo de Narváez — nineteen ships (one small ship sank en route), at least eight hundred soldiers, more than twenty cannons, eighty horsemen, 120 crossbowmen, and eighty harquebusiers — to capture Cortés. Spanish accounts claim Moteuczoma learned that Narváez had landed before Cortés did, which was probably true, and that he sent emissaries to greet him. The first word of Narváez's arrival did come by Aztec messengers, but a conspiracy between Moteuczoma and Narváez to attack Cortés and force his withdrawal is improbable in light of the king's weak response to his own seizure and continued imprisonment.[14]

Although Velásquez had known of Cortés's disobedience since the previous summer, an expedition sent in reprisal could not sail before the favorable winds of spring. Thus, it was not until around 20 April 1520 that Narváez and his men landed at San Juan de Ulúa with orders from the governor to seize Cortés and return him to Cuba. When Cortés learned of this, he marched to the coast, reached Narváez's camp at Cempohuallan about 27 May, and prepared to attack.

Narváez had more than eleven hundred men, yet in a strange

move, Cortés took only 266 Spaniards with him. This left Narváez with a huge numerical advantage that Cortés could easily have overcome simply by taking some of his Indian allies, too. Why he did not is unclear. Perhaps the Tlaxcaltecs refused to go, being concerned only with toppling Tenochtitlan and having no interest in Narváez. But they were probably left behind for other reasons. Perhaps Cortés did not want them to see that Spaniards could be defeated in battle or to show them a far larger Spanish force with which they might seek a more advantageous alliance. But because Cortés left his horses in Tenochtitlan, it is likelier that he planned to avoid actual combat and gain his ends through treachery.

Once he arrived on the coast, Cortés launched a surprise attack after midnight, resulting in the capture of Narváez and the surrender of his men. Narváez's swift defeat by vastly inferior forces might seem to be a testament to Cortés's great military skills, but there is significant evidence that Cortés had negotiated, or was in the midst of negotiating, an arrangement to settle their dispute peacefully, so Narváez was not expecting an attack. Cortés had also sown seeds of dissension within Narváez's camp, and when the attack came, many of the defenders did not fight, nor were the cannons used. Narváez was thereafter imprisoned in Vera Cruz and his men joined Cortés, although with widely varying degrees of enthusiasm.[15]

Meanwhile, events in Tenochtitlan had not gone as smoothly for the Spaniards as they had on the coast. When Cortés left for Vera Cruz, he placed Pedro de Alvarado in charge in Tenochtitlan. Alvarado was left in command of a force of eighty soldiers, including fourteen harquebusiers and eight crossbowmen, as well as five horses, some cannons, and all the remaining powder. The Spaniards' quarters were fortified and stocked with a large quantity of maize brought from Tlaxcallan. During Cortés's absence, Alvarado massacred thousands of Aztec nobles during the festival of Toxcatl. He maintained that the Aztecs had planned to attack the Spaniards, but this was almost certainly untrue, despite dissension among the Indians and general hostility toward the Spaniards for holding Moteuczoma prisoner.

The most important of the eighteen monthly festivals, the feast of Toxcatl involved human sacrifice and a dance and procession by warriors carrying a figure of the god Huitzilopochtli. The festival was a major celebration of Aztec war gods, and the participating warriors were dressed in their finery rather than in functional combat gear. If Alvarado actually believed there was a threat — and he claimed to have extracted this information from some Indians by torture — it was not real. Alvarado's limited forces would have had a minimal chance of succeeding in a conventional battle against the Aztecs, so he wanted the advantage of striking first.[16]

The festival of Toxcatl was held in the courtyard before the Great Temple, which was accessible through only four entrances. Alvarado blocked these, then entered with his fully armed Spaniards and began slaughtering the Aztecs. Unarmed and trapped inside, most were killed, but some escaped over the walls. How many died will never be known with certainty, but the sixteenth-century priest Diego Durán estimated that the courtyard held eight thousand to ten thousand nobles, and most of them were killed. When word of the massacre spread, the people gathered their arms and attacked the Spaniards, killing seven, wounding many, and driving the rest back to their fortified quarters.[17]

Once behind their defenses, the Spaniards managed to drive the Aztecs back with artillery fire. The Aztecs could certainly have destroyed Alvarado's forces, but the cost would have been high, so they besieged the Spaniards without attempting an all-out effort to destroy them. This decision might have been a result of several factors: the Aztecs' disarray following the loss of so many leaders, their observance of a mourning period following their funerals, the continued imprisonment of Moteuczoma, and their uncertainty over unseating a reigning king. In any case, once besieged, Alvarado sent two Tlaxcaltecs to tell Cortés what had happened.

Taken at face value, Alvarado's explanation of this event is puzzling. The Spaniards had been in Tenochtitlan for over half a year and had seen other such monthly festivals, many far bloodier than this one, yet had not been alarmed. Why did this one precipitate a massacre?

None of the participants left an alternative explanation, but the circumstances suggest Cortés's involvement. He no longer trusted Moteuczoma and feared he might ally with Narváez. And despite the enormous reversal of fortune the massacre caused, Cortés never punished Alvarado for precipitating the attack, though he brutally punished other infractions of his orders. These circumstances suggest that Cortés himself ordered the massacre to eliminate Moteuczoma's supporters but wished it to take place after he was gone so he could deny culpability, as he had in the past. Moreover, he had the perfect model to follow: the Cholollan massacre.

In Cholollan, killing the pro-Aztec king and nobles had left the pro-Tlaxcaltec faction in power, giving Cortés a powerful ally at his rear. Perhaps Cortés felt he could achieve the same thing in Tenochtitlan. After all, he had left a Spanish force behind, he already held the Aztec king, and he had left behind a Tlaxcaltec force similar to the one in Cholollan. But he misunderstood that although Tenochtitlan's nobles held different political opinions, they were undivided in their loyalty to the city.

The Cholollan massacre had been masterminded by Tlaxcaltecs who were acutely aware of the nobles' loyalties, and it succeeded for that reason. The Toxcatl massacre occurred in a markedly different political environment that the Spaniards failed to understand, and it failed for that reason. In short, Cortés learned the wrong lesson from Cholollan. The Tenochtitlan massacre did decimate the Aztec forces, killing not just thousands but the very best soldiers — the seasoned veterans and noble warriors who participated in the festival. The slaughter both reduced the number of elite troops now facing the Spaniards and destroyed much of the army's command structure, which, at a loss of only seven men, was a major coup for the Spaniards. Politically, however, it turned the tide against both the Spaniards and Moteuczoma.[18] Even with superior firepower and a much higher kill ratio, the Spaniards could not hope to prevail against the great crush of Aztecs inside Tenochtitlan. To this point, they had been shielded by Moteuczoma, whom they held prisoner. But every time he acted on behalf of the Spaniards and against Aztec interests, Moteuczoma's position was further undermined, for he lost more and more noble support. Moteuczoma's eventual loss of authority was probably inevitable, but the Toxcatl massacre was the ultimate outrage, and his support vanished virtually overnight. Thus, whatever military gains Alvarado enjoyed from the massacre were purchased at a tremendous political cost.

When Cortés received word of the tumult in Tenochtitlan, he sent a message to Alvarado that he was returning and began the march with an army swollen by men from Narváez's force. His troops now numbered more than thirteen hundred soldiers, ninety-six horses, eighty crossbowmen, and eighty harquebusiers. At Tlaxcallan, Cortés was joined by two thousand Tlaxcaltec warriors, and the entire party marched by way of Tetzcoco, reaching Tenochtitlan on 24 June 1520 and entering the city unopposed.[19]

Tenochtitlan's streets were completely deserted, perhaps to show Aztec opposition and displeasure, as the Aztecs claimed, but allowing Cortés back into the city had military implications, too. Outside, he could move freely, use his horses effectively, receive military and logistical support from his allies, and retreat to safer areas if need be. Once inside Tenochtitlan, all these advantages were forfeited. Cortés must have recognized the potential danger but must have felt he could rectify the situation with Moteuczoma's help — suggesting either a fundamental misunderstanding of Aztec kingship or a failure to grasp how badly the situation had deteriorated.

Augmented by Narváez's men, the force that returned to Tenochtitlan was much larger and better armed than the one that had left, and Cortés felt he was now in a much stronger position. Spaniards now made up perhaps a fourth of his entire force. But only Moteuczoma had held the Aztecs at bay previously, and he no longer could: for the first time since he reached Tenochtitlan in November, Cortés faced a strictly military challenge. He rejoined the forces left inside Tenochtitlan, but now the city was a trap. Cortés could repulse virtually any Aztec assault on his stronghold with his artillery, but he was also cut off. Some messengers made their way in and out of the city, but large groups could not, and Cortés was cut off from allied support, food, and additional supplies of shot and powder.

The Spaniards were besieged in their quarters for twenty-three days. The causeway bridges were raised to cut off a Spanish retreat, and Aztec soldiers controlled the city. Resistance was so fierce that Spanish sallies in groups as large as four hundred men were attacked and forced back with serious losses. The Aztecs continued to assault the Spaniards' quarters, and all of Cortés's attempted forays were forced back. The Aztecs had seized the offensive: any Spanish notion that they had ever had the upper hand vanished as they realized they had not dominated the Aztecs but had merely been tolerated by them.[20]

Spanish arms and tactics were proving insufficient under this withering assault, and in a desperate bid to shift the tactical balance Cortés decided to build three war machines — large, movable towers that could each protect twenty to twenty-five men who could fire out through loopholes. However, these machines did not prove decisive and were destroyed in battle; moreover, Spanish attempts to burn the city were thwarted by the crisscrossing canals. Having failed in all of his military efforts, Cortés tried to negotiate a withdrawal, but to no avail. He then brought Moteuczoma onto the roof to order his people to stop the attack, but the king was struck down.[21]

Spanish and Indian accounts of Moteuczoma's death conflict.

The Spaniards claimed he was struck by Aztec stones while attempting to stop his people's attacks on Cortés's men. Because the Aztecs deeply disapproved of his actions and had repudiated his leadership, this version is possible. But Aztec accounts claimed that Moteuczoma was killed by the Spaniards. Whether or not they did so to gain a four-day respite while the people mourned their king, holding Moteuczoma prisoner had now become a liability rather than an asset. His captivity could still inspire Aztec attacks, but if he were released, he would be ignored at best and could unite his people against the Spaniards at worst. There was little to be gained by keeping Moteuczoma alive and much to be gained if he died, so the Aztec version, too, is plausible and, in light of both earlier and later Spanish actions, probable.[22]

Following Moteuczoma's death and cremation, Cuitlahua, king of Ixtlapalapan, son of King Axayacatl and brother of Moteuczoma, was elected king, but the formal investiture did not take place until 16 September, almost three months later. Cuitlahua had consistently opposed the Spaniards, so Cortés released an Aztec prisoner with a message that Moteuczoma's nephew, who was with the Spaniards, should rightfully be the king, not Cuitlahua, arguing from the principle of hereditary succession that prevailed in Europe. Even in his current predicament, Cortés was trying to manipulate the political situation by dividing Aztec loyalties — or, more likely, he still failed to grasp the dynamics of Aztec kingship. This effort failed, and the assault continued.[23]

Food, water, and gunpowder were all running out: the Spaniards had to escape or die. This show of weakness would certainly affect Cortés's political alliances, but the choice now was flight or death, so Cortés decided to sneak out of Tenochtitlan late at night when the Aztecs would be least alert. The Spaniards were in the center of the city and would have to fight their way out no matter which direction they went. Tlaxcallan was the Spaniards' objective, so a retreat directly east would be shortest. But this would require crossing almost 25 kilometers (15.5 miles) of Lake Tetzcoco, as well as making their way through the dike that enclosed the western portion of the lake. This would have to be done while under attack if they were discovered, which was virtually certain, because a water escape would require dozens, if not hundreds, of canoes, many more than could be secured secretly. And even if this route were feasible, taking it would require abandoning all the horses and probably the cannons as well.[24]

Because a canoe escape was infeasible, the Spaniards had to choose among the three major land routes along the causeways. The north causeway went to Tepeyacac, the smallest of the three termini and thus probably the least dangerous, but this route required the longest march through Tenochtitlan. The south causeway went to Coyohuacan and Ixtlapalapan, but the water was deepest along this route and the exit towns were hostile. The western route, which Cortés used, went to Tlacopan, also a large, hostile city, but it required the shortest march inside Tenochtitlan and thus offered the least chance of detection. Because the Spaniards would be vulnerable strung out along a road, carrying all their supplies and accompanied by their allies, prisoners, and dependents, marching undetected was crucial. The Spaniards would be leaving their fortifications, which was all that had stood between them and the Aztecs.

The Aztecs had removed the causeway bridges and widened and deepened the openings to keep the Spaniards from fleeing, so Cortés ordered a portable wooden bridge to be built that could span these breaches. According to Spanish accounts, they began their escape just before midnight on 30 June. A heavy rainstorm hid their movements. They crossed one breach but reportedly were seen at the second by an Aztec woman getting water, and she raised an alarm. Attacked on the causeway and from canoes on either side, the Spaniards abandoned their bridge and fled, for they could not form defensive formations or even see the arrows shot at them in the dark. Cortés finally reached Tlacopan, but many Spaniards had been killed, along with their noble prisoners, most of the

Citlaltepec •

Lake Zumpango

• Xoloc

• Zacamolco

Tepotzotlan •

⊙ Xaltocan
Lake Xaltocan

Teotihuacan •
Otompan •

Cuauhtitlan •

Tenanyocan •

Teocalhueyacan •

• Tetzcoco

Tepeyacac •

Lake Texcoco

Azcapotzalco •

Tlacopan •

Popotlan
• Tlatelolco

Chapoltepec •
• Tenochtitlan

Dyke of Nezahualcoyotl

Chimalhuacan •

• Tepepolco

• Coatepec

Mexicatzinco •
Ixtlapalapan

Coyohuacan •
Huitzilopochco • Colhuacan

Lake Xochimilco

Cuitlahuac
⊙

Xochimilco ⊙

Lake Chalco

• Chalco

Mizquic •

Tlalmanalco •

N

🔺 No longer occupied
in sixteenth century

0   10 mls
|—————————————|
0   10 km

3. The Valley of Mexico, c. 1520

Tlaxcaltecs and Huexotzincas, and some horses; and all the cannons were lost.[25]

Some Spaniards were cut off and could not get out of Tenochtitlan, so they turned back, returning to their quarters, where they were again besieged for some days before they were all killed. The Spaniards who escaped had actually passed out of the city proper before they were seen and the alarm was raised.

Though long accepted, this venerable account strains credulity. The Spaniards did sneak out of the capital on the night of 30 June, but it seems odd that the bulk of the forces that made it out were men from Cortés's original army, whereas most of Narváez's men, who had become increasingly disgruntled and had proved not to be effective fighters, had not. The events following the Toxcatl massacre had again been educational for Cortés. His earlier optimism that a thousand Spaniards needed only a few thousand allied soldiers to prevail had been shattered by his being consistently pushed back in Tenochtitlan. He now recognized that large Spanish forces of the size he might muster were not the key; large allied forces were. And he recognized that he no longer needed all the Spanish soldiers he had, especially if they were neither trustworthy nor good fighters.

It was doubtlessly Cortés who placed these very men at the rear of the column, but was it fate that made the woman shout the alarm before they could cross the causeway? Spanish accounts claim the woman raised the alarm, but how plausible is this claim? The Aztecs neither used the lake or canals as a toilet nor drank the brackish water, so is it plausible that an Indian woman had awakened at midnight to draw water from the brackish western portion of the lake? All this allegedly happened in the middle of a rainstorm violent enough to hide the sight and sound of thousands of Spaniards and Tlaxcaltecs marching through the middle of Tenochtitlan, yet the woman did not stay home and simply collect fresh rainwater in a pot. Was this implausible account merely a cover story for Cortés's raising the alarm after he and his trustworthy men had reached a point where they could escape but those he neither trusted nor needed could not? Whatever the case, Cortés was again left with his best fighters and most trustworthy men while having lost most of those he considered liabilities — at a point when he would have to depend on far larger allied armies, so his smaller Spanish force would be less important anyway.

At dawn, Cortés and his remaining men reached Popotlan, near Tlacopan, but were surrounded by attacking Aztecs. The Spaniards were then driven toward Tlacopan and finally rested at Otoncalpolco, where they were met by the people of Teocalhueyacan. The alarm had been raised in all the surrounding towns, but the people of Teocalhueyacan nevertheless aided the Spaniards.[26]

Although the Spanish accounts usually speak only of the Tlaxcaltecs, Tlaxcallan was only the most prominent of several allied cities and provinces that also included Huexotzinco, Atlixco, and Tliliuhqui-Tepec, all of which were represented in the forces supporting Cortés. The people of Teocalhueyacan were Otomis, but under Aztec pressure many of them had migrated east and settled in Tliliuhqui-Tepec, with which Cortés had allied. Indeed, this source of assistance may have been known to Cortés before he left Tenochtitlan and was perhaps a key factor in determining his route.[27]

From Teocalhueyacan the Spaniards had to march around the lakes to reach Tlaxcallan. Although Cortés might have received some aid from the Chalca cities, he would also have been more vulnerable to attack from causeways and canoes in the densely populated southern end of the valley than in the less populous north. Moreover, the land rose much more sharply from the lakes in the southern end of the valley, and the Spaniards would have been funneled along a narrower strip of land where their movements would have been easily anticipated and Aztec attacks more effective. Consequently, the Spaniards marched north from Teocalhueyacan, under constant assault.[28]

They had lost all their cannons and most of their crossbows but were able to keep the attackers at bay with short cavalry charges. That night the Spaniards reached Tepotzotlan, which was abandoned, and they left the next morning, spending the following night in Citlaltepec. They reached Xoloc the next night and fought a major battle near Zacamolco the following day, but they fared poorly and had to withdraw.[29]

Although the Spaniards were under assault to varying degrees throughout their flight, the fighting was relatively light during most of the transit around the northern lakes. Part of this may be attributed to the customary four days of mourning in Tenochtitlan for the nobles killed during Cortés's flight, including Cacama and the sons and daughters of Moteuczoma, but four other factors may have played an even larger role. First, the northern end of the valley simply held fewer people, so the local forces available to fight the Spaniards there were smaller. Second, little surplus food was available in the north this early in the agricultural season to support either Spaniards or Aztecs. Indeed, the Spaniards found so little food that they ate horses killed in battle. Third, Aztec troops and supplies could be brought by canoes from Tenochtitlan, but the lakes were still very low and travel was difficult, if not impossible. And fourth, the Aztecs could not have marshaled large offensive armies, because it was the rainy season and most of the men were still engaged in agricultural pursuits. So although considerable forces could be mobilized against the Spaniards in and around major towns, at this time the Aztecs were not equipped to dispatch and support large forces for any appreciable period or at any significant distance. Thus, throughout much of the Spaniards' flight from Tenochtitlan, most of the soldiers they fought were drawn from the cities they passed near, and in the north these were small and few.[30]

Once they completed their transit of the north, the Spaniards reentered more populous areas and were again attacked in force. They could not simply transfer Old World tactics to fight the Indians, because they were typically outnumbered and surrounded. Instead, during most of these clashes they drew up into defensive formations, which minimized the problem of coordinating movements and maximized the effectiveness of their weapons. Harquebuses and crossbows both had greater range than Indian weapons, allowing the Spaniards to engage the enemy while still beyond the reach of return fire, and had greater effect, so the Spaniards could more easily disrupt opposing troop formations and throw the attackers into disarray. But more important were the horses.

Groups of armored horse lancers mounted rapid charges into advancing formations. Whereas gaps created by crossbow and harquebus fire could often be closed before the opposing sides met, cavalry charges created gaps that could be exploited by follow-on troops. Thus, Spanish successes were less a matter of individual superiority than of technological and organizational superiority: they were better able to maintain their protective formations while disrupting those of their enemies and attacking their exposed flanks.

The Aztecs nevertheless persisted in their practice of surrounding the Spaniards, in part because of their training but also because it was an effective, though costly, strategy. They could not prevent a breakout, but the Aztecs typically attacked in several different commands, so even though the Spaniards could disrupt one, the rest remained intact. Moreover, even when the Spaniards broke through, their rear elements were less able to withdraw as a cohesive unit, leaving the weakest Spanish units to face the most cohesive Aztec ones. Thus, even though encirclement could not contain the Spaniards, it was effective against the withdrawing Spanish forces.

After retreating from the battle near Zacamolco, the Spaniards the next day reached Otompan, where Aztec troops had gathered, and fought another fierce battle before marching on. The next day they entered the territory of Tlaxcallan, having lost more than 860

Spanish soldiers, five Spanish women who had arrived with Narváez, and over a thousand Tlaxcaltecs in the five days of flight from
Tenochtitlan. Desperately needing a safe haven, they marched toward the city of Tlaxcallan, uncertain and anxious about the reception they would receive.[31]

CHAPTER 7

FLIGHT AND RECOVERY

During their flight from Tenochtitlan, the Spaniards were at their most vulnerable. They had left their fortifications, they had lost their cannons, many crossbows, and a number of horses, their supplies were running out, and they were strung out along a march through enemy territory. Yet the Aztecs did not mount a sustained assault. Certainly, logistical and manpower limitations hindered their movements; the war season was still five months away and Aztec forces had not been assembled and retrained for war, so large armies were unavailable to assault Tlaxcallan. But the political disarray of Tenochtitlan's leadership was probably the main factor that permitted the remnants of Cortés's force to slip away. Because the Spaniards were in flight and seemed to be no further threat, the Aztecs turned their attention to the more immediate problem of shoring up support among their tributaries.

Escape, however, was only part of Cortés's problem. Having fled in the face of certain defeat, his political alliances were now unsure. He had been able to create political ties through his military superiority—often perceived rather than demonstrated—but this had now been shown to be false. Thus, as he marched toward Tlaxcallan, Cortés was anxious over his reception. He ordered the Spaniards not to seize anything from the people there, despite their desperate need. When they reached the town of Huei-Otlipan, the Spaniards were received and fed, but for pay rather than from tributary obligation. Clearly, Cortés's political standing had changed, and Tlaxcallan's rulers debated their continued alliance.[1]

Opinion was divided in Tlaxcallan, as it was in Tenochtitlan. General Xicotencatl had always opposed the Spaniards and was even more opposed after they fled Tenochtitlan, though perhaps primarily for domestic political purposes. Had Tlaxcallan been a defecting Aztec ally, it probably would have shifted its allegiance back. But Tlaxcallan was an independent enemy state and had few options. Its own political position had been eroding long before Cortés arrived: it was now more tightly encircled by Aztec tributaries, and neither Cholollan nor Huexotzinco was fully trusted. Short of becoming an Aztec ally — and likely a subservient one — Tlaxcallan's best choice was to continue its support for the Spaniards.[2]

After several days the rulers of Tlaxcallan and Huexotzinco came to Huei-Otlipan to greet Cortés and re-cement the alliance. Then together the parties marched to the province's capital on 11 July 1520. Once there, the Spaniards were relatively safe. Cortés's remaining 440 Spaniards, twenty horses, twelve crossbowmen, and seven harquebusiers were all wounded, and they rested there and tended their wounds for approximately three weeks.[3]

Even in Tlaxcallan Cortés's security was not absolute. The Aztecs could penetrate the province, as they had previously, but because Tenochtitlan remained in turmoil, this did not happen. Tlaxcaltec support, however, was not a foregone conclusion, and the Tlaxcaltecs exacted major concessions from Cortés for their continued help should he defeat the Aztecs. These included the right to tribute from Cholollan, Huexotzinco, and Tepeyacac (all of which had previously been Aztec tributaries), command of a fortress to be built in Tenochtitlan, an equal division of the spoils the Spaniards would receive from the towns and provinces conquered, and perpetual freedom from tribute themselves.[4]

Meanwhile, in Tenochtitlan, Moteuczoma and many other rulers were dead, and though Cuitlahua had been chosen king, he had not yet consolidated his position. This left the entire Aztec empire in uncertainty. Usually, when the Aztecs conquered other cities they left the local kings to rule as before, as long as they fulfilled their new tributary obligations. Without the conquerors' instituting major structural changes in the tributary towns, their allegiance to Tenochtitlan was essentially voluntary, based on their perception of the Aztecs' ability and willingness to back up their demands by force should the towns default on their obligations. This efficient system required little military or administrative expense by the Aztecs to maintain the flow of tribute into their capital. But the perception of Aztec power that undergirded this compliance depended primarily on the king.

An established Aztec king's ability to enforce his will was rarely challenged, but new rulers had to prove themselves. Thus, between his selection and coronation, each king-elect normally led his army on a campaign — in part to secure sacrificial victims for his investiture ceremony but more practically to demonstrate his military prowess and resolve. A successful demonstration would re-cement Aztec vassal ties without the need for actual reconquest throughout the empire.

Cuitlahua could not immediately demonstrate this prowess. As a result, many Aztec tributaries were divided over whether to continue their obedience or to rebel, especially now that Tlaxcallan and the Spaniards offered a powerful alternative alliance partner. This uncertainty reached the highest ranks, with nobles falling into conflicting factions. Cuitlahua could not demonstrate his prowess until the war season began some months hence, and he died of smallpox before it arrived.

Cortés's situation was very different from Cuitlahua's. He had lost men and arms, but he had learned that his own forces by themselves were not powerful enough to undertake major offensive actions, so he was not crippled by the loss of men in the flight from Tenochtitlan. His future lay in relatively small numbers of Spaniards backed up by massive allied support, so that superior

Spanish weapons could punch holes through Aztec lines that could then be exploited by the allies. The loss of hundreds of Spaniards in Tenochtitlan only marginally affected this tactic. Moreover, as long as Tlaxcallan remained loyal, Cortés had no empire requiring attention in the wake of his defeat. There was nevertheless an urgency to his actions. He had to renew his efforts immediately in order to avoid defections of both Indians and Spaniards, and he had to succeed before Velásquez could send another force against him.

One factor working in Cortés's favor was disease. A member of Narváez's party who reached Mexico was infected with smallpox, and the disease swept into the Valley of Mexico, touching off an epidemic such as the Aztecs had never seen before. Some 40 percent of the population of central Mexico died within a year. The smallpox plague reached the Valley of Mexico after mid-October, lasted sixty days in Tenochtitlan, and burned itself out by early December. And among its victims was Cuitlahua, who died on 4 December, having ruled for only eighty days.[5]

Smallpox was unknown in indigenous Mesoamerica, and the native populations, lacking previous exposure and therefore immunity, were devastated by the disease. Initial infection is followed by an incubation period of about twelve days, during which there are no obvious symptoms. Then begins a three- to five-day period of fever, headaches and backaches, prostration, and vomiting, followed by the onset of the smallpox rash. At this point the worst symptoms seem to subside, but it also signals the beginning of the infectious phase. The rash lasts for about eight days, after which scabs form and then fall off six days later. Five days into the rash, the fever returns. The disease runs its entire course from infection to recovery in about twenty-six days, conferring permanent immunity on survivors. Death, if it occurs, usually happens toward the end of the disease cycle, in the last four or five days.[6]

If Cuitlahua indeed died on 4 December, he must have been infected as early as 10 November and been unable to perform his royal functions after about 22 November. Thus, the empire would have been effectively leaderless during the crucial period when the Aztecs would normally have been preparing for war. And beyond its effects on Cuitlahua, the pathology of smallpox would have given rise to successive outbreaks in Tenochtitlan every two to three weeks throughout the epidemic, incapacitating even the survivors for more than two weeks each and further disrupting the Aztecs' ability to plan.[7]

Smallpox unquestionably affected the course of the conquest, but not simply as a result of massive Aztec deaths. The smallpox epidemic spread and devastated the Indian populations friendly to the Spaniards as well, so the net effect was to reduce the numbers on both sides. The epidemic did make a difference on the leadership of the two sides. Aztec leaders were devastated, and though new ones emerged, they lacked both the experience of their predecessors and the time needed to consolidate their rule and reaffirm tributary allegiances. Leaders on the pro-Spanish side were lost, too, but they were replaced by loyal supporters. The Spaniards themselves had greater immunity and did not die from the epidemic. Thus, the Spanish leadership remained intact, and the devastation allowed Cortés to consolidate his support among the newly installed leaders while the Aztec leadership was divided and in tatters.

Cortés's men were nevertheless dispirited. Many of them, especially those who had come with Narváez, wanted to retreat to Vera Cruz before the Indians rose against them. Cortés cajoled and placated them but refused to withdraw. Leaving central Mexico would mean an eventual return to Cuba or Spain, where his life was still in danger, and he was determined to reassert his power and dominate the Indians of the region.[8]

While recuperating in Tlaxcallan, Cortés must have given his defeat great thought, and at least one thing was clear. Despite his initial confidence and the bolstering it received with the addition of Narváez's men and equipment, his strategy of controlling Tenochtitlan from within had been hopelessly flawed. To conquer Mexico, Cortés would have to secure his line of communication with Vera Cruz, which was his only source of resupply for Spanish arms; he had to neutralize any threat to his rear before attempting another advance on Tenochtitlan; he had to re-cement his Indian alliances through demonstrations of force; and he had to secure a reliable source of food. Previously, all this had been guaranteed by Moteuczoma, but the Aztec political apparatus had irrevocably slipped from Cortés's grasp, and he lacked the forces to confront the Aztecs directly. To remedy this situation, he decided to chip away at any Aztec tributaries that threatened him or his future plans. Badly depleted of both men and equipment, he sent to Vera Cruz for any soldiers remaining there and all the gunpowder and crossbows. These were delivered, but only seven men were available, four of whom were sailors who were less skilled as soldiers.[9]

The Aztec empire was particularly vulnerable to factionalization. Not only were tributaries often divided internally, but their allegiance to the Aztecs extended only as far as their own interests converged. Anything more was based on fear of Aztec reprisals. This factionalization had been brought home to Cortés at Teocalhueyacan, where he had been helped even while under assault from the Aztecs. If the Spaniards could conquer an Aztec tributary and promise protection from reprisals, a shift in allegiance was simple and consistent with traditional patterns of alliance formation in Mesoamerica. A campaign to the east of the Valley of Mexico would meet relatively small forces and, if successful, could achieve many of the Spaniards' military objectives, demonstrate their political power, ease the process of convincing others to become allies, and simultaneously deprive the Aztecs of support from these towns.

While Cortés was besieged in Tenochtitlan, a party of Spaniards from Vera Cruz had been attacked and killed in the province of Tepeyacac, an Aztec tributary. He seized on this as a pretext for retaliation, an opportunity to acquire tribute, and a starting point for his renewed war with the Aztecs. More importantly, this attack may have been undertaken to fulfill Cortés's pledge to the Tlaxcaltecs and to ensure their support for his war on Tenochtitlan. Cortés then asked for Tlaxcaltec assistance in punishing the towns of Tepeyacac, Quecholac, and Tecamachalco.[10]

Spanish accounts claim that the Aztecs anticipated these attacks and sent troops throughout the region, but this is improbable and smacks of Spanish self-aggrandizement. Although some forces might have been sent, it was still well before harvest, so the Aztecs would have been unable to field large numbers of soldiers. Besides, Cortés's march on Tepeyacac began only a month after he fled Tenochtitlan, and given the turmoil there from Cuitlahua's succession, the loss of so many Aztec leaders, the beginning of the smallpox epidemic, and the Aztec belief that the Spaniards had fled in total defeat, it is unlikely any large-scale, sustained, coordinated offense began or could have begun. In any case, such a strategy would have been inherently flawed. If the Aztecs had been able to raise a large force, they should have taken the offensive, marched against the Spaniards in Tlaxcallan, and crushed them there. Reinforcing their tributaries would merely dilute Aztec forces, because too few men could be sent to each town to ensure that an assault would be repulsed. Without significant forewarning of the Spaniards' target, such a defensive strategy would have been doomed.[11]

Around 1 August, Cortés marched against Tepeyacac with 420 Spaniards, seventeen horses, six crossbowmen, and two thousand Tlaxcaltecs, but with no cannons or harquebuses — which highlights the crucial importance of horses in these battles. He took food for only one day, eliminating the need for a large support contingent. This suggests great confidence that he would win quickly, and it was true that the risk was minimal, because the Spaniards were close enough to Tlaxcallan that supplies could be sent quickly or their forces could return.[12]

This was the rainy season, when the men of Tepeyacac would

be dispersed in agricultural pursuits and unprepared for war, but the same was true of the Tlaxcaltecs and may well account for their low participation. The Mesoamerican tradition of flower wars might also have helped the Spanish attack. If the Spaniards made an impressive show of strength, many towns might capitulate and become allies of Cortés without military conquest. Both this traditional behavior and the season made for an easy campaign and a quick Spanish victory.

Cortés camped three leagues from Tepeyacac and sent the town a message to surrender, which was rejected. Cortés then engaged Tepeyacac's army on a plain and, led by his horsemen, routed it with no Spanish deaths. Tepeyacac's rulers then pledged fealty to the Spaniards, after which Cortés and his allies continued their conquest of the region, completely subduing it in a matter of weeks.[13]

Cortés recognized that these conquests were only as secure as his presence, so he founded and fortified the town of La Villa de Segura de la Frontera at Tepeyacac. This settlement would secure Cortés's gains and serve as a base from which the Spaniards could reinforce their allies and retaliate against their enemies. Having done this, Cortés controlled most of the major towns along the main route from Cholollan to Ahuilizapan, where the trail descended to the Gulf coast and Vera Cruz.[14]

While Cortés was pacifying the region, he received word that a resupply ship for Narváez had arrived from Cuba and been captured. Its captain, Pedro Barba, was a friend of Cortés's, and he, thirteen soldiers, and two horses were sent to Tepeyacac, followed eight days later by nine men, six crossbows, and one horse from a second ship similarly taken.[15]

In the autumn of 1520 King Cuitlahua attempted to block further Spanish expansion by sending troops to Cuauhquecholan and Itzyocan, south of Cholollan straddling the main pass into present-day Morelos and thence into the Valley of Mexico (see map 2). Cortés sent a force of Spanish and Tlaxcaltec soldiers —

thirteen horsemen, two hundred foot soldiers, and thirty thousand Indian allies — to fight them, ostensibly at the secret request of the towns' rulers. They passed near Huexotzinco, where Cortés was told that the kings were plotting against him, so he had them seized but later released. A Huexotzinca rebellion was possible, especially because a large force of Aztecs was now only a day's march away, but it was improbable. This seizure might have reflected Spanish anxiety over the reliability of their allies, but more likely it was partial fulfillment of Cortés's agreement with the Tlaxcaltecs to give them control over Huexotzinco.[16]

When the Spaniards neared Cuauhquecholan, some of its factionalized rulers met them and disclosed how the Aztecs were positioned. In the ensuing battle, the Aztecs fled. They fell back to Itzyocan, reinforcing the Aztec troops there, but to little avail; the Spaniards defeated them. The unrepentant rulers of both towns were replaced, and the new kings pledged their fealty.[17]

Word then reached Cortés at Segura de la Frontera that another ship had reached Vera Cruz, soon followed by two more. Their companies added 145 men and nineteen horses to Cortés's forces. Attacks against Spaniards continued in many towns, however, and Cortés was engaged in fighting troops loyal to the Aztecs throughout the region.[18]

By this time, smallpox had swept throughout central Mexico, killing vast numbers of Indians. While Cortés's strength was growing, Tenochtitlan was again in political turmoil. After Cuitlahua died, Cuauhtemoc, son of King Ahuitzotl, became king of Tenochtitlan in February 1521. His inauguration followed Cuitlahua's death by more than two months, during which both Tenochtitlan and the empire were without a ruler. Moreover, the crisis Cuauhtemoc confronted gave him no time to consolidate his rule. In an effort to secure the loyalty of his vassals, he gave lavish gifts to some rulers and remitted the tribute of others, following a policy initiated by Cuitlahua. But this failed to have the desired effect and may even have been perceived as weakness. Without demonstrating his strength and broadening his political base throughout the empire, Cuauhtemoc's domestic support remained fragile and he was less able to act decisively at home, which might account for his failure to strike at the Spaniards in Tlaxcallan. Thus, the Aztecs faced the Spaniards with an able leader but one who did not enjoy the unquestioned support of all his tributaries.[19]

Although smallpox struck Cortés's allies as well as his enemies, it did not lessen his military strength relative to Tenochtitlan's, because proportionately the same numbers died everywhere. It did strengthen Cortés politically. Not only was Tenochtitlan in disarray from two royal successions in eighty days, but the kings of many other cities, including Tlaxcallan, also contracted the disease and died. Cortés seized this opportunity and selected men loyal to him as their successors. Thus, while the plague weakened the Aztecs, it strengthened the Spaniards. Having secured himself politically and militarily, Cortés now turned his attention to his return to Tenochtitlan.[20]

CHAPTER 8

THE RETURN TO TENOCHTITLAN

After Cortés fled Tenochtitlan, the Aztecs took no action against the badly mauled Spaniards aside from sending a few reinforcements to allies near Tlaxcallan. In retrospect, a massive strike before the Spaniards could recuperate was perhaps the Aztecs' best option. But social and political circumstances made other courses of action more appealing to them.

As we have seen, Tenochtitlan was in political turmoil as Cuitlahua became king, followed by Cuauhtemoc eighty days later, and neither king was able to consolidate his rule effectively. Smallpox raged throughout the city and the region, killing multitudes, including many kings and nobles. Attention and manpower were diverted to repairing the destruction already caused in Tenochtitlan, and the Aztecs might well have believed the Spaniards would never return—at least not until they began their depredations to the east, when it was too late.

Whatever effect this social disruption had on Aztec decision making, there were also sound strategic reasons for adopting a defensive posture. The Aztecs could muster an enormous army in and around the Valley of Mexico, but logistical constraints kept them from dispatching all but a portion of it for any appreciable distance. Thus, the force they could send to Tlaxcallan might not have been large enough to defeat the Spaniards, who were reinforced by virtually the entire adult male population of the region. Besides, any troops dispatched to Tlaxcallan would inevitably include many of the king's noble supporters. Their absence might weaken him politically during these turbulent times and perhaps even open the city to attack in the army's absence.

Moreover, how far and how many forces could be sent depended on their logistical support, which in enemy territory was very limited. This constraint affected the Tlaxcaltecs as well as the Aztecs, so first Cuitlahua's and then Cuauhtemoc's decision to remain in the Valley of Mexico was prudent. There, the military situation was reversed: remaining in Tenochtitlan meant the king had access to all his soldiers while forcing his enemies to bear the expense and manpower reductions involved in coming to him.

This decision also affected the Spaniards' tactical capabilities, especially their use of horses and formations. The Aztecs were painfully aware of how effective the Spaniards' defensive formations could be in open combat, so withdrawing to Tenochtitlan gave them many advantages. First, remaining in and around Tenochtitlan minimized Aztec logistical constraints and allowed them to assemble the largest feasible army, leaving the difficulties of mounting and supplying an army far from home to the Spanish forces. Second, the withdrawal allowed them to bring food into the city far more easily and cheaply than the Spaniards could supply themselves and their allies by land. Third, it gave the Aztecs much greater mobility, because their canoes enjoyed shorter interior lines of communication throughout the valley, whereas the Spaniards would be forced to march around the valley along the shore. Fourth, the Aztecs could mobilize, concentrate, and support troops by canoe at any point around the valley, leaving the Spaniards without a secure rear area and forcing them to defend themselves everywhere at once. Fifth, with their great canoe fleets, the Aztecs would not be hemmed in by any land assault and could reinforce their own land forces, greatly complicating any Spanish attack. Sixth, horses would be of little use against the island city of Tenochtitlan; any attack would have to move along the causeways, where horsemen had little room to maneuver, could be attack from canoes on either side, and could more easily be hemmed in and defeated. Seventh, the Spaniards' ability to disrupt Aztec formations would be limited because of the depth of their lines on the causeways, and the Aztecs could adopt effective countermeasures. And eighth, channeling the offensive along the causeways also minimized the number of allied troops that could support the Spaniards, greatly reducing this advantage. In sum, withdrawing to Tenochtitlan would minimize Cortés's main advantages and force him onto the offensive, which would require him to take greater risks and inevitably lead to higher Spanish losses.

Thus, the Aztec decision to await the Spaniards in the Valley of Mexico rather than attack them in Tlaxcallan offered the advantages of cheap and unseverable logistical support, the largest possible army, and unrestricted mobility and striking power anywhere in the valley, all balanced against the Spaniards' uncertain political support and diminishing logistical support. As events bore out, this strategy ran into unanticipated complications. The main one was that the decision was undertaken with military concerns paramount; it gave the Aztecs defensive protection, concentration of force, and offensive striking power. But the strategy entailed considerable political risks, because it left the surrounding cities unprotected, subject to Spanish predation or conquest, and ultimately subject to defection as an act of self-preservation. It is likely that the Aztecs recognized this danger, for they brought the kings from the surrounding cities into Tenochtitlan, even if they underestimated the willingness of the remaining nobles to support the Spaniards. Perhaps they were sacrificing these cities, knowing that they could not defend them all. They must have found the risk acceptable, recognizing that everything depended on who won the battle for Tenochtitlan: if they won, the kings of nearby cities would return home with Aztec backing and reassert control; if they lost, who ruled at home would not matter. In light of military events up to that point, the Aztec decision to withdraw into their capital was sound.[1]

Cortés's forces were rested, more Spaniards had joined him from the coast, and his supply of horses, gunpowder, and crossbows were all increased, though they remained below preflight levels. Cortés had already begun the essential first phase of his return to Tenochtitlan, conquering Aztec tributaries east of the Valley of Mexico, securing their allegiance, generating logistical support, if not manpower, and guaranteeing the safety of the road to Vera Cruz. All this strengthened Cortés, but the actual conquest of Tenochtitlan demanded a fundamentally different strategy from the one he had employed previously.

During the first battle for Tenochtitlan, Cortés's forces had been trapped inside the city, cut off from outside support, and assailed from all sides. As time and supplies ran out, he had been forced to act even though conditions were unfavorable, and it had cost him dearly. He had acted from his belief that he could prevail with his Spaniards and a few thousand allies — perhaps not militarily but politically, by playing one faction off another. But that had failed in Tenochtitlan, and Cortés's main strategic goal now was no longer political destabilization but conquest. Accordingly, he marshaled a vastly larger army, big enough to reverse the previous situation, cut the Aztecs off from outside support, besiege their capital, and force them to fight under conditions dictated by the Spaniards.

Tenochtitlan was a large and powerful city, protected by its island location, and initially Cortés had too few men to march in and surround its army. Yet he could achieve essentially the same result by expanding the theater of operations from the city itself to include the entire valley. He could not count on decisively defeating or allying with all the towns in the valley, but he could still cut Tenochtitlan off if he could control the lake, and this he could accomplish by using superior European ships.

Before he began his return to Tenochtitlan, Cortés ordered a Spaniard named Martín López to direct the cutting and shaping of wood to construct thirteen brigantines, which he could do in the safety of Tlaxcallan by virtue of his new, stronger alliance. He also sent to Vera Cruz for the anchors, sails, and rigging he had stripped from his ships before they were grounded, as well as equipment taken from subsequent arrivals. A thousand Indians carried the rigging to Tlaxcallan, accompanied by Spanish blacksmiths and more harquebuses, powder, crossbows, and other arms from a newly arrived ship, as well as three horses and thirteen additional soldiers.[2]

The Tetzcoco region had suitable stands of timber, and Cortés might have built his ships there, where they could have been easily launched into the lake. But when he began his shipbuilding, he did not control that area. Moreover, building them in the Valley of Mexico would have revealed his plans to the Aztecs at a time when they might still have been able to take effective action against them. It would also have subjected the shipbuilders to Aztec attacks throughout their lengthy construction, forcing Cortés to divert large numbers of Indian allies from offensive actions to defend the construction. By building the ships in Tlaxcallan, the workers needed little defense, which freed most of the Tlaxcaltec soldiers for combat in the Valley of Mexico and greatly simplified Cortés's logistical problems, because the laborers were fed at home. Thus, building the ships in Tlaxcallan was safer and cheaper, allowed the use of laborers who otherwise could not contribute to the war effort, and still permitted the Spaniards and their allies to begin the war before the ships were completed. All that now remained to put Cortés's plan into action was secure logistical support.

On 28 December 1520, Cortés had eight or nine cannons, forty horsemen, and 550 Spanish soldiers, 80 of whom were crossbowmen or harquebusiers. With this force and ten thousand Tlaxcaltec soldiers, Cortés began his return march to the Valley of Mexico via Tetzmollocan. Before he left, the lords of Tlaxcallan allowed themselves to be baptized, for they were now inextricably committed to the enterprise, their fate tied to Cortés's. The Spaniards could take full advantage of large numbers of allied soldiers. Now, any breach Cortés's men opened in the enemies' lines could be exploited by his allies, and their sheer number would keep the Spaniards from being encircled, as had been their fate previously.[3]

Late December was already within the central Mexican war season, so Cortés could expect to meet considerable resistance, but the postharvest period also guaranteed plentiful supplies and large allied forces. En route to Tenochtitlan, Cortés defeated an enemy force in a pass into the valley and reached Coatepec, near Tetzcoco, just two days after leaving Tlaxcallan. But his real advantage lay in a new alliance with the Tetzcocan prince Ixtlilxochitl, who had come to Tlaxcallan and forged an alliance with Cortés. If Cortés succeeded in taking control of Ixtlilxochitl's home city, then the Spanish-Tlaxcaltec force could not only reenter the Valley of Mexico but also be guaranteed an adequate supply of local foodstuffs. The next morning, with Cortés and Ixtlilxochitl at the head of the army, Tetzcocan nobles approached the Spaniards and invited them into Tetzcoco in peace.[4]

Tetzcoco's failure to oppose Cortés's entry was the legacy of years of political divisions. When the city's ruler, King Nezahualpilli, died in 1515, he left legitimate sons but no chosen successor. One son, Tetlahuehuetzquiti, was unsuited to rule, but others were, including Coanacoch and Ixtlilxochitl, who were brothers and sons of the king by another Aztec wife. Moteuczoma, however, put his nephew Cacama on the throne, and Ixtlilxochitl fled to Metztitlan, where he raised an army, returned, and conquered the area north of Tetzcoco, ultimately reaching an uneasy accommodation with Tenochtitlan. Although the region was divided, Cacama remained on the throne in Tetzcoco with Aztec support. However, he had opposed Moteuczoma's acquiescence to Cortés and had been captured and subsequently killed during the Spaniards' flight from Tenochtitlan. Following the deaths of both Cacama and Moteuczoma, Tetzcoco was ruled by Coanacoch, although the details of his accession are sketchy. He became king following the death of Cacama, perhaps through Aztec imposition.

But however Coanacoch reached the throne, Tetzcoco must have remained divided, and when Cortés arrived with his new ally, Ixtlilxochitl, the balance of power shifted against him. He and his followers fled by canoe to Tenochtitlan.[5] Following Coanacoch's flight, another of King Nezahualpilli's sons, Tecocol, allegedly became ruler and head of the Spanish-backed faction, although at least the Tetzcocans who followed Coanacoch and the Aztecs still regarded Coanacoch as the legitimate king. Tecocol was reportedly a willing Spanish ally who ordered his people to fortify the city and make arms, including cotton armor, for the Spaniards. But because no more than two months elapsed between Tecocol's claimed accession and his death, it is likely that his kingship was a convenient fiction. The time span was too brief for the selection and coronation of a new king. The claim that Tecocol had acceded, however, placed the onus on him for usurping Coanacoch's legitimate rule while allowing his successor to avoid that taint.

As subsequent events would show, once the kings of outlying towns withdrew to Tenochtitlan, they were cut off and lost power. Whenever thrones were vacated, either by death or by flight, new rulers took over. But despite Cortés's claims that he installed the new rulers, he lacked the knowledge or power to do so. Rather, existing contenders for the throne seized on Cortés's presence to shift the political balance toward their own faction in order to take power. Many of these new rulers doubtless lacked the complete support of their subjects, but they also lacked coordinated opposition. In the case of Tetzcoco, this shift in rulers may have been engineered, at least in part, by Ixtlilxochitl, who had gone to Tlaxcallan and accompanied Cortés on his return to the Valley of Mexico. When Tecocol died conveniently and suspiciously around the first of February, Ixtlilxochitl succeeded him.[6]

Through these political maneuvers, Tetzcoco, the second city of the empire, fell bloodlessly into Spanish hands, giving Cortés the ideal base for his attack and virtually eliminating any logistical

limits on bringing additional troops from Tlaxcallan. The Spaniards were lodged in royal palaces in Tetzcoco, as they were in all
cities, friendly or hostile. This was a fortuitous conjunction of
political symbolism and practicality, because these were the only
quarters that were both defensible and large enough to house all
the Spaniards.

This return to the Valley of Mexico with the support of Ixtlilxochitl marked a new phase in the conquest of Mexico. The basic
pattern had been set by the Tlaxcaltecs, who engineered the place-
ment of friendly rulers on the thrones of conquered or intimidated
cities near their confederacy east of the Valley of Mexico. But they
had been unable to do the same in the Valley of Mexico. Successfully backing reliable royal candidates with sufficient support
to remain in power required thorough knowledge of all the major
power contenders and brokers, which was also aided by local
political connections, and they lacked those in the Valley of Mexico. Thus, once the Spaniards were back in the Valley of Mexico, it
was Ixtlilxochitl who became crucial, not merely for local military
support and supplies but also for his connections to, and understanding of, the major political players in the various cities. After
Tetzcoco's alliance with Cortés, the kings of adjacent subordinate
towns dependent on Tetzcoco pledged their loyalty as well. Their
own pro-Spanish factions were now significantly strengthened,
and their pledges of loyalty reflected this. The Spaniards now
dominated the area around Tetzcoco all the way to the base of the
Ixtapalapa peninsula to the south (see map 3). And Cortés would
have been keenly aware of the shifting importance of his two most
important allies.[7]

Long hostile to Tenochtitlan, the Chalca cities were subject to
Aztec control from Ixtlapalapan, near the tip of the Ixtapalapa
peninsula, but they were likely Spanish allies, as Cortés knew.
Leaving three thousand to four thousand Indian allies and half the
Spaniards in Tetzcoco, Cortés marched against Ixtlapalapan with
the rest, supported by more than seven thousand Tlaxcaltecs and

twenty nobles from Tetzcoco. Two leagues from Ixtlapalapan, the Aztecs attacked the Spaniards simultaneously from land and canoes, but Cortés forced them back to the city. Breaking through their lines, he entered and occupied it. Whether this was a Spanish victory or an Aztec feint, Cortés's forces were now unknowingly in a vulnerable position. Much of Ixtlapalapan had been built out into the lake, and though protected by dikes, the city was actually below water level. Once Cortés's forces were quartered inside, the Aztecs broke the dikes and flooded the city. The violent flooding put Cortés's army to flight, and some men drowned, though most escaped to higher ground. All the gunpowder was ruined, the spoils were lost, and the Spaniards finally withdrew to Tetzcoco under constant attack by Aztecs who landed by canoe along the line of march. Isolated on a peninsula with only one avenue of advance or retreat, the Spaniards were exposed to constant assault by Aztec forces. Cortés's first major battle since reentering the Valley of Mexico ended in defeat.[8]

Cortés reached Tetzcoco, but all was not well with his men. Confronted by this military defeat and aware that the continual arrival of ships at Veracruz offered them an avenue of escape, several Spaniards now wanted to leave and allegedly plotted to assassinate Cortés. He seized the main conspirators, but many important people were implicated. Cortés could not afford an open division among the Spaniards; it would weaken him in the eyes of his Indian allies, with potentially disastrous consequences. So he focused only on the leader, Antonio de Villafaña, one of Narváez's men, and hanged him rather than punishing the other conspirators, using Villafaña's execution to keep them in line.[9]

Despite continued unrest, Cortés controlled the divisions within his camp, so the Aztecs faced an apparently unified opponent. The Spaniards, by contrast, did not. The Indians were divided by preexisting antagonisms, by new ones that had emerged with the arrival of the Spaniards, and frequently by political divisions within towns that hobbled their leaders' ability to act decisively.

Dividing the Aztecs was crucial to Cortés's success, and throughout the campaign he followed a carrot-and-stick policy of mercilessly attacking his enemies while forgiving the past transgressions of those who became his allies, greatly exacerbating existing divisions within and between cities. Had Narváez been able to march inland and establish an independent presence, the Aztecs or others might have been able to divide the Spaniards in a similar fashion. But Cortés kept Spanish divisions below the surface. Although many still wanted to return to Cuba, there were no Spanish attempts to negotiate a separate peace with the Aztecs. The remaining dissidents wanted to change the agenda, not split it.

Spanish political tactics had little effect if Indian kings had solid local support or if they were supported by Tenochtitlan and were close enough that Aztec influence was decisive. Otherwise, Spanish pressure frequently warped the local political hierarchy. Spanish support often proved crucial, and some kings pledged allegiance to bolster their domestic power. If they resisted, Spanish and allied support was often enough to oust the king and enthrone more favorable challengers, although this was typically an Indian initiative rather than a Spanish stratagem. Such changes reinforced the allied towns' ties to the Spaniards, because these rulers now depended on continued Spanish support to retain their thrones. At the same time, the rapidly shifting political landscape diminished Aztec influence and complicated the Aztecs' efforts to maintain allies.

More towns, including Otompan, pledged loyalty to the Spaniards. Others, such as the Chalca cities, that wanted to ally with Cortés could not because of the presence of Aztec troops. Cortés's concern for the Chalca area extended beyond his need for additional allies. This area straddled the road to the Gulf coast, which he had to keep open for more men and arms (although these could have been funneled to the north) and for food from both Chalco and Tlaxcallan (which could not). The Aztecs recognized this and attacked the area repeatedly. Cortés dispatched one of his lieutenants, Gonzalo de Sandoval, with fifteen to twenty horsemen, two hundred Spanish soldiers, and all the Tlaxcaltecs to Chalco, but the Aztecs attacked the Tlaxcaltecs at the rear and inflicted heavy casualties before being driven off. In the main clash at Chalco, the Aztecs used long lances against the horses, but the battle took place on a level plain where the horses could be used to greatest effect, and the Spaniards prevailed. Sandoval returned to Tetzcoco from Chalco with two sons of the king, who had recently died of smallpox. Cortés installed the elder as king of Chalco and the younger as king of Tlalmanalco.[10]

Cortés then sent Aztec captives to Cuauhtemoc with a message of peace, as he had done throughout the campaign, but this overture was spurned because it was essentially a demand that the Aztecs surrender and become Spanish vassals. The Aztecs continued to mount raids by canoe against defecting lakeshore towns, but these were suppressed by Spanish retaliation.[11]

When Cortés could fight his enemies on open terrain, he was generally successful, but his successes gave him the same problem that had plagued the Aztecs earlier. So many towns on the eastern side of the lakes were now allies that the Spaniards could not defend them all, and dividing his forces among the many towns would leave none strong enough to repulse a determined Aztec assault. Therefore, Cortés kept his forces in Tetzcoco and dispatched them as needed, which typically meant the Spaniards responded after the damage was done and might not respond at all when there were multiple calls for help. The allied cities were forced to become actively involved, providing intelligence about Aztec plans and armed defense of their homes.

As long as the Aztecs could strike from canoes throughout the valley, further Spanish expansion only compounded Cortés's problems. Unless he could stop these attacks, the pro-Spanish rulers of allied towns would be in danger of insurrection. Cortés could not defend all his allies by simply responding to Aztec initiatives; he had to take the offensive and strike directly at the source — Tenochtitlan.

To realize this objective, Cortés dispatched a force under Sandoval to Tlaxcallan to fetch the timber being cut for the ships. When Sandoval was almost there, he met a group of eight thousand to ten thousand Tlaxcaltecs bringing the timbers toward Tetzcoco, guarded by an equal number of soldiers and accompanied by two thousand more carrying food. Sandoval's men joined them, guarding the front and sides while the Tlaxcaltecs guarded the rear. Marching north around the mountains and avoiding the still unsettled Chalca area, this party reached Tetzcoco around the first of February after four days' march, and construction of the brigantines began.[12]

On 3 February, Cortés marched north against Xaltocan, which had rejected his peace entreaties. Located in the lightly populated north, Xaltocan was not a serious threat to the Spaniards. It was well removed from the major area of operations, offered little danger to the Spaniards beyond small-scale, canoe-borne sniping, and could easily have been bypassed and isolated had Cortés's purpose been primarily military. But Xaltocan was similar to Tenochtitlan in being built on an island, cut by canals, and connected to the mainland by a causeway. Xaltocan presented the same problems in miniature that Cortés would face in Tenochtitlan. Because he had assembled a force two to four times larger than he had dispatched against any of the more significant and formidable cities in the southern portion of the valley, the assault was probably undertaken to test his forces and tactics.[13]

Xaltocan had been reinforced from Tenochtitlan, and these troops attacked the Spanish forces from canoes in the canals. The lakeshore near Xaltocan was cut by creeks and canals, rendering the horses almost useless. Because the causeway into the town had been destroyed, the Spaniards could not enter, but the two sides exchanged fire. The Indians were unharmed because their canoes were armored with thick wooden bulwarks. Frustrated, Cortés was about to withdraw when two Indians from Tepetezcoco, who were enemies of Xaltocan, told him that most of the causeway had not actually been destroyed; rather, the people of Xaltocan had merely allowed more water in to cover it. On learning this, the Spaniards found the causeway, crossed into Xaltocan, and conquered the town.[14]

Recalling their disastrous experiences in Tenochtitlan, the victorious Spaniards were nevertheless afraid to remain in Xaltocan as long as the Aztecs controlled the water, so they left to camp on the mainland. This was not a major tactical success, given Cortés's overwhelming numerical superiority, but it did graphically demonstrate the effectiveness of water barriers and the Aztec control of the lakes that the Spaniards would have to overcome if they hoped to conquer Tenochtitlan.[15]

From Xaltocan Cortés marched around the lakes to Cuauhtitlan, Tenanyocan, and Azcapotzalco, all of which had been abandoned. None of these cities was large enough to defend itself against the Spaniards, so rather than mounting a costly and ultimately futile resistance, their inhabitants withdrew to Tlacopan, concentrating their forces there. In the eastern valley, such towns had often capitulated in the face of Spanish attack, because they were beyond effective Aztec help and had closer ties to centers such as Tetzcoco. But in the west the Aztecs were able to implement a coordinated strategy, pulling smaller populations into larger centers where they could defend themselves, limiting the number of places Tenochtitlan had to defend, and complicating Cortés's situation by removing populations he might have controlled through supportive rulers and whose cities he might then have used as bases of operations.[16]

At Tlacopan Cortés was met by a large army and newly constructed barricades and ditches. His horses were able to break through and force the Aztecs to retreat only with great effort. The Spaniards entered, sacked, and burned the city before Aztec rein-

forcements poured over the causeway from Tenochtitlan. Cortés
attacked these as well and they were apparently forced back, but
this was an Aztec stratagem to entice the Spaniards into a compromised position. Once the Spanish troops were fully on the causeway, the Aztecs turned and attacked them while canoe-borne
troops assailed them from both sides, squeezing the Spaniards
from three sides. Exposed and vulnerable, Spanish cavalry and
swordsmen could engage only those directly in front of them on
the causeway. This Aztec tactic minimized the effects of Spanish
weaponry and maximized the effectiveness of their own, forcing
Cortés into an immediate retreat and leaving several Spaniards
dead and many wounded.[17]

Cortés remained under constant attack in Tlacopan for five or
six days before withdrawing to Tetzcoco. Throughout the withdrawal, the Aztecs attacked the Spaniards' rear. The Spaniards
were tired, and it was much more difficult to maintain a solid front
during a march than while attacking, which allowed the Aztecs to
inflict greater damage. Moreover, the baggage and supplies were
in the rear, offering an easier target for sorties aimed at the logistical weakness of Mesoamerican armies. The entire campaign had
lasted fifteen days, ending on 18 February when Cortés returned to
Tetzcoco. Although it inflicted damage on the Aztecs, it did so at
considerable cost in a series of battles that otherwise achieved little
of permanent significance.[18]

Following Cortés's return, more rulers from nearby towns arrived to swear fealty to him, but the Chalca cities remained under
Aztec attack. Cortés's men were exhausted, so he sent Sandoval to
Chalco with a force of Spaniards, a few Tlaxcaltecs, and a company of Tetzcocas, all of whom had remained in Tetzcoco and had
not taken part in the northern campaign. Once in Chalco, Sandoval
added local soldiers and attacked the Aztecs near Chimalhuacan,
but the Aztecs fell back to some passes where they were able to
fend off the Spaniards. Because they had merely withdrawn to the
south, the Aztecs remained a threat to the Chalca cities once the

Spaniards left. So Sandoval followed them to Huaxtepec, where, thanks to the cavalry, his forces defeated them again. He then marched to the fortified town of Yacapitztlan, and after hard fighting—mostly by his Indian allies—he won again and finally returned to Tetzcoco. After the Spaniards withdrew, however, the Aztecs again attacked Chalco by canoe. But with aid from Huexotzinco, the Aztecs were repulsed without Spanish assistance.[19]

The Gulf coast road was still not secure, but more ships reached Vera Cruz on 24 February, landing men and arms that ultimately reached Cortés. If the Aztecs severed this intermittent but sizable flow of men and arms, Cortés's position would significantly worsen, with political complications for both Spaniards and Indian allies. Simply repelling the Aztecs was insufficient, because they would pull back and wait for the Spaniards to leave. The Aztecs and their allies had to be eliminated from the adjacent areas, too. Thus, Cortés assembled a great force and on 5 April marched against the Aztecs at Yauhtepec, well to the south of the Chalca cities, reaching it on 11 April. There he assaulted two hilltop strongholds. After two days he was still unable to scale them in the face of thick fire, so he climbed an adjacent, undefended hill and fired his cannons and harquebuses into the Aztecs' positions until they surrendered. Cortés then marched on and conquered Cuauhnahuac on 13 April.[20]

This campaign secured the area south of the Valley of Mexico, reducing the fear of an attack from that direction. The conquests also effectively cut Tenochtitlan off from further support from the south by eliminating the conquered cities as a source and by cordoning off loyal towns farther south with a swath of Spanish-controlled territory.

The next day Cortés marched back toward the Valley of Mexico, reaching the city of Xochimilco on 16 April. This city, too, had been heavily fortified, and Cuauhtemoc threw large forces against Cortés, keeping up the attack from canoes well into the night. At daybreak on the eighteenth, the Aztecs again attacked the Spaniards' encampment, and Cortés's badly mauled troops were finally forced to withdraw.[21]

The next day, when more Aztec reinforcements arrived, Cortés began his retreat to Tetzcoco, going first to Coyohuacan while under constant attack. Coyohuacan was deserted, and the Spaniards remained there a day before burning its main buildings and then marching toward Tlacopan under constant attack. The Spaniards continued their march, passing the deserted cities of Azcapotzalco, Tenanyocan, and Cuauhtitlan, retracing the route they had taken during their earlier incursion and reaching Tetzcoco on 22 April.[22]

Cortés claimed this campaign had been for the purpose of learning the layout around Tenochtitlan in preparation for his brigantines, but this seems unlikely. He had earlier stayed in Tenochtitlan for eight months and was surely familiar with the city and its environs. The incursion's more probable purpose was to assess the political and military climate of the area and to determine which towns would resist. And although the Spaniards' arms and horses had proved decisive outside the valley, they were consistently forced back when battles took place near the lakes, where the Aztecs could use the great mobility of their canoes for attack and reinforcement. This was about to change.[23]

CHAPTER 9

CONQUEST AND DEFEAT

Control of the lakes in the Valley of Mexico would be crucial to the conquest of Tenochtitlan. Cortés's ships had been under construction for several weeks, and although they had been attacked repeatedly by canoe-borne Aztecs, the assaults were unsuccessful because the assembly site lay half a league from the lakeshore. Fear of attack, rather than lack of materials or laborers in the Valley of Mexico, was probably why Cortés had ordered all the timbers for the ships made in Tlaxcallan and then carried overland to Tetzcoco. Now the ships were ready to be launched.

Twelve of the ships were each 12.8 meters (42 feet) long and 2.4–2.7 meters (8–9 feet) abeam. They drew 0.6–0.8 meter (2.0–2.5 feet) of water, had 1.2 meter (4 feet) of freeboard at the waist and 1.8–2.1 meters (6–7 feet) at the forecastle and the poop, were nearly flat bottomed, and were about equally divided between one and two masts. The thirteenth, the flagship, was slightly larger, at 14.6 meters (48 feet). In order to launch these ships from their landlocked construction site, Cortés ordered a canal built. Forty thousand Tetzcocas dug for seven weeks to construct a canal 3.7 meters (12 feet) wide and equally deep, and the ships were launched on 28 April. This was toward the end of the dry season, when the lakes were at their lowest, which must have greatly restricted the movement of Cortés's ships. Their flat-bottom design minimized this problem, but throughout the conquest the brigantines were concentrated in the deepest water in and around Tenochtitlan.[1]

The launching of the ships was to be coordinated with Cortés's main offensive, so he also ordered other preparations. Each allied town in the valley was to make eight thousand copper arrowheads, based on Spanish examples, to be affixed to wooden shafts, and within eight days more than fifty thousand of these excellent crossbow bolts were produced. Each crossbowman was also given two bow strings. The horses were all shod, and the lancers all practiced. At this point Cortés sent requests to Tlaxcallan for twenty thousand warriors and to his allies in the valley to be ready to help.[2]

The Spaniards now had 86 horsemen, 700 foot soldiers, and 118 crossbowmen and harquebusiers. From this number Cortés selected crews for the thirteen ships, each holding twelve oarsmen (six to a side), twelve crossbowmen and harquebusiers, and a captain, for a total of twenty-five men per ship plus artillerymen, because each ship had a cannon mounted in the bow. Although seaborne guns are not as steady or accurate as land guns, placing them on ships — presumably in swivel mounts on the railings — gave these cannons great mobility, allowed them to be adjusted to changing circumstances and targets far more quickly than field cannons, and permitted vigorous pursuit if the enemy withdrew.[3]

The remaining land forces were divided into three armies. Pedro de Alvarado was given command of thirty horsemen, eighteen crossbowmen and harquebusiers, 150 Spanish foot soldiers, and a force of twenty-five thousand Tlaxcaltecs and was dispatched on 22 May 1521 to Tlacopan. Cristóbal de Olid was placed in command of twenty crossbowmen and harquebusiers, 175 Spanish foot soldiers, and a force of twenty thousand Indian allies and dispatched to Coyohuacan. Gonzalo de Sandoval commanded twenty-four horsemen, fourteen harquebusiers, thirteen crossbowmen, 150 Spanish foot soldiers, and a force of more than thirty thousand Indian allies from Huexotzinco, Cholollan, and Chalco and was dispatched to Ixtlapalapan. Throughout this final phase of the conquest, Spaniards composed less then 1 percent of the forces arrayed against the Aztecs; more than 99 percent were Indians. And although Spanish accounts generally minimize the contributions of their allies, the role of Indian leaders was crucial. In addition to the linguistic barriers, only native leaders could command their troops in battle and ensure their cooperation. Although Indian allies reinforced the Spaniards, they necessarily operated as independent forces under their own leadership.[4]

Their support, however, was not unquestioning. In a generally neglected incident, the Tlaxcaltec leader, Xicotencatl the Younger, was seized by Cortés, accused of treason, and hanged. Cortés had summoned the rest of his Tlaxcaltec allies when was ready to begin the assault on Tenochtitlan. Two armies made the three-day march — one of sixty thousand Tlaxcaltecs commanded by Xicotencatl the Younger and another composed of Tlaxcaltecs, Huexotzincas, and Chololtecs under the command of his rival, Ocotelolco's general, Chichimecateuctli. But on the night he arrived, Xicotencatl reportedly deserted, either for a women he had left behind or to seize control in Tlaxcallan. Reportedly, Chichimecateuctli learned of this and informed Cortés, who sent five Tetzcocan nobles and two Tlaxcaltec nobles to force Xicotencatl's return. When he refused, Cortés sent five Spaniards and five Tetzcocans, who seized him, and he was hanged, which is variously recorded as having occurred at Tlaxcallan or Tetzcoco.[5]

Neither explanation rings true. If Xicotencatl loved a woman in Tlaxcallan, he could easily have brought her with him, and if he was returning there to seize control of the government, he would hardly have left his army behind. And once his death was a fait accompli, Cortés's allies in Tlaxcallan accepted the proffered excuse of treason.

Treason was apparently a capital offense in Tlaxcallan, as it was among the Aztecs, but treason involves betrayal, which was not the case with Xicotencatl. Indeed, desertions in the face of changing political realities were common and typically went un-punished. Xicotencatl's hanging was an exception that demands explanation.[6]

The event can be best understood by examining its political context. Cortés was now significantly less dependent on Tlax-callan than he had once been. He had already gotten his shipbuild-ing supplies and assembled the brigantines, and he was receiving supplies, political intelligence, and a significant number of sol-diers from Tetzcoco and its dependencies. Nevertheless, he still needed Tlaxcaltec support. The smallpox epidemic of the previous December, however, had killed Maxixcatl, ruler of the Tlaxcal-tec province of Ocotelolco, and had upset the balance of power in Tlaxcallan. Maxixcatl had been succeeded by his twelve- or thirteen-year-old son, don Lorenzo Maxixcatl,[7] but the replace-ment of Cortes's primary Tlaxcaltec ally by a young and inex-perienced boy left the de facto ruler, Xicotencatl the Younger, the dominant political force in Tlaxcallan. Cortés perceived Xicoten-catl's opposition to the Spaniards to be a pro-Aztec stance rather than the internal political position that it was. Accordingly, Xico-tencatl's execution was most likely contrived by Cortés with the apparent assistance of Chichimecateuctli, who was the main bene-ficiary of that death.[8]

Having eliminated a political threat, Cortés next targeted three cities. Though significant, they were by no means the only impor-tant cities or even the largest. Their primary significance was loca-tional: each controlled access to a major causeway linking it to Tenochtitlan. Severing these conduits would both stop the flow of men and materiel into Tenochtitlan and bottle up the Aztecs inside.

The Spanish and allied armies left Tetzcoco on 22 May 1521, during the waning days of the city's smallpox epidemic. Alvarado and Olid marched north together around the lakes, passing through Cuauhtitlan, Tenanyocan, and Azcapotzalco before reaching Tla-copan. From there they marched to Chapoltepec, routed its de-fenders, and cut off the aqueduct that supplied Tenochtitlan.

As the most powerful city in Mesoamerica, Tenochtitlan had never before had its economic lifelines threatened like this. But the city was uniquely vulnerable.[9] Whatever else a city might be, it is a large population that cannot feed itself. Every city has to draw food in from outside to feed its populace, and defensively this is its Achilles' heel. A landlocked city in Mesoamerica could draw in basic foodstuffs from a hinterland little more than a single day's journey away. The cost of food is not merely the expense of production plus a profit but also the cost of transportation, and because this meant the labor of an adult male for each 23 kilograms (50 pounds) carried, it was much higher in Mesoamerica than in Europe, where draft animals and carts carried large loads at more reasonable rates. As a result, most cities in Mesoamerica were relatively small: their populations could grow no larger than the number that could be reliably fed.

Tenochtitlan, however, was home to more than 200,000 people, vastly more than any other Mesoamerican city. It owed its great size to its unique location in the middle of an interconnected series of lakes, which allowed Tenochtitlan to take advantage of the only truly efficient form of transportation available in Mesoamerica — canoes. Whereas a single porter could carry a 23-kilogram load, a single canoer could easily pole 920 kilograms (2,000 pounds) at the same speed. This meant that Tenochtitlan enjoyed a vastly different situation from those of most other cities in Mesoamerica. Rather than drawing goods into the center from a maximum radius of, say, 26 kilometers (16 miles), as would have been the case for a landlocked city, Tenochtitlan could draw in food from a similar radius, not from the city center but from the entire lakeshore. The cost of overland shipment remained the same, but once foodstuffs reached the lakeshore, the cost of transport from there to Tenochtitlan by canoe was only 2.5 percent of the cost for an equivalent distance overland, a negligible amount. Thus, the capital could afford to draw in food from a vastly larger hinterland than could landlocked cities.

Increasing the area on which Tenochtitlan could draw, however, was easier in theory than in practice. Much of that land was
already occupied by other cities, and many of these were allies or
tributaries from whom more could not easily be extracted. To deal
with this dilemma, Tenochtitlan turned to *chinampas* — artificial
fields constructed in the lakes of the Valley of Mexico, which were
only a couple of meters deep. To construct chinampas, the builders
drove stakes into the lake bed to form enclosures into which soil,
taken primarily from the lake bottom, was dumped. These excava-
tions both created deeper canals between the fields and yielded
very fertile soils. The end product was a series of artificial islands
of exceptional fertility that required no irrigation because they
rose about half a meter above the lake level and the crops' roots
easily reached the water table. Because they were so low on
the warm water, the chinampas were also relatively unsusceptible
to the frosts that strike the rest of the valley from September
through May. Therefore, year-round cropping was possible, aided
by the night soil that was shipped to the fields in canoes from
Tenochtitlan.

Large-scale chinampa construction in the Valley of Mexico
was an Aztec innovation that began after the late 1450s. The southern two lakes, Lakes Xochimilco and Chalco, were devoted to
chinampas, which were relatively uniform size and laid out in a
regular pattern, indicative of state planning. Adding the 9,500 hec-
tares (over 2.3 million acres) of the chinampas in these two lakes
to the agricultural potential of the Valley of Mexico went a long
way toward supplying Tenochtitlan's needs. But still more food
was required by the growing capital, and it could come only from
the lands of the Aztecs' allies.

Tenochtitlan could not directly compel its allies to send more
food, because it depended on them for soldiers and other political
support. But it did manipulate the economy of central Mexico to
achieve this end. Each allied city produced much of its own needs,
including textiles, pottery, and stone tools, which it then sold to its

own dependent communities in return for agricultural products. These city-states were thus relatively self-sufficient economic systems that needed neither to buy nor to sell much in Tenochtitlan. Tenochtitlan did not intervene in this system directly, but it did harness its tribute system to alter the economies of neighboring cities to suit its own needs. Tenochtitlan received enormous quantities of finished materials as tribute from its dependencies, such as gold jewelry and cotton mantles. Part of it was redistributed among the nobles, but much of it was sold through the market. Because tribute goods were essentially free — beyond the costs of war — they could be sold at or below their cost of production. No producer could compete with this politically subsidized trade, and the inhabitants of nearby cities were effectively forced out of the trade in these items.

Because neighboring towns could not compete with Tenochtitlan in the sale of manufactured goods received in tribute, their production of such goods declined. The sole area in which the towns could compete was agriculture, because not even Tenochtitlan could afford to import food from great distances. Thus, during the decades of Aztec dominance, manufacturing in the other cities of the Valley of Mexico declined while their agricultural production increased. By dominating the market in manufactured goods, the Aztecs effectively forced their nearby allies away from self-sufficient economies and toward an integrated, valley-wide economy in which they acted as the agricultural hinterland of Tenochtitlan's industrial and commercial core.

Despite its enormous population, especially for Mesoamerica, Tenochtitlan managed to secure a reliable agricultural hinterland. To the extent they could, the Aztecs had insured themselves against famine, but these measures were responses to ecological reversals, not to war. Most of Tenochtitlan's foodstuffs — whether from their own chinampas, purchased in trade, or secured as tribute — remained outside the city proper. Tenochtitlan lacked sufficient storage facilities to maintain its own warehouses, and most food entered the city only as needed. Sieges were rare and short-lived in Mesoamerica, and as large as Tenochtitlan was, no one in Mesoamerica could threaten it with one. But the Spanish brigantines cut Tenochtitlan off in an entirely unexpected way from food supplies that were otherwise available and plentiful.[10]

The same was at least partly true of its water supply. Although Tenochtitlan was an island city, the lake was brackish, and all drinking water had to be brought in. Much of it came in by canoe, carried in pottery jars, but a significant portion flowed into the city from the springs at Chapoltepec along an aqueduct built by King Ahuitzotl in 1499. Cutting this flow was a major, though not decisive, blow to the Aztecs, and it signaled the initiation of Cortés's strategy of starving out the defenders rather than defeating them solely on the battlefield.

Having struck the first blow against the flow of subsistence goods into the capital, the two Spanish captains returned to Tlacopan and tried to march across the causeway to Tenochtitlan. Any battle on the causeways would nominally have favored the defenders, because their width restricted the number of soldiers who could actually engage in combat, greatly prolonging the fight and working against the side with the poorer logistical support — usually the attacker. Throughout the battle for Tenochtitlan, however, normal Mesoamerican conditions did not entirely apply. Relatively few Spaniards attacked each causeway, but a greater proportion of their most effective troops was actively involved, and they used superior weapons. Thus, restricting the fighting to several long corridors was not as disadvantageous to the Spaniards as it normally would have been, though it did mean they bore the brunt of the combat and could not employ their allies as effectively as in open combat. Fighting on the causeways did reverse the normal defensive advantage, however, presenting the Spaniards with a limited front of massed troops who were ideal targets for their fire. Cannons could kill and disrupt the Aztec front, but because of their relatively slow rates of fire, most of the fighting was hand to hand, pitting the Spaniards' steel swords, pikes, and armor against the Aztecs' wood and obsidian swords and spears and their cotton armor.

Despite a clear one-to-one technological superiority, the Spaniards were continually threatened by the sheer mass of the Aztec defenders. The danger of being trapped and killed by the crush of Aztec soldiers was constant, so the Spaniards stressed mobility. This allowed them to use their weapons to greatest advantage, probably by repeatedly advancing for hand-to-hand combat and falling back while the cannons, harquebuses, and crossbows were fired to disrupt the Aztecs. Moreover, the Aztecs could not attack the rear, because it was protected by large numbers of Indian allies, allowing the Spaniards to concentrate on their front.[11]

The Aztecs tried to fight in their own way but were forced to adjust their tactics in response to Spanish weaponry. Cannons were particularly devastating because they could kill from a distance that Aztec weapons could not reach. But the Aztecs soon learned that the cannons could fire only in a straight line, so they began to dodge from side to side instead of marching in straight lines, and they ducked when the cannons were about to fire rather than remaining erect. Moreover, if a cannon fired from far enough away that the Aztecs could dodge the shot, it was also too far away for the Spanish forces to exploit the breach it caused. Instead, the Aztecs had enough time to reform and meet any assault. Their countermeasures, however, were limited by the causeways that funneled them in masses toward their Spanish foes, so the Aztecs responded by building barricades that offered protection from crossbow and harquebus fire, although cannons could demolish them after a few shots.[12]

The Aztecs were most effective with their naval assaults. Canoe-borne soldiers attacked the Spaniards on the causeways, firing arrows, darts, and slingstones into the Spaniards' flanks while thick wooden planks protected them from all but cannon fire. The Spaniards returned fire with their crossbows, harquebuses, and cannons, when they could be spared from their frontal assault. But these weapons fired slowly, and the canoes did not offer densely packed targets and remained beyond the reach of Spanish swords and pikes. Thus, the Spaniards faced enemies on three sides, two of which were beyond effective retaliation. The situation was sufficiently bad that the Spaniards quickly limited their use of horses on the causeways, because their mobility was severely restricted anyway.[13]

The initial Spanish assault was forced back with heavy losses, and Olid took his army and marched south to Coyohuacan and set up camp. The forces of Olid and Alvarado had been repulsed when they were together, and now that they had separated, neither force was in a position to take the offensive. The two remained in their respective camps, fighting only to ward off Aztec attacks.[14]

Meanwhile, Sandoval began his march on 30 May, going south through mostly friendly territory until he reached Ixtlapalapan. He attacked and burned the city, and most of its defenders fled in canoes. At the same time, Cortés launched his fleet and sailed to Tepepolco, a fortified island near Tenochtitlan. He landed 150 men and captured the island, but, alerted by smoke signals from its hilltop, a large force of Aztec canoes counterattacked. Cortés's small force was no match for the approaching Aztecs and he abandoned the island to meet them at sea, where he had the advantage of Spanish ships. In this first naval engagement, the brigantines proved convincingly superior, sailing through and overturning the canoes, which then fled into canals that were too narrow for Cortés's ships to follow.

He next sailed his fleet toward Coyohuacan, where Olid's forces were under attack. Landing thirty men and three cannons, Cortés seized the small site of Xoloco on the Ixtlapalapan causeway and camped there for the night. The next day he reached Coyohuacan, helped drive off the attacking canoes, and made a breach in the causeway so his ships could pass through and defend both sides. This breach was made by Indian laborers, whose role is

virtually ignored in the Spanish accounts, despite the fact that
more of the success of the siege of Tenochtitlan was owed to
engineering on a massive scale by tens of thousands of allied
Indian laborers than it was to combat.[15]

Once the breach was made, Cortés's brigantines passed through,
accompanied by thousands of allied canoes. Once inside, they
quickly destroyed or dispersed the Aztec fleet. After the deploy-
ment of Cortés's ships along the western and southern causeways,
Sandoval's forces marched in relative safety from Ixtlapalapan to
Mexicatzinco, where a causeway ran to Coyohuacan. The Aztecs
responded by sending a fleet of canoes to sever the causeway and
prevent the two forces from linking up.[16]

As the Aztecs attempted to destroy the causeway to Mexicatzinco, Cortés sailed to reinforce Sandoval. Keeping ships on
both sides of the causeways was essential, because otherwise the
Aztecs would concentrate their canoes on the side opposite the
brigantines. Thus positioned, they could fire freely at the Spaniards on the causeways. Placing ships on both sides kept the canoes
at bay but tied up twice as many ships as would otherwise have
been necessary. Nevertheless, it allowed the Spanish forces to
move, albeit with great difficulty, and Sandoval's army fought its
way across the Mexicatzinco causeway to join Olid at Coyohuacan
on 31 May.[17]

It is unclear why Sandoval moved from the Ixtapalapa peninsula to Coyohuacan. If he had destroyed the peninsula as an enemy
base, he could then have supported other Spanish operations. But
because he had mostly stayed in his own camp until the brigantines
arrived, and because there were subsequent hostilities in the area,
Sandoval's movement probably indicates a failure of Spanish
strategy. Unsupported, his army was too small for major offensive
actions, as were Alvarado's and Olid's. Sandoval had to join Olid's
forces or at least move onto the causeway, where, with the help of
the brigantines, he could limit the areas of engagement and minimize his disadvantages. Sandoval and Olid took the bases of the

causeways from Ixtlapalapan and Coyohuacan, respectively, and marched to the juncture where the two causeways merged into a single one leading to Tenochtitlan. From there, only one force could be used effectively on the narrow causeway, so Sandoval's army was pulled back and sent to Tepeyacac to capture the still open northern causeway.

Throughout the siege, the Spanish ships greatly complicated Cuauhtemoc's planning. Aztec defensive efforts had been concentrated along the narrow fronts where causeways ran, but now the Spaniards could land forces virtually anywhere around the Valley of Mexico. In actuality, the Spaniards' ability to do this was limited, because each ship held few men and none could carry horses. But the threat forced the Aztecs to prepare for defense everywhere, diluting their efforts on the active fronts. Perhaps the ships' greatest importance, however, was their ability to bring artillery into range of many areas of Tenochtitlan not previously threatened.

In response to these Spanish initiatives, the Aztecs built traps for both men and ships. The relatively shallow lakes allowed the Spaniards to wade across breaches between segments of the causeway in many places, but they also enabled the Aztecs to dig pits in the lake bottom that could not be seen from above. Spaniards who fell into them could drown or be more easily captured by men in canoes. A similar approach was used against the ships. The Aztecs placed sharpened stakes in the lake floor to impale the ships, especially near the water traps, in case the Spanish fleet came to the aid of floundering soldiers.[18]

Protected by ships on either side of the causeways, Spanish forces were able to advance along them. But they could control only their immediate areas and were unable to consolidate their gains. As soon as they moved, Aztec forces reoccupied abandoned positions, deepened and widened the breaches in the causeways, and built even stronger defenses.[19]

The Spaniards' initial strategy had been to attack along the causeways during the day and withdraw to the relative security of their camps at night. But because the Aztecs reoccupied the areas thus abandoned, the Spaniards spent much of their time and resources retaking the same places day after day. They could not afford this costly and wasteful practice and soon changed tactics. Instead of withdrawing for the night, they would advance along the causeways until they reached a wide place and set up camp there. They also began posting guards at heavily defended barricades and bridges to prevent the Aztecs from rebuilding and reoccupying them. Although this complicated Aztec efforts, it did not completely frustrate them. Nevertheless, with these changes, the Spaniards began making more progress along the causeways.[20]

Logistics became increasingly important to both sides as the campaign wore on. The Spaniards were accompanied by large numbers of Indian women who ground maize and prepared food, and these women became targets of Aztec attacks. Although the attacks generally failed, they forced the Spaniards to divert resources to protect their camps. Tenochtitlan was particularly vulnerable logistically. The attack had begun in the spring, well before harvest, so supplies were at their lowest of the year. Famine was taking hold in the city.[21]

The Spaniards had already cut the aqueduct from Chapoltepec, and their occupation of the main causeways cut off the shipment of food and water into the city by foot. Moreover, the brigantines kept canoe traffic to a minimum during the day. Just as the few hundred Spanish soldiers served as shock troops for their tens of thousands of Indian allies, so the brigantines typically sailed in twos or threes and played a similar role for the thousands of allied war canoes. Without the support and screening of allied canoes, the brigantines could break up Aztec fleets but could not exploit their gains and risked being overcome by swarms of Aztec canoes when they could not outrun them.[22]

With sails, oars, and favorable winds, the brigantines were faster than the Indian canoes, but so many Aztec craft tried to reach Tenochtitlan for resupply that a blockade was hopeless without the help of allied canoes. The perimeter of Tenochtitlan offered at least 24 kilometers (15 miles) of shoreline where canoes could land, and the causeways doubled or tripled that perimeter. The few brigantines launched at night or diverted from combat during the day could not intercept the thousands of canoes plying the lakes. Patrolling farther from the city and causeways greatly increased both the distance each brigantine was responsible for and the likelihood that canoes would slip through. Sailing closer minimized patrol distances and maximized the likelihood of interdicting blockade runners, but it also increased the ships' vulnerability to attack and to stakes hidden in the water. Moreover, Aztec canoes could cross areas too shallow for the brigantines to follow. Thus, large fleets of allied canoes played a crucial role in this effort. Without them, the Spaniards' blockade of Tenochtitlan would have failed.

Cortés kept two of his brigantines on patrol at night to interdict supply-laden canoes, even though darkness increased the risks of navigating the shallow and trap-strewn lakes and reduced the number of ships available for military support during the day. The two ships succeeded in stopping some canoes from reaching Tenochtitlan, but in response the Aztecs set up an ambush.[23]

Hiding thirty of their largest war canoes among the reeds growing in the lake, the Aztecs dispatched two or three supply canoes as a lure. When the brigantines spotted them, they gave chase, and the canoes fled past the hidden war canoes. The Aztecs had driven sharpened stakes into the lake bottom along the route they expected the Spanish ships to follow, and when they did, the Aztec canoes attacked en masse. Trapped between the attacking canoes and the stakes, all the Spaniards were wounded, one captain was killed, and his ship was captured. The Aztecs had already learned to be wary of the brigantines, which reduced their combat effectiveness, and the Spaniards on the brigantines were now learning equivalent lessons.

The Spaniards, however, ultimately prevailed in the naval struggle. When the Aztecs tried this ploy again, Cortés was prepared, having learned of the plan from some Indian captives. As before, canoes lured the Spanish ships past forty hidden Aztec canoes. But the Spaniards reversed the Aztec ploy and pretended to flee when attacked, drawing the Aztecs with them past a place where Cortés had stationed six brigantines. These counterattacked and destroyed the canoes, putting an end to that Aztec ploy. Despite this naval success, ships could harass and contain, but they could not win the struggle for Tenochtitlan. They played a vital role, especially in reducing the Aztecs to starvation, but the war was ultimately won by the land forces.[24]

The struggle for the causeways continued. Anyone who charged ahead of the rest or was otherwise separated was easily captured, so the Spaniards were forced to move only as units. Although they were prevailing on the causeways, they often pursued Aztecs across breaks in the causeways, only to have them turn and push the Spaniards back, pinning them against the open breach, where they were unable to maneuver. After a few such setbacks, Cortés ordered his forces not to advance unless the breaches were filled in first. The Aztecs were left with little choice except to continue building barricades and widening breaches, as well as implanting stakes to hinder the movement of the brigantines.[25]

Tenochtitlan was not alone in opposing the Spaniards: there were many loyal towns in the Valley of Mexico. But their support shifted with the tide of battle. The people of Xochimilco, Cuitlahuac, Mizquic, Colhuacan, Mexicatzinco, and Ixtlapalapan all responded to Cuauhtemoc's call for help and brought their canoes to support the Aztecs, but the Xochimilcas and Cuitlahuacas turned on the Aztecs, taking advantage of the situation to loot. In response, the Aztecs attacked the Xochimilcas and Cuitlahuacas, killed many, and took others captive. The prisoners were then taken before Cuauhtemoc and Mayehua, king of Cuitlahuac, who were both in Tenochtitlan, and each sacrificed four of the rebellious leaders. Mayehua's rule may well have been contested within his city because he had fled to Tenochtitlan, and Aztec control over towns that they no longer dominated directly was slipping badly.[26]

Foot soldiers bore the brunt of combat on the causeways because the many breaches and barricades thwarted the horses and
rendered them virtually useless. But as the Spaniards advanced and
the breaches were filled, Alvarado, moving along the western
causeway from Tlacopan, ordered his cavalry brought forward.
The horsemen should have excelled in leading the advance on the
causeways, but the Aztecs attacked from all four sides simultaneously, and they were helpless against fire from the canoes.[27]

The best defense the Aztecs could have adopted against the
cavalry was a formation so closely packed that the horses could not
charge through it. But this would have required extensive retrain-
ing, for which the Aztecs had no time, and even if they had, such
close formations would have been even more vulnerable to Spanish firepower. Although the Aztecs could not mount an organizational defense, they could and did adopt technological defenses,
including the use of extra-long lances to spear the horses before
they reached the front lines. They also shifted from combat in open
areas that favored horses to confrontations in broken terrain where
horses could not charge, and they achieved the same effect in
Tenochtitlan by placing barricades and boulders in open plazas. As
a last resort, Aztec soldiers escaped the horses by jumping into the
canals, where they could not follow.[28]

Although the Aztecs failed to come up with a completely effective response to Spanish tactics, they adopted a combination of
responses that kept the Spaniards off balance. Surrounding the
enemy was a standard Aztec tactic that was at least partly successful against the Spaniards. Guns and cavalry ensured that the Spaniards could break through virtually any Aztec line, but these could
not be brought to bear everywhere simultaneously. So even if the
Spaniards broke through, the Aztecs could salvage something from
the encounter by attacking the enemy's withdrawing and frequently disorderly rear elements. They also made astute use of
feigned withdrawals and ambushes, often drawing the overconfi-
dent Spaniards forward before cutting them off and counterattack-

ing. Once caught in such presses, many Spaniards jumped or fell
off the causeways, often into hidden pits or the waiting hands of
Aztecs in canoes. The Aztecs often found themselves in similar
situations, but for them, jumping into the water offered safety.
Despite the Spaniards' overall progress, these Aztec successes
made the Spaniards more cautious and greatly slowed their march
into Tenochtitlan.[29]

The effectiveness with which the Indian allies had supported
the Spaniards in open areas was largely absent in the causeway
battles. There, the allies became liabilities if the Aztecs attacked
from all directions, because when the Spaniards were forced to
withdraw under fire, they were hindered by the great press of their
own allies. To remedy the problem, Cortés allegedly ordered them
off the causeways. The accuracy of this report, however, is questionable. Although battles had limited fronts, fighting without Indian support would still have been suicidal. Doing so would have
allowed the Spaniards to bring their weapons to bear in all directions, given them greater mobility, and thus minimized the effectiveness of Aztec traps, but this is an unlikely scenario. With the
Spaniards divided into at least three armies, manning thirteen
ships, standing guard at night at their base camps, and recuperating
from wounds, they could not have launched an unaided attack,
even on the causeways. Therefore, any allies ordered off the causeways were doubtless those engaged in filling breaches, not the
indispensable combat troops.[30]

Spanish victories were not limited to the battlefield. Each success reverberated throughout the Valley of Mexico as towns previously allied with Tenochtitlan shifted their loyalty to the Spaniards.
This was particularly true of towns in the southern portion of the
valley, including Ixtlapalapan, Huitzilopochco, Colhuacan, and
Mizquic. The Spaniards claimed these towns provided little real
support, which suggests either that they were positioning themselves politically in the event of a victory by Cortés or that the
nobles left behind when their kings fled had switched to the Spanish

side, but the people may have been less certain, leaving the towns militarily paralyzed. Nevertheless, spurred by gain, the townspeople did intercept supplies bound for Tenochtitlan, and they could be ordered to provide laborers and bring food for the Spaniards. Whether or not the allegiance of these lakeshore towns was wholehearted — and it was probably encouraged by the presence of Spanish ships — it did reduce active support for the Aztecs.[31]

The Aztecs were being slowly but inexorably pushed back along the causeways, and they recognized that they had to take the offensive or they were doomed. Throughout the campaign, the Aztecs had attacked the Spaniards' camps, but now Cuauhtemoc ordered a simultaneous night attack from land and water on all three Spanish camps. Night attacks were difficult to coordinate and control, but the Aztecs knew precisely where the Spanish camps were. Moreover, they knew that the brigantines were less useful at night. The attacks were carried out on two successive nights, but although a number of Spaniards were killed, the Aztecs failed to dislodge the armies.[32]

Even though they were generally victorious, the Spaniards could not sustain open combat, especially if they could not use their horses. Even if they killed many Aztecs for each Spaniard lost — twenty-five to one was the ratio claimed before their previous flight from Tenochtitlan — they would ultimately lose a war of attrition. Instead, they customarily adopted a defensive posture when attacked in order to fend it off, and took the offensive only when it favored them. For example, they took the offensive on the causeways, where they could minimize the effects of the Aztecs' vast numerical superiority and maximize the effectiveness of their own weapons and tactics, but they maintained defensive postures around their camps. When Cortés was attacked during the Aztecs' coordinated night campaign, he remained in his camp and fought a defensive battle, conserving his men, maximizing the effects of his weapons, and forcing the Aztecs to fight where they could not bring their superior numbers to bear. This forced the Aztecs to take the greater chances and consequently to suffer more casualties.[33]

Cuauhtemoc then decided to concentrate all his forces against a single camp and for this purpose chose Alvarado's at Tlacopan. A larger force might succeed against Spanish firepower through the sheer crush of numbers. But Cuauhtemoc decided to attack at dawn, which was typical in Mesoamerican warfare because sunrise provided the maximum amount of daylight for fighting and a means of coordinating widely dispersed assaults without clocks or other readily available timepieces. Whether or not Cuauhtemoc was forced into a daylight attack by the complexity of commanding and coordinating so large a force, the timing also helped the Spaniards, allowing them to use their brigantines effectively and to repulse the Aztecs.[34]

The campaign continued as before, although the Spaniards did experience setbacks. During an assault on 30 June, the Aztecs feigned a withdrawal and Cortés pursued them, neglecting to fill a breach before he crossed, something that was easier to do now that fewer allies accompanied these assaults. The Aztecs sent their war canoes into the breach and then turned and attacked, catching the Spaniards between the two forces. Cortés was wounded in the leg and was seized and being dragged off by several Aztecs when he was rescued by his men. Sixty-eight other Spaniards were captured alive, and eight horses were killed.[35]

More Spaniards were captured than killed in this battle, because they had been surrounded and cut off. In a battle between opposing fronts, taking captives was much harder. Steel armor also made it difficult to kill the Spaniards except by wounding them in the neck and head, so taking them alive was often easier than killing them outright. But perhaps even more important, taking captives alive fit Mesoamerican traditions of rewarding soldiers' exploits.

Ten of the Spanish captives from this battle were taken to the

Great Temple in Tenochtitlan and sacrificed. Their severed heads were then sent to the battlefront and thrown at the Spaniards, which must have demoralized them. After the Spaniards withdrew to their camps for the night, they could hear the drums from the Great Temple and see the other captured Spaniards being made to dance in front of the image of the Aztec god Huitzilopochtli before their hearts were cut out. Aside from religious significance, the Spaniards were sacrificed for psychological effect, both on Cortés's forces and on the Aztecs' allies. The sacrificed Spaniards were flayed and their faces — beards attached — were tanned and sent to allied towns as tokens of Aztec success, as proof of Spanish mortality, and in order to solicit assistance and warn against betraying the alliance.[36]

Buoyed by this success, the Aztecs attacked each of the Spanish camps throughout the next four days. The loss of so many Spaniards following the assault on his camps was a major setback for Cortés. The tide of battle had seemingly turned against him, and ever sensitive to the political situation, his Indian allies began defecting. Most of the soldiers from Tlaxcallan, Cholollan, Huexotzinco, Tetzcoco, Chalco, and Tlalmanalco returned to their homes, leaving only token forces with the Spaniards. Ixtlilxochitl stayed, because Coanacoch was still alive in Tenochtitlan and his own fate was tied to Cortés's. Moreover, he advised Cortés to continue interdicting the supplies for Tenochtitlan, which he could do because the brigantines still controlled the lakes.[37]

After the main assault on his camps, Cortés returned to the offensive, but with reduced allied support, it slowed enormously. The Spaniards' situation improved, however, when they discovered a way to break the stakes the Aztecs had planted in the lake bed without impaling their ships. Now they could sail relatively unimpeded, and with the help of the brigantines, the Spaniards repulsed the attacks that continued for the next two weeks.[38]

As it became clear that the Aztecs had failed to destroy the Spaniards completely, allied troops began to return from Tetzcoco,

Tlaxcallan, Huexotzinco, and Cholollan to re-ally with the Spaniards. Díaz del Castillo wrote that the Spaniards' allies left because the god Huitzilopochtli had told them the Spaniards would now be defeated, and when this failed to happen, they returned. Such claims may actually have been made, but the allied withdrawal from and subsequent rejoining of the battle reflects the same pattern of support based on the changing tide of battle and on the perception of power that permeated Mesoamerican political alliances. Now the Spanish forces again advanced on the city, and Cortés sent another entreaty for peace to Cuauhtemoc, which also went unanswered.[39]

The Spanish forces had moved close enough to Tenochtitlan to reach and destroy a spring the Aztecs used for drinking water, even though it was brackish. The Aztecs in turn dug a new well and arranged for the Xochimilcas to bring water into the capital by canoe at night. In response to Cortés's peace demand, the Aztecs renewed their attacks, forcing the Spaniards off the causeways and into their camps, where they were again besieged for six or seven days.[40]

Throughout the siege, the Aztecs received little help from tributary cities beyond the Valley of Mexico. In some cases this may have been motivated by general hostility toward Aztec domination, but such a motive is unlikely in towns whose kings owed their rule to Aztec support. One reason for the lack of support is that the Spanish invasion had created hostile zones cordoning off the loyal towns from the Valley of Mexico. Another reason few allied cities sent help to Tenochtitlan was because doing so would have stripped them of their armies and left them vulnerable to Spanish attack. But as a result of Aztec successes and apparent Spanish vulnerability, trouble erupted in some of the outlying areas. Cortés received word from Cuauhnahuac, one of his allied towns, that it was under attack by troops from Malinalco, an Aztec ally. The direct military consequences of this clash would have been minimal for the Spaniards, regardless of who won, even if the Malinal-

cas then marched against Cortés, because they would increase
Aztec forces but not otherwise shift the strategic balance. The political effects of this attack, however, were potentially enormous.[41]

The Spaniards were being battered, but Cortés could not permit an Aztec victory against towns loyal to him, even if they were
beyond the Valley of Mexico and not directly involved in the war.
If he did, the snowball effect could rapidly strip him of his allies if
they felt his protection was inadequate. In fact, this assault appears
to have been a clash between traditional enemies and had nothing
to do with the siege of Tenochtitlan. But whether or not Cortés
thought it did, he could not afford to ignore it. Accordingly, he
dispatched eighty foot soldiers, ten horsemen, and Indian allies
under the command of Andrés de Tapia. This force met the Mali-
nalcas between their city and Cuauhnahuac, routed them, and returned to the Valley of Mexico ten days later. Two days after that,
Cortés learned that the Matlatzincas, in the Valley of Tolocan to the
west, had mounted an army, also against a traditional foe. He again
sent eighteen horsemen, a hundred foot soldiers, and a large force
of Indian allies, this time under the command of Sandoval, to meet
them. Sandoval found them on a plain after two days' march,
routed them, and pursued them to Matlatzinco, which he sacked
and burned.[42]

The Aztecs renewed their attacks, but now, with fewer troops
in reserve, they could no longer reopen the canals as quickly as the
Spaniards filled them. Both sides were being worn down, and
hunger gripped the city as the Aztecs ran low on food and water.
The lake supplied some food, but fishing could continue only
surreptitiously, because the brigantines and allied canoes targeted
anyone they caught doing so. Although Aztec combat losses could
not be replaced, the Spaniards, too, were losing men, and by mid-
July their gunpowder was almost exhausted. At that point, more
Spanish ships reached Vera Cruz with fresh supplies of gunpowder, crossbows, and soldiers that quickly made their way to
Tenochtitlan.[43]

When the Spaniards finally reached Tenochtitlan itself, the Aztecs once more changed their tactics. Now, instead of facing Spanish gunfire with vulnerable formations, they attacked the Spaniards' flanks from the buildings lining the streets, regaining the edge their canoes had provided earlier. In response, Cortés ordered all his allies to send their farmers to the city with their tools to raze the buildings on both sides of his advance, using the rubble to fill the breaches in the causeways and provide a more easily traversable, continuous surface. This was a major shift: breaches in the causeways had previously been filled by allied soldiers, but this much larger operation now used ordinary laborers, freeing soldiers for combat once they were inside Tenochtitlan and more of them could be used effectively than they could on the causeways.[44]

When Cortés finally entered Tenochtitlan to stay, the Aztecs withdrew north to Tlatelolco (map 4). This area was presumably safer because Spanish troops had been more successful in advancing into the city from the south, but the move may also have been influenced by Spanish naval operations. The Spaniards used their ships to fire into Aztec positions and to land small parties of soldiers, which greatly complicated Aztec defensive planning. Because Tlatelolco's causeways were still intact, the brigantines were less a threat there. Nevertheless, the Spanish advance continued, reaching the great market of Tlatelolco around 1 August.[45]

Spanish horsemen entered the marketplace unexpectedly and, exploiting the element of surprise, rode down and lanced many Aztecs. The Aztecs resisted and, though forced back, fought the Spaniards from the roofs of the adjacent houses. They could not stand up against the cavalry charges, but they would sally forth to fight, and when pushed back they retreated to the houses. Once inside the houses, they smashed holes in the rear walls and escaped; it was too dangerous for the Spaniards to follow. But this was only a holding action and did not signify a successful defense against Spanish attack.[46]

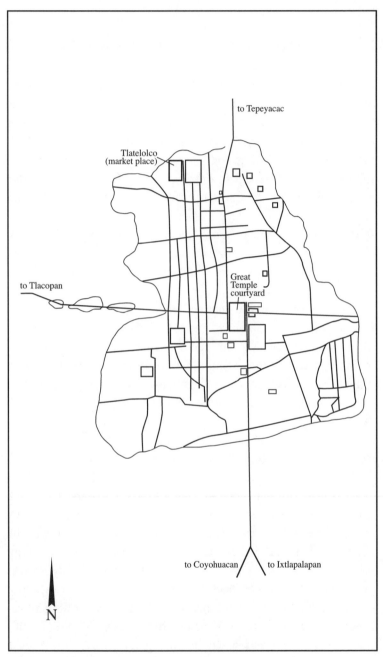

to Tepeyacac

Tlatelolco
(market place)

to Tlacopan

Great
Temple
courtyard

to Coyohuacan / \ to Ixtlapalapan

N

4. Layout of Tenochtitlan, c. 1520

Spanish tactics were not always successful, either. Although the Spanish cavalry was devastating on open plains, its role was greatly restricted in urban combat. The mobility of the horsemen was limited on the causeways, and they were attacked from the sides with virtual impunity in the city streets. But once the Spaniards entered large plazas, horses were again formidable weapons. To counter this, the Aztec defenders scattered stones and boulders throughout the plazas to prevent the horses from galloping, and they concentrated on attacking the Spaniards as they withdrew. The Spaniards, in response, turned the Indian tactic of feigned withdrawal and ambush against the Aztecs themselves, until they stopped attacking the withdrawing forces altogether.[47]

Meanwhile, on behalf of the allied forces, Ixtlilxochitl captured his brother, Coanacoch, who was leading the loyalist Tetzcocas. With their leader now in Cortés's hands, those Tetzcocas fighting on the Aztec side shifted to Ixtlilxochitl's side—a major setback for Cuauhtemoc. Within four days, all three Spanish armies had advanced to the Tlatelolco marketplace and controlled seven-eighths of the city. Their increased control allowed the Spaniards to move freely between their camps, greatly easing their efforts to coordinate the offensive.[48]

The supply of gunpowder was again low, so when one soldier volunteered to build a catapult to bombard Cuauhtemoc's quarters, Cortés ordered him to proceed. After four days of construction, the completed catapult was taken to the marketplace and fired, but it was a failure—the stones rose no higher than the catapult itself. Even though it failed, this incident illustrates the continued reliance Cortés placed on heavy artillery and its ability to strike from a distance, safe from Aztec retaliation.[49]

Hand-to-hand fighting continued, but now that the battle was inside the city, more soldiers were involved, including allied forces, who fought independently. The Indian allies had been a major asset when they supported Spanish-led assaults, but it was a different story when they faced Aztec troops alone. Without Spanish arms to break up Aztec formations, the Tlaxcaltecs and Tetzcocas met the Aztecs on equal terms and were soundly defeated. During these clashes, the Aztecs could maintain their formations and fight conventionally and without peer. Even in the final days of the battle for Tenochtitlan, when they were exhausted and hungry and their best soldiers were already dead or wounded, the Aztecs were still able to cut off and kill many enemy Indians when they attacked without Spanish support. The Aztecs' conventional superiority was so striking that the Spaniards sometimes disguised themselves as Indians and marched in the middle of their allies in order to entice the Aztecs into attacking what appeared to be an Indian force unsupported by Spanish arms. If the Aztecs did attack, the Spaniards would fire their weapons before the Aztecs realized what was happening.[50]

Throughout the conquest, the Aztecs captured weapons. But cannons and presumably harquebuses were destroyed rather than used when they fell into Aztec hands, because the Aztecs lacked powder and could not master the weapons' complexity, having no similar ones of their own. For instance, when the Spaniards first entered Tenochtitlan's central plaza, they placed a cannon atop the gladiatorial sacrifice stone and fired at the Aztecs in the courtyard. They then fled when counterattacked, leaving the cannon behind. The Aztecs seized the abandoned cannon and dropped it into the lake, where it could not be recovered. The Aztecs did use crossbows against the Spaniards at one point, but their shots went wide, either because they were unskilled with this weapon or, more likely, because the crossbows were fired under duress by captured Spaniards and their poor performance was deliberate. Where direct analogies to native arms existed, however, the Aztecs were quick to master captured Spanish weapons, especially swords. Some were mounted on long poles like lances and scythes; others were used as swords by elite warriors. Too few steel swords were captured, however, to have a decisive effect on any of the battles.[51]

In early August, Cuauhtemoc finally requested a meeting with Cortés, and negotiations began, during which the Aztecs ate lavishly in an effort to convince the Spaniards that their food was plentiful. A lull in the fighting held for several days as negotiations continued, but Cuauhtemoc always sent nobles instead of appearing himself. Whether Cortés actually negotiated in good faith or not, he nevertheless blamed the failure of the talks on the Aztecs and resumed his attack. In a last-ditch effort to inspire the defenders, Cuauhtemoc dressed an elite warrior in the late King Ahuitzotl's attire to lead the attack. But despite initial success, the effort ultimately failed, and on 13 August the Spaniards easily broke through the last Aztec defenses.[52]

Even though the Aztecs had exhausted all their weapons, resistance continued, and Cortés ordered the brigantines to sail through the canals among the houses. He also ordered a general search for Cuauhtemoc so he could be captured alive. After this final land assault, the Aztecs surrendered.[53]

The eventual outcome of the battle for Tenochtitlan had been apparent to the Aztecs for some time, and their leaders had discussed what they should offer the Spaniards in tribute and how they should surrender. Accounts of the final surrender differ in Spanish and Indian versions. According to Spanish accounts, once the city was lost, Cuauhtemoc fled with a fleet of fifty canoes, and Sandoval ordered the brigantines to pursue. The ship commanded by García Holguin overtook Cuauhtemoc's canoe, which stopped after being threatened with cannon fire, and the king surrendered and asked to be taken to Cortés. Captured along with Cuauhtemoc were his wife and about thirty nobles, including the king of Tlacopan.[54]

Aztec accounts claim that Cuauhtemoc and his advisers had already decided to surrender and were en route to do so when Holguin seized their canoe, which seems a likelier sequence of events. The city was defeated and in Spanish hands, and there was no place for Cuauhtemoc to go, nor was there any purpose in his going anywhere. In any case, Tenochtitlan lay in ruins and Cuauhtemoc was taken prisoner after the three-month siege.[55]

Despite the surrender, the Spaniards' allies continued to attack the Aztecs, killing thousands and stealing their property. The massacre in Tenochtitlan continued for four days. It was a revealing event, not for what it says about Mesoamerican warfare but for what it demonstrates about Cortés's lack of control, despite his claims to the contrary. In Mesoamerica, defeat did not necessarily mean sacking the vanquished. Rather, victory was conceived as a gradient: the more effort required to subdue the enemy, the greater their punishment would be. A town was usually sacked only if it resisted to the end. Thus, the fate that befell Tenochtitlan was not atypical of defeat in Mesoamerica generally: it had resisted to the last, and sacking the city and massacring its inhabitants were well within normal expectations. But this was not necessarily the accepted chain of events for European warfare. Under the prevailing conventions of martial conduct, inhabitants of surrendered towns were not supposed to be abused, although this ideal was seldom achieved.[56]

What the sacking and massacre of Tenochtitlan meant, then, is problematical. From a Spanish perspective, Cortés's inaction might be interpreted as rewarding his Indian allies before asserting control. But the destruction diminished the city's wealth and was decidedly against Cortés's interests, which suggests not a willingness to allow it to happen but an inability to prevent it. From an Indian perspective, these acts were the logical culmination of a determined, though ultimately unsuccessful, resistance. Which interpretation is correct is uncertain, but if the massacre took place in keeping with Mesoamerican military practice, it suggests that the Indian allies, not the Spaniards, were in control. The alternative explanation, that Cortés orchestrated the massacre, shows the Spaniards in no better light, because although sackings and massacres were common in Europe, they typically grew from the commanders' inability to control their troops. Thus, either interpretation of the massacre in Tenochtitlan suggests that Cortés lacked the power to maintain control over his allies.

By now Tenochtitlan was filled with the dead, although most had died of starvation rather than from combat. With Cortés's permission, the survivors marched out of the city over the next three days, after which he ordered the aqueduct repaired and the dead removed and buried. Cortés had defeated the Aztecs with a surviving force of nine hundred Spaniards, eighty horses, sixteen pieces of artillery, and thirteen brigantines. But the pivotal role had been played by his 200,000 Indian allies, even though they went virtually unacknowledged and certainly unrewarded. Perhaps a thousand Spaniards were killed throughout the conquest of Mexico, a small number in comparison with the unknown numbers of Aztecs and Indian allies, which surely ran into many tens of thousands on each side.[57]

CHAPTER 10

Aftermath

The conquest of Mexico was not the victory of a Spanish jugger-naut. The Spaniards themselves were never more than fifteen hundred strong, and in the final stage of the conquest, the siege of Tenochtitlan, they amounted to less than 1 percent of the total forces and perhaps less than one-half of 1 percent. Moreover, it was a campaign fought not according to a master plan from the outset but in fits and starts, and it was very much a learning experience for both sides. All participants initially regarded the others as something different from what they really were: the Spaniards saw the Indians as inferior and easily defeated, and the Indians viewed the Spaniards as powerful and perhaps supernatural, if not invincible. Although these perceptions changed with harsh experience, they patterned the behavior of both sides, leading to miscalculations that profoundly affected the meeting of Old and New Worlds.

The Spanish arrival presented groups such as the Cempohualtecs and Tlaxcaltecs with new political opportunities that they ultimately seized. Both Indians and Spaniards sought alliances in their own fashion. The Indians frequently gave the Spaniards the daughters of kings and nobles in efforts to link the two sides through elite marriages. But the Spaniards failed to recognize the significance of these acts and accepted the women largely as concubines. For their part, the Spaniards claimed to seek alliances through religious conversion, but these claims and their actions were both motivated primarily by political purposes, to justify the war.

The Spaniards did not vigorously pursue religious conversions. Combatants on both sides prayed to their gods, but meaningful conversion in the sense that Roman Catholic religious doctrine was transmitted, understood, and believed almost surely did not occur during the conquest period. Whatever conversion effects did take place would have satisfied both the Spaniards' legal and religious obligations, but Christianity was still culturally impenetrable to the Indians, and true comprehension was not what the conquistadors sought. Rather, public conversions were political statements and took place only after an alliance had been established and the Indians could no longer back out. This happened at Cempohuallan after the attack on the Aztecs for which the Indians would be blamed, and at Tlaxcallan after the Spaniards had fled Tenochtitlan, renegotiated their alliance, and promised the Tlaxcaltecs vassalage over adjacent city-states.

Despite its superficiality, the Christianization of Indian rulers was the price of Spanish assistance and meant a breach in traditional patterns of authority. Conversion pried rulers away from the local priesthood and made them dependent on Spanish support because, unaided, the rulers could not withstand the internal opposition that their conversions generated. Public conversion did not signal an actual change in belief but rather a political alliance from which there was no escape.

Thus, a pattern arose of apparent conversion of allied rulers to Christianity. Conversion would alienate the native priesthood and at least some of the populace, but it nevertheless occurred when the loss of internal support was offset by the power and political support gained from the Spaniards. By contrast, religious conversions did not take place in Tenochtitlan, not because the Aztecs were more devout but because they stood at the political apex in Mesoamerica. They did not need Spanish support to maintain their position and so were not compelled to undergo public conversion. Only the Aztecs did not need Spanish power to advance their political position in the existing power structure of Mesoamerica, which is why only they rejected even the superficial trappings of Christianity.

Thus, neither a Spanish religious imperative nor an Aztec loss of faith explains the success of the conquest. The fate of both Aztecs and Spaniards was tied to their respective political situations, and each had little choice but to follow the courses they selected. The Aztecs could resist or lose their empire; the Spaniards could conquer Mesoamerica, be killed by the Aztecs, or be tried for treason in Cuba. The main protagonists were on a collision course, and although both sides chose that course, neither saw the consequences clearly. Circumstances and events forced decisions on them, but the costs and consequences were beyond their anticipation.

Cortés unquestionably brought new and effective military technologies to the confrontation. Steel swords, metal armor, harquebuses, crossbows, cannons, horses, and ships all gave the Spaniards a great technological advantage. The Aztecs successfully altered their tactics and countered some of these innovations, but they could not counter them all. Instead, the Aztecs' main advantage lay in the size, skill, and organization of their military. Although casualties would have been high, early in the conquest the massive Aztec armies could have crushed the Spaniards through numbers alone, despite the technological imbalance.

What made the conquest of Mexico possible was not the Spaniards' military might, which was always modest, but the assistance of tens and even hundreds of thousands of Indian allies — laborers, porters, cooks, and especially soldiers. The Spaniards were so few that it was not their technology alone that was important but the way it was coupled with Indian forces. Spanish arms could disrupt opposing formations in a way native arms could not, but victories were typically won by large numbers of allied troops who could exploit the breaches. The Spaniards' most serious threat was the way they could convert relatively unimportant groups into a significant offensive force. This was a world-shattering alteration of the political landscape, but the Aztecs did nothing about it, either because they failed to recognize it in time or, perhaps, because of ineffective political leadership and tributary control problems. The self-serving accounts of the conquistadors notwithstanding, the conquest was not simply a matter of Spanish brains versus Indian brawn.

Spanish technology was important, but the key to the success of the conquest was acquiring the native allies who magnified the effects of those arms. Doing this required a thorough understanding of the political organization of Mesoamerican states and empires, the nature of rule and patterns of royal succession, and the individuals and factions involved. Cortés may have had some grasp of the situation, but not the detailed knowledge or understanding necessary to determine which faction to attack and which to support: only the Indians had this knowledge. The political manipulations that funneled men and materiel to the Spaniards were engineered by the Indians in the furtherance of their own factional interests, first by the Tlaxcaltecs and then by the Tetzcocans. The Tlaxcaltecs could have destroyed the Spaniards, either in their initial clashes or after the Spaniards' flight from Tenochtitlan, and some factions wanted to do so. But the Tlaxcaltec leaders saw the advantages of an alliance, given their own imperiled position vis-à-vis the Aztecs, and *chose* to ally with Cortés. The conquest was not primarily a conflict between Mexico and Spain but one between the Aztecs and the various Mesoamerican groups supporting Cortés. It was centered on issues internal to Mesoamerica. Cortés neither represented the forces of Spain nor had formal Spanish backing. Instead, he fought on his own behalf in hope of eventual Spanish royal support and legitimation.

The Aztecs fought a Mesoamerican war and lost. They chose to defend their capital on the assumption that they would gain a defensive military advantage and that the stringent logistical constraints on Mesoamerican warfare would work in their favor. But Spanish technology and, more importantly, regional political shifts stripped them of their advantages. If the conquest of Mexico was an Indian victory over Indians, however, rather than a Spanish victory over Indians, why did all the Indians fare so poorly thereafter? The answer can be found largely in the different goals pursued by the Indians and the Spaniards.

To the extent that it was actually his conquest, Cortés conquered Tenochtitlan, but he did not conquer the entire Aztec empire. Most Aztec allies did not participate in the battle: some were neutralized by the Spaniards or cordoned off from the main theater of operations, but most failed to fight because the Aztec empire was not a tightly integrated political entity that could command participation from its parts. Nevertheless, the fall of Tenochtitlan did signal changes for its tributaries. When a Mesoamerican empire fell, its constituent cities continued as before, but they were now independent or had new overlords. Much the same would have been expected when the Aztecs fell, and certainly their defeat meant that former tributaries were freed. But it also left the tributaries vulnerable and isolated. As a result, they were easily defeated during the subsequent Spanish pacification operations, much of which was again accomplished with the help of Cortés's Indian allies.

The Spaniards' encounter with the Indians was not simply "culture contact," in which beneficial innovations were freely adopted or merged into the existing cultures. It was a conquest, signaled by military defeat and greatly affecting the cultural realm. The conquered Mesoamericans' very notions about the nature of the world were not merely questioned but suppressed, subordinated, or destroyed, and alien cultural ideas were imposed, at least superficially, even if they were not internalized. The defeat of Tenochtitlan left the Spaniards with a victory they could claim, and they seized the political and economic power with which they could impose their culture. Defeat left the Aztecs and the rest of Mesoamerica with little alternative but to adapt: they had lost the power to maintain their own culture at anything above the local level.

But most of Cortés's Indian allies were concerned primarily with local conditions. Their burdens were eased by the overthrow of the Aztecs, and so they benefited. However tumultuous the overthrow was, the Indians saw it as relatively minor, because this type of political restructuring was common and normally signaled a change in the hierarchy rather than in the system itself. The situation of most former tributaries improved significantly after the conquest: they now kept goods previously owed as tribute to Tenochtitlan, they had access to European goods, and they were no longer threatened by Aztec retaliation. Certainly during the early years following the conquest, Cortés's allies were far stronger than he was. But he successfully played his most powerful allies off against each other, leaving none in a position to dominate the postconquest era alone, and traditional enmities and prerogatives kept them from allying against the Spaniards. Whatever benefits they gained from the conquest were short term.

The conquest meant very different things to the Spaniards and to the Indians. To the Indians who allied with Cortés, it meant the removal of an enemy or a tributary lord, which benefited them. The Indian allies used the situation to improve their immediate circumstances by removing the Aztec threat. They foresaw only what they could — an overthrow similar to others in Mesoamerica that shifted the existing situation in ways more favorable to themselves.

The Spaniards, by contrast, saw the conquest as a means of bringing all the Indians under their rule. They had a longer-term view based on their experiences in Europe, and to them the conquest meant the removal of the only significant competing Mesoamerican power, which left the Indians fully exposed to the expansion of Spanish control. The Indians could only have assumed the continuation of a hegemonic imperial system, which is what they had known, and could not have anticipated the territorial one the Spaniards were to impose. The Spaniards focused on what was to become the national level — the control of all groups in Mesoamerica, the imposition of centralized rule, and the collection of tribute on a massive scale. For them this was one more step in their imperial success, but for the Indians it was a world-shattering event, although this was not immediately clear to all of them.

The Tlaxcaltecs aided the Spaniards in the continued conquest of other areas in Mesoamerica, presumably because they thought it was to their advantage. But these conquered areas felt no particular allegiance to Tlaxcallan, so the Tlaxcaltecs were conquering areas that the Spaniards then controlled and used against them. The Spaniards failed to comply with the terms of their preconquest agreement with Tlaxcallan, in which Tlaxcallan was promised control over Huexotzinco, Chollollan, and other cities that had been its allies previously. But making these cities tributaries would have given Tlaxcallan a substantial empire in the east, one that would have dominated all communication with the Gulf coast. The Spaniards failed to aid in subjugating these cities, and the Tlaxcaltecs could not do so alone. Thus, although they remained strong in their own territory, the Tlaxcaltecs were not a significant threat elsewhere, and the Spaniards faced no major challengers.

Nevertheless, they feared an Indian rebellion. In the early years after the conquest, armed Spaniards were ordered to Tenochtitlan, eventually renamed Mexico City, to repel an imagined threat, and the social, religious, political, and economic life of the Indians was allowed to continue as before. Spanish priests did not reach New Spain, as Mexico was now called, until June 1524, three years after the conquest, and only after more colonists with additional arms arrived in Mexico did the Spaniards subdue all the other groups and truly consolidate their control. It was not until 1525, after the first priests arrived, that the Spaniards struck directly at native society and began destroying Indian temples, books, and images of gods. By that time it was too late for an Indian rebellion to succeed.[1]

Mexico was conquered not from abroad but from within. The Spaniards were important and quickly took full credit, even when they served only as the most visible — not the most crucial —

element. The Aztecs did not lose their faith; they lost a war. And it was a war fought overwhelmingly by other Indians, taking full advantage of the Spanish presence but exploiting their unique inside understanding of Mesoamerican political dynamics, which Cortés could never master. The war was more a coup or at most a rebellion than a conquest. Conquest came later, after the battles, as the Spaniards usurped the victory for which their Indian allies had fought and died.

CHAPTER 11

CONSEQUENCE AND CONCLUSION

The conquest had major consequences for the indigenous societies of Mexico, now colonized as New Spain, many of which are still felt to the present day. The Spaniards made some changes deliberately, and their consequences could have been reasonably well anticipated, as in the areas of religion and political organization. Other changes had unexpected consequences, as in the introduction of Old World animals and alterations in the indigenous economy. Still other transformations were unintentional, such as depopulation and changes in social organization.

The indigenous practice the Spaniards sought most to overturn was religion, or at least that is the goal most vividly reflected in the accounts penned by Spanish priests. Although conversion efforts may have been grounded in honestly held religious convictions, they also had a political purpose. Only by following through on the religious conversion of the Indians could Spain justify its actions according to its own laws as well as in the eyes of the Church, whose approval was ultimately needed for political legitimacy. Thus, an important result of religious conversion was to shore up the colonial regime politically. It also had the effect of simultaneously undercutting Indian rule. As the native religious hierarchy crumbled, so, too, did a crucial support of the native social structure and its political regime.

During the first years of nervous coexistence, the Spaniards uneasily tolerated native religion, but once they grew strong enough to enforce their will, they suppressed native religious practices as completely as they could. Temples and idols were destroyed along with the other main outward manifestations of polytheistic native religion. Within a single generation, the indigenous priesthood was virtually extinct. Private beliefs were more difficult to eradicate, but public observances largely ceased or continued only in the guise of acceptable Christian rituals.

In the early 1530s, Bishop Zumarraga began an ecclesiastical inquisition in Mexico in an attempt to eradicate native beliefs. A number of Indians were tried and convicted of heresy and burned at the stake, among them several prominent political leaders. This penalty, however, applied only to Indians who had converted to Christianity and then lapsed back into "paganism." The Indians immediately grasped the idea that if they never converted, they could not be tried for heresy, and the public burnings caused an almost immediate cessation of conversions. In the face of this monumental failure, it was decreed that the Indians were not subject to the Inquisition at all, and conversions resumed; the attention of the Inquisition was reserved for Protestants, Jews, and backsliding and heretical Catholics of European ancestry.

Many of the native conversions were peaceful, however, especially after the eradication of native priests. The Church, especially the Franciscan, Dominican, and Augustinian orders, played a prominent religious role, constructing churches in virtually every significant Indian town during the sixteenth century. It also played a major political role in native affairs. Nevertheless, many native beliefs bore striking similarities to those of the Roman Catholic Church and inevitably permeated orthodox beliefs, resulting ultimately in a highly syncretic religion.[1]

The Spaniards were less intent on completely restructuring native political life, although they did cause drastic changes, initially at the highest levels, but these soon permeated even the lowest levels of indigenous society. The threat of an Indian rebellion was constantly in the Spaniards' minds, especially during the first half of the sixteenth century. The effectiveness of Indian soldiers and arms was unquestioned, and the Spaniards employed them as late as the 1540s against hostile Indians elsewhere. Although no Indian rebellion materialized in central Mexico, the continuation of indigenous states and empires was a threat to Spanish control, and they were quickly destroyed. This left the town (*cabecera*) and its dependencies (*sujetos*) to be governed by native rulers as the highest remaining level of political organization among the Indians.[2]

Native rulers governed legitimately under indigenous political notions of rule, as the Spaniards acknowledged. But the Spaniards soon labeled native rulers *caciques,* a term imported from the Indies, and this inappropriate application led to considerable confusion. Unlike *tlatoani* (native ruler), a word that had a definite social meaning in Aztec society, *cacique* did not, and many illegitimate pretenders made their way to power under that rubric, undermining the position and privileges of the traditional elites. By the mid-sixteenth century, Indian towns had largely adopted Spanish political forms, including town councils, councilmen, judges, and other officials. In many places, elected Indian governors who served fixed terms eventually replaced the caciques, who then declined in importance, often retaining only vestigial rights and privileges. Governance at a regional or national level increasingly lay solely in Spanish hands. Despite the presence of Indian officials, control even at the town level was increasingly exercised by Spanish clergy or landowners who permitted the Indians to operate only within prescribed limits.[3]

Spanish-induced changes were not limited to religion and politics, of course, but the Spaniards did not seek to effect the changes in many other aspects of Indian life that their presence nevertheless caused. The initial Spanish intention was to leave the native economic system largely intact and merely tap it for goods and labor, as Indian rulers had done. Thus the native tribute system was immediately reoriented to supply the new Spanish overlords as well. But all aspects of native life were affected by one of the most devastating, though unintentional, changes caused by Spanish contact — depopulation.

When Cortés landed in 1519, central Mexico (which extends from the desert north of Mexico City to the Isthmus of Tehuantepec) held an estimated 25.2 million people. Eighty years later, at the end of the sixteenth century, the population had dropped by 95 percent, to just over a million. Some of these losses were occasioned by warfare, but the vast bulk were the result of Old World diseases to which the Indians had no immunities. Many epidemics followed the Spaniards' arrival, notably smallpox in 1520–21, followed by major outbreaks of typhus in 1545–48 and 1576–81. Numerous other diseases, including measles, influenza, and mumps, also swept through Mexico, and the lowlands, where the anopheles mosquito lived, were savaged by malaria as well.[4]

Massive depopulation affected virtually all Indian institutions and practices. Notable among these were residence patterns. Prehispanically, residence was apparently extended, with households including husband and wife, children, parents, and various collateral relatives. After the massive depopulation, many households reverted to consisting of nuclear families — just husband, wife, and offspring. The population loss was so severe that many towns were no longer viable, and twice in the sixteenth century, particularly in the 1590s, the Spaniards forcibly gathered the remaining Indians into fewer, larger towns where they could be more effectively controlled.[5]

Just as residence patterns were changed by the demographic collapse, so, too, was the broader native social system. Whereas preconquest native communities had an upper noble, or ruling, class, lower nobles, commoners, and serfs, as well as slaves, marked social compaction took place after the conquest. The Spaniards lumped all nobles into a single class (*principales*) that nevertheless tended to dominate political offices, and everyone else now occupied a single commoner class (*macehuales*), until the rights and privileges of the principales were so eroded that a meaningful distinction no longer existed in the seventeenth century.[6]

The drastic population decline affected all aspects of life in New Spain, and nowhere were its effects more apparent than in the economic realm. Except in the somewhat nebulous case of rebellion, slavery had been outlawed, but labor, not land, remained the real cornerstone of wealth in the New World. For favored Spaniards, a labor supply was ensured through the *encomienda,* a grant by the king not of landownership per se but rather of the right to the labor of the Indians on the land. Obligatory labor was not an alien concept in Mesoamerica; political dependents often paid their rulers in both goods and services. The Spanish imposition of the encomienda labor obligation was added to the existing political obligations of the commoners and exercised through native rulers who increasingly served as middlemen between the Indian commoners and their Spanish masters.[7]

For demographic reasons, the indigenous tribute system proved satisfactory for the Spaniards at first. In the smallpox epidemic that struck during the conquest, approximately 40 percent of Mesoamerica's population died. The mortality was not spread equally across the population, however. Most who died were infants, children, the aged, and the infirm, which left an unusual population profile. The largest percentage of those who survived were adults, so even though the total population was now significantly smaller, it was, in fact, healthier in economic terms. Not only was much land vacated through death, so that the remaining Indians could abandon more marginal areas, but those who survived were healthy adults and were therefore more productive. Whereas a preconquest married man might have been supporting a relatively large number of dependents, he now had far fewer mouths to feed. As a result, much of what an Indian man could produce could be siphoned off as surplus, and it was this that funded the early Spanish fortunes.

Because it was based on a demographic aberration, however,

this economic prosperity was destined not to last. Those who survived the epidemic had children at a normal rate, and because adults of child-bearing age made up such a large percentage of the epidemic survivors, they reproduced in extraordinarily large numbers for the population as a whole. As a result, within fifteen years there were vastly more dependents than before — both a large number of new children and an increasing number of adults who were growing older and becoming less economically productive themselves. By the early 1540s the native population was probably — for a brief time — as large or larger than it had been immediately after the conquest, but it was not an economically healthy population. Because so many of the Indians were young or old, the ratio between the number of economically productive adults and their dependents was significantly lower. The adults doubtless worked just as hard as before, but they had so many more mouths to feed that less and less of what they produced could be supplied as surplus.[8]

Population changes were not the only factors affecting the economy of New Spain. In addition to diseases, the Spaniards introduced new plants, such as wheat, lettuce, and numerous fruits. Some of these provided significant additions to the native agricultural complex, but wheat and sugarcane had the greatest effects, which were largely negative for the Indians. Wheat offered no nutritional advantages over native staples such as maize, but it was the traditional bread crop of Spain, and the Spaniards began cultivating it almost immediately. It was both a cultural preference and an important social marker — Spaniards ate wheat, Indians ate maize. But wheat required both irrigation for multiple crops and twice as much labor as maize for comparable caloric yields, so when Spaniards took land out of maize cultivation and planted wheat, it was a net loss in agricultural productivity. Sugarcane, introduced via the Indies, also played a significant role in New Spain. Cultivated and then processed, sugarcane promised great financial returns when shipped back to sweet-poor Europe. But again, it required irrigation and intensive cultivation, so although sugarcane was a major cash-crop export for the Spaniards, it also took much of the best land out of subsistence cultivation.[9]

Even more important than the new crops were the many animals introduced into New Spain. Among these were horses, cattle, donkeys, sheep, goats, pigs, and chickens, all of which affected native society. The larger animals offered, for the first time, a more efficient means of transportation than had hitherto been available in Mesoamerica, although they did not become widespread or available to Indians on a general basis until late in the sixteenth century. But even in Spanish hands these draft animals had an enormous effect on the political economy of New Spain, because food could now be brought into cities from unprecedented distances. Cities that had previously not competed with each other for foodstuffs now did so, and Mexico City was especially predatory. Using its formidable political power as the capital of New Spain, Mexico City poached on the agricultural produce of other cities, often mandating its importation as a matter of law. The net effect was to drive many Indian farmers off the land altogether, because they were now required to transport and sell their produce at prices far below market levels, effectively subsidizing life in the capital at the expense of people living elsewhere.[10]

Some European animals added to the food supply, however, and still others, such as sheep, provided new materials for clothing, augmenting the indigenous cotton. The chicken was perhaps the most useful animal introduced, at least initially, because it was added without disrupting the native plant and animal complex. But many of the other animals, especially horses, cattle, sheep, and goats, ended up competing with Indians for land. This competition would doubtless have been controlled had the Indians been allowed to incorporate the animals however they best suited their needs. But most of the larger animals were owned by Spaniards and were allowed to graze freely, often in the Indians' agricultural fields.[11]

In addition to the direct destruction of crops, the introduction of large numbers of domesticated animals led to massive overgrazing, which destroyed much of the ground cover. The effects of this were felt particularly in the Valley of Mexico, where large-scale timbering was also going on, largely as a result of the reconstruction of Mexico City. These twin plagues of deforestation and ground-cover destruction led to massive runoffs of the summer rains: less water was now held in the plants and soil, and the runoff swept much of the valley's topsoil into the lakes, raising their bottoms and flooding the nearby cities. To remedy this, toward the end of the sixteenth century the Spaniards embarked on a plan to drain the lakes, in the expectation that this would alleviate the problem and also open vast new tracts of fertile land for farming and grazing. But draining the lakes undermined the canoe-based transportation system that had fed the capital. Now, much costlier mule trains and ox carts had to be used, leading to higher prices, and the drained areas became alkali flats from which noxious clouds of dust blew during the windy season to plague the city.

In 1575, New Spain began to enter a depression that was to last almost a century. It was the result of Spanish miscalculation, mismanagement, and studied lack of concern for the long-term consequences of their actions. The first Spaniards enjoyed unprecedented prosperity as a result of the favorable native demographic profile already mentioned. Over the rest of the century, the number of Indian laborers inexorably declined, but a fall-off in production was only one part of the problem. New Spain was bound together economically by vast numbers of human porters. In comparison with Old World technologies, this was an inefficient means of moving products overland, and the porters' rapid replacement by wagons and mules would seem logical. But that would have meant major capital investments, not only in wagons and draft animals but also in constructing roads suitable for their use, because Indian roads frequently were inadequate. From the perspective of the Spaniards, they could coerce Indian labor or use porters as part of their tribute obligations at little or no cost. So despite its inefficiency, the porter system continued to dominate trade and the movement of goods to market in New Spain.[12]

Mexico's rapid depopulation inevitably doomed this labor-intensive form of transport, and there was nothing the Spaniards could do about it. In addition, the Spaniards failed to use their laborers to construct roads suitable for mule trains and ox carts during the early years, when there were still enough Indians to do so. The demographic collapse, with all its consequences, was either unforeseen by the Spaniards or was perceived as being too far in the future. Faced with a choice of using their laborers for ends that might prove beneficial in the long run or employing them to generate immediate wealth, the Spaniards chose short-term gains. Toward the end of the century, there were no longer enough Indians to serve as porters and keep the economy of New Spain alive, nor had adequate roads been built on a European model. Mules and wagons were available and could have provided adequate transportation, at least in theory, but without suitable roads, they were slow and costly. Most consumers could not bear this added expense, and production reverted to locally needed and consumed products. Only such luxuries as silver were still exported from throughout New Spain. It was now too expensive for most other goods to be shipped great distances, and New Spain's economy declined as the country broke into a series of balkanized regions between which there was little exchange.[13]

By the end of the sixteenth century, the Indians, though still a majority, were but a fraction of their previous numbers. The political system was in the hands of Spaniards, and the Indians enjoyed only local control. Their economy was enormously transformed by the introduction of new plants and animals, by the alteration of their marketing system, and by new values that elevated goods such as gold and silver while undermining the traditional value of other items, such as feathers and mineral pigments. Their religion was in tatters and they now worshiped in Catholic churches, although they retained many of their own beliefs and practices in new guises. Their intellectual traditions were destroyed. Native writing systems were replaced by the Latin alphabet, and indigenous books were destroyed as works of the devil. Their vigesimal (base-20) counting system was replaced by the European decimal system, and the native calendar was quickly replaced by the European one, on both religious and economic principles, for matters such as labor demands and markets were now determined according to the European system.

Those who fought on the Spaniards' side during the conquest, especially the Tlaxcaltecs, had their own reasons for doing so. Each group or faction acted in what it felt to be its own best interests in deciding whether or not to ally with the Spaniards. But none would have knowingly sought the fate that ultimately befell them all, so it is doubtful that any of the Indians who allied with the Spaniards foresaw the world-shattering changes the conquest would bring. Within a few short decades, most of what made up the Indian world was gone, swept away by disease, war, religious zealotry, and Spanish political and economic control. The Tlaxcaltecs and others were in a difficult political position when they allied with the Spaniards, but they would never have participated in their own cultural destruction merely to ensure the physical destruction of their enemies. Indian participation in the conquest was self-interested but short-sighted, and the victors' immediate gains were quickly swept away by the unstoppable tide of Spanish domination.

BRIEF SKETCHES OF
THE PARTICIPANTS

Acamapichtli ("Reed-fist"). A noble from Colhuacan, he was chosen as the Aztecs' first king, ruling from 1372 to 1391.

Aguilar, Gerónimo de (1489?–1531?). Settled in Santo Domingo, lost in a shipwreck in 1511, and washed ashore in Yucatan, where he was held by the Mayas until rescued by Cortés in 1519.

Ahuitzotl ("Otter"). Either the son or the grandson of Moteuczoma Ilhuicamina, he was the eighth Aztec king, ruling from 1486 to 1502.

Alfonso IX (1171–1230). King of León from 1188 to 1230.

Alvarado, Pedro de (1485–1541). A member of both Grijalva's and Cortés's expeditions to Mexico, he led the Toxcatl massacre in Tenochtitlan, commanded one of Cortés's three armies, and was dubbed Tonatiuh, the Aztec sun god, because of his blond hair.

Anonymous Conquistador. An anonymous member of the conquest of Mexico, known only through his chronicle of that event.

Avila, Alonzo de. Conquistador who came to Mexico with Cortés and led the land forces during the battle at Potonchan.

Axayacatl ("Water-mask"). Either the son or the grandson of Moteuczoma Ilhuicamina, he was the sixth Aztec king, ruling from 1468 to 1481.

Barba, Pedro. Captain of a ship sent to resupply Narváez, he arrived late and was captured. He then joined his friend Cortés in the conquest of Mexico.

Cacama ("Secondary-ear-of-maize"). He became king of Tetzcoco in 1515 on the death of his father, Nezahualpilli, with the help of his uncle, Moteuczoma Xocoyotl. After Moteuczoma collaborated with the Spaniards, he plotted against him but was taken prisoner and died in 1520 during Cortés's flight from Tenochtitlan.

Charles V (1500–1558). Holy Roman emperor under that name from 1519 to 1556 and king of Spain under Charles I from 1516 to 1556.

Chichimecateuctli ("Lord of the Chichimecs [barbarians, lit., people from Chichiman, i.e., Breast-area-place]"). Commanding general of the military forces of Ocotelolco, Tlaxcallan; implicated in the death of Xicotencatl the Younger.

Chimalpopoca ("He-smokes-like-a-shield"). The son of Huitzilihuitl, he was the third Aztec king, ruling from 1417 to 1427, when he was assassinated, allegedly by Maxtla.

Coanacoch ("Serpent-ear-pendant"). A son of Nezahualpilli, he became king of Tetzcoco in 1520 after the death of Cacama. When Cortés returned to Tetzcoco, Coanacoch fled to Tenochtitlan and led loyalist Tetzcocas against the Spaniards until he was captured by his brother, Ixtlilxochitl.

Cocozca ("Necklaces"). A son of Nezahualpilli, he was placed on the throne of Tetzcoco in 1520 with Spanish backing after the imprisonment of Cacama. He was apparently assassinated by his brother, Coanacoch, after the Spaniards fled Tenochtitlan.

Columbus, Christopher (1451–1506). Italian: Cristoforo Colombo; Spanish: Cristóbal Colón. A Genoese sailor, he was the first European to reach the Americas, on behalf of Spain. He led four separate voyages there, in 1492–93, 1493–96, 1498–1500, and 1502–1504.

Córdoba, Francisco Hernández de. Led Governor Velásquez's first expedition of exploration and discovered Yucatan for Spain. He died in Cuba in 1517 from wounds sustained at Chanpoton during the expedition.

Cortés, Hernan (1485?–1547) Born in Medellín, he emigrated to Hispaniola in 1504 and led the third Spanish expedition to Mexico, which culminated in its conquest.

Cuauhtemoc ("He-descends-like-an-eagle"). The son of Ahuitzotl, he was the eleventh and final Aztec king, ruling from 1520 until Cortés conquered Tenochtitlan. He was killed by the Spaniards in 1525.

Cuitlahua ("Excrement-owner"). The son of Axayacatl, he was the king of Ixtapalapan before succeeding his brother, Moteuczoma Xocoyotl, to become the tenth Aztec king. He ruled for only eighty days in 1520 before dying of smallpox.

Díaz del Castillo, Bernal (1495–1583). Born in Medina del Campo, he emigrated to the New World in 1514 and was a member of the Mexican expeditions of Córdoba, Grijalva, and Cortés.

Duero, Andrés de. Secretary to Governor Velásquez of Cuba and a secret partner with, and advocate for, Cortés as leader of the third expedition to Mexico.

Durán, Diego (1537?–1588). Born in Seville, he emigrated to New Spain in 1542, became a Dominican in 1556, and chronicled Aztec religion and history.

Escalante, Juan de. Conquistador with Cortés's expedition who was left in charge of the Spanish garrison at Vera Cruz when Cortés marched to Tenochtitlan.

Grijalva, Juan de (1480?–1527). Born in Cuéllar, he accompanied his uncle, Diego Velásquez de Cuéllar, on the conquest of Cuba in 1511. In 1518 he led the second expedition to Mexico.

Guerrero, Gonzalo. Lost in a shipwreck, presumably in 1511 with Gerónimo de Aguilar, he washed ashore in Yucatan, where he was held by the Mayas. He married, rose to high position in Maya society, and refused to return to Spanish society when Cortés landed in Yucatan in 1519.

Holguín, García. Conquistador in command of one of the brigantines in the Valley of Mexico; he captured Cuauhtemoc.

Huitzilihuitl ("Hummingbird-feather"). The son of Acamapichtli, he was the second Aztec king, ruling from 1391 to 1417.

Itzcoatl ("Obsidian-serpent"). The son of Acamapichtli and uncle of

Chimalpopoca, he was the fourth Aztec king, ruling from 1427 to 1440.

Ixtlilxochitl ("Black-eyed-flower"). A son of Nezahualpill who rebelled against the imposition of Cacama on the throne of Tetzcoco. He raised an army and took control of the northern part of Tetzcocan territory. He later allied with Cortés, became king of Tetzcoco after Tecocol died, and was a pivotal leader in the conquest of Tenochtitlan.

Juanillo. A Maya Indian captured during Córdoba's expedition to Mexico. He was baptized and taken to Cuba to learn Spanish but died before he could serve as translator in subsequent expeditions.

Lares, Amador de. The king's accountant in Cuba and a secret partner with, and advocate for, Cortés as leader of the third expedition to Mexico.

Malinche (probably a corruption of Malinalli, "Grass"; baptized as Marina). One of twenty women given to Cortés by the Mayas after their defeat at Potonchan. Speaking both Yucatec Maya and Nahuatl, she (along with the Maya-speaking Aguilar) served as a linguistic link between Cortés and the Aztecs. She was also the mother of Cortés's son, Martín.

Maxtla ("Breechcloth"). Son of Tetzotzomoc, he assassinated his brother and seized the throne of the Tepanec empire on the death of his father. He was defeated by the Aztecs under Itzcoatl in 1428.

Mayehua ("Glove"). King of Cuitlahuac, he fled to Tenochtitlan and fought on the Aztec side during the Spanish seige.

Melchorejo. A Maya Indian captured during Córdoba's expedition to Mexico. Baptized and taken to Cuba to learn Spanish so he could serve as translator in subsequent expeditions, he escaped from Cortés's men at Potonchan and returned to the Mayas.

Moteuczoma Ilhuicamina ("He-frowned-like-a-lord He-pierces-the-sky-with-an-arrow"). The son of Huitzilihuitl, he was the fifth Aztec king, ruling from 1440 to 1468.

Moteuczoma Xocoyotl ("He-frowned-like-a-lord The-younger"). The son of Axayacatl, he was the ninth Aztec king, ruling from 1502 to 1520, when he was killed while held hostage by the Spaniards.

Narváez, Pánfilo de (1480?–1528). He was placed in command of a large fleet by Governor Velásquez and ordered to capture Cortés and return him to Cuba. He landed on the Veracruz coast on 20 April 1520 but was defeated and captured by Cortés on 28 May 1520.

Nezahualpilli ("Fasted-noble"). King of Tetzcoco from 1472 to 1515.

Olid, Cristóbal de. Conquistador who commanded one of Cortés's three armies during the seige of Tenochtitlan.

Sandoval, Gonzalo de. Conquistador who commanded one of Cortés's three armies during the seige of Tenochtitlan.

Santiago. St. James, who was credited with appearing to lead Spanish forces in battle both in the reconquest of Spain and in the conquest of Mexico.

Tecocol ("Someone's-anger"). Son of Nezahualpilli who became king after the flight of Coanacoch. A Spanish ally, he died around the first of February 1521.

Tentlil ("Black-at-the-lips"). The Aztec governor of the Totonac area, he resided at Cuetlachtlan and was the first Aztec official to greet Cortés when he landed on the Veracruz coast.

Tetlahuehuetzquiti ("He-causes-people-to-laugh-at-things"). Son of Nezahualpilli, he was not considered fit to rule when his father died in 1515.

Tetzotzomoc ("Fractured-stone"). Ruler of the Tepanec empire from 1367 until his death in 1426.

Tizoc ("White-chalk-pulque-drinker"). Either the son or the grandson of Moteuczoma Ilhuicamina, he was the seventh Aztec king, ruling from 1481 to 1486, when he was assassinated after five years of neglectful leadership.

Velásquez de Cuéllar, Diego (1465–1524). He accompanied Columbus on his second voyage to the New World in 1493 and conquered Cuba in 1511–14, becoming its first governor. He authorized the first voyages to Mexico by Córdoba in 1517, Grijalva in 1518, and Cortés

in 1519, as well as an unsuccessful punitive expedition led by Pánfilo de Narváez in 1520 to capture Cortés.

Villafaña, Antonio de. Conquistador who reached Mexico with Narváez's expedition. He joined in the conquest of Mexico and later led
a conspiracy against Cortés, but it was discovered and he was
hanged.

Xicotencatl ("Person-from-Xicotenco [Place-at-the-edge-of-bumble-
bees]"). A Tlaxcaltec general who resisted Cortés's entry into Tlaxcallan. Always opposed to the Spaniards, even after Tlaxcallan's
alliance with them, he was later hanged by Cortés in Tetzcoco for
allegedly conspiring with the Aztecs against him.

Zumarraga, Juan de (1468–1548). A Spanish Franciscan, he became
the first bishop of Mexico in 1528.

NOTES

INTRODUCTION

1. For example, see the works of Brundage (1972:252–90), Collis (1972), Davies (1974:233–83), Gibson (1966:24–28), Innes (1969), Johnson (1987), Kirkpatrick (1967:66–100), MacLachlan and Rodríguez (1980:68–76), Madariaga (1969), McHenry (1962:35–46), Merriman (1962, 3:458–502), Miller (1985:66–93), Moreno Toscano (1981), Parkes (1969:39–58), and White (1971:159–262).

2. For example, Leon-Portilla 1966; Sahagún 1975, 1978.

3. Brundage 1972:252; Collis 1972:55–60; Davies 1974:239, 258–60; Innes 1969:116; Kirkpatrick 1967:71–72; Leon-Portilla 1966:13; MacLachlan and Rodríguez 1980:69; Madariaga 1969:16, 118–19; McHenry 1962:35, 40, 41; Merriman 1962, 3:475, 478; Miller 1985:78; Moreno Toscano 1981:313; Padden 1967:118, 122–25; Parkes 1969:50; Todorov 1984:118–19.

4. Carrasco 1982:150–51, 200–203; MacLachlan and Rodríguez 1980:72; Padden 1967:205–207; Vaillant 1966:238.

5. Madariaga 1969:185–86; Merriman 1962, 3:479; Vaillant 1966:238.

6. Davies 1974:252; Elliott 1966:65; Parry 1966:85.

7. Davies 1974:251; Madariaga 1969:177; Merriman 1962, 3:478.

8. Collis 1972:91; Davies 1974:250–51; Elliott 1966:65; Gardiner 1959; Kirkpatrick 1967:67; MacLachlan and Rodríguez 1980:70; Mer-

riman 1962, 3:478; Padden 1967:156; Todorov 1984:61; Vaillant 1966:238–39; White 1971:169, 171; Wolf 1970:154.

9. Wolf 1970:154–55.

10. Baxby 1981:13; Hopkins 1983:205–206; Innes 1969:179; McNeill 1977:183; Padden 1967:206; Todorov 1984:61.

11. Todorov 1984:118–19.

12. Lockhart 1993.

CHAPTER 1. THE SPANISH BACKGROUND TO THE CONQUEST OF MEXICO

1. Chaunu 1979:85–89; Elliott 1966:44–45, 1984:152–53; Gibson 1966:4; MacKay 1977:55, 60–63; O'Callaghan 1975:91–92; Ramsey 1973:51–78; Rowdon 1974:35–36; Wright 1969:39–40.

2. MacKay 1977:15, 50, 66.

3. Chaunu 1979:85–89; Cipolla 1965:78–81; Elliott 1984:152–53; O'Callaghan 1975:338–39, 343–45.

4. Chaunu 1979:98; Parry and Sherlock 1971:14–17.

5. Alonso el Sabio 1972, 2:228, 2001, 2:440; Castro 1971:416–19; Elliott 1966:55, 57; Pagden 1990:13–36; Ramsey 1973:238, 266–67.

6. Powers 1988:16, 112; Quatrefages 1988:6–7; Ramsey 1973:56.

7. Jones 1987:93, 114–21, 141.

8. Jones 1987:150–54, 175–78, 190.

9. Quatrefages 1988:3–4, 6, 12–13, 18; Rowdon 1974:58.

10. Jones 1987:173, 184–85, 190–91.

11. Elliott 1966:62–65; Ramsey 1973:258–60.

12. Elliott 1966:75–76; MacKay 1977:96; MacLachlan 1988:1–12; Pagden 1990:13–36.

13. Elliott 1984:162–63; Sauer 1966:20–28; Wilson 1990:43–52.

14. Denevan 1976a:291; Lockhart and Schwartz 1983:36; Parry and Sherlock 1971:3; Sauer 1966:37, 48. I use the population figure of six million as a reasonably accepted estimate of the West Indian population,

but more focused and detailed analyses have cast doubt on it. For instance, Rosenblat (1954, 1:102) put the Caribbean population significantly lower, at 300,000, although he was consistently and, I believe, unacceptably low for the rest of Native America as well. In a more recent publication, Rosenblat (1976:44–45) put the population of Hispaniola at 100,000 in 1492, whereas Cook and Borah (1971:408) estimated it to have been some eight million. But see Henige 1998 for a critique of population estimates generally.

15. Wilson 1990:17–20.

16. Sauer 1966:50–59; Wilson 1990:22, 32.

17. Lockhart and Schwartz 1983:62–63; Sauer 1966:71.

18. Cook and Borah 1971:401; Elliott 1984:166.

19. Elliott 1984:166; Lockhart and Schwartz 1983:79; Parry and Sherlock 1971:9–10.

20. Boyd-Bowman 1973:2–3, 6–8; Elliott 1984:169; Parry and Sherlock 1971:11–12.

Chapter 2. Mesoamerica and the Aztecs

1. For a fuller discussion of the role of warfare in the development of Mesoamerica as a culture area, see Hassig 1988 and 1992, on which this account is based. Teotihuacan's dates are modified according to Cowgill 1996.

2. For a discussion of *tlamemes,* see Hassig 1985:32 and passim.

3. Carrasco 1984.

Chapter 3. The Discovery of Yucatan

1. Díaz del Castillo 1908–16, 1:8, 11–12, 1977, 1:41, 43; Martir de Angleria 1965, 1:397–98, 1970, 2:6.

2. Alonso el Sabio 1972, 2:228, 2001, 2:440; Díaz del Castillo

1908–16, 1:14, 1977, 1:45. Where the data conflict, I follow the dating of Wagner (1942a:26, 1942b:47–48, 1944) for the expeditions of Córdoba, Grijalva, and Cortés, respectively.

3. Colón 1984:274; Cook and Borah 1971:376–410; Díaz del Castillo 1908–16, 1:14–16, 1977, 1:45–46; Wilson 1990:94–96.

4. Díaz del Castillo 1908–16, 1:20, 1977, 1:49.

5. Spanish accounts report that the Mayas used *macanas.* This is the same word they applied to the Aztec *macuahuitl,* or broadsword, but they had picked up this Taino word in the West Indies, where it referred to a digging stick. Although it clearly referred to a sword in Mexico, it may simply have meant agricultural implements wielded like weapons by commoners, rather than actual swords.

6. Brereton 1976:37; Burne 1955:28; Foley, Palmer, and Soedel 1985:104; Payne-Gallwey 1986:14–20, 37; Pope 1965:91; Pope 1923:334–40; Rodgers 1939:108; Salas 1950:183.

7. Brereton 1976:37; Contamine 1984:143, 147; Pope 1965:91; Salas 1950:207, 209, 213. See also the illustrations of the step-by-step reloading procedure in Gheyn 1986 [1607]:9–181.

8. Pope 1965:91.

9. Díaz del Castillo 1908–16, 1:17, 1977, 1:47.

10. Díaz del Castillo 1908–16, 1:18, 1977, 1:47; Martir de Angleria 1965, 1:401, 1970, 2:9.

11. Díaz del Castillo 1908–16, 1:18, 20–21, 1977, 1:48–49; Martir de Angleria 1965, 1:402, 1970, 2:10.

12. Acosta 1954:236–37, 1970–73, 2:508–10; Durán 1967, 2:467–503, 1994:460–494; Muñoz Camargo 1966:169–72; Sahagún 1975:1–8, 1989:31–33.

13. Díaz 1942:69–70, 72, 1950:5, 7, 10; Martir de Angleria 1965, 1:403, 1970, 2:12; Oviedo y Valdés 1942:88–94, 96–99, 1959, 2:118–25. I am not relying on the account of Grijalva's expedition written by Díaz del Castillo (1908–16, 1977), because its reliability is disputed. Wagner (1942b:18–21) questions whether he was even there.

14. Díaz 1942:73–74, 1950:11–13; Oviedo y Valdés 1942:99–102, 105–106, 1959, 2:125–29. Díaz (1942:73, 1950:11) says five cannons,

but Oviedo y Valdés (1942:99, 104) reports only three — two medium-sized bronze cannons and one of iron.

15. Pope 1965:58; Rodgers 1939:337.

16. Arnold 1978:243; Contamine 1984:147; Rodgers 1939:339–40; Salas 1950:216; Stone 1961:160, 162; Tarassuk and Blair 1982:54; Vigon 1947:37, 46.

17. Díaz 1942:74, 1950:13; Oviedo y Valdés 1942:106, 1959, 2:129.

18. Díaz 1942:75, 1950:13–15; Oviedo y Valdés 1942:112, 1959, 2:134.

19. Díaz 1942:75–76, 1950:15; López de Gómara 1964:15–18, 1965–66, 2:16–19; Martir de Angleria 1965, 1:405–406, 1970, 2:16. See Oviedo y Valdés 1942:111 and 1959, 2:133–34, for a detailed list of the clothing and gifts presented to Grijalva.

20. Díaz 1942:76–77, 79–80, 1950:16, 19–21; Oviedo y Valdés 1942:114, 1959, 2:135–36.

21. Díaz 1942:80–82, 1950:21–24; Oviedo y Valdés 1942:125, 130, 132–33, 1959, 2:141–42, 145–46.

22. Acosta 1954:238, 1970–73, 2:513; Alva Ixtlilxóchitl 1969:3, 1975–77, 1:450; Sahagún 1975:5–6, 1989:34–36.

23. Acosta 1954:238, 1970–73, 2:513; Durán 1967, 2:513, 1994:502; Sahagún 1989:37.

24. Acosta 1954:238, 1970–73, 2:514; Durán 1967, 2:507, 1994:497; Sahagún 1975:5, 9, 1989:37–38, 41.

25. Boyd-Bowman 1973:3–5; Gibson 1975:292; Lockhart 1972:19–20, 31–36; Mörner 1976:747–48; Sauer 1969:198; Wagner 1944:3–5.

26. Díaz del Castillo 1908–16, 1:70, 1977, 1:81; López de Gómara 1964:19, 1965–66, 2:19–20.

27. Díaz del Castillo 1908–16, 1:90, 1977, 1:94; López de Gómara 1964:20–21, 1965–66, 2:21; Martir de Angleria 1965, 411, 1970, 2:26; Tapia 1950:31–33, 45–47, 1993:19–20, 26–27.

28. Chaunu 1979:96–97; Chaunu and Chaunu 1955–59, 7:28–29; Haring 1918:208.

29. Cortés 1963:11, 1971:11; Díaz del Castillo 1908–16, 1:85,

92, 1977, 1:91, 96; López de Gómara 1964:23, 1965–66, 2:23; Tapia 1950:36, 1993:22; Vigon 1947:473. Wagner (1944:157) suggested that the field guns were *culebrinas*, capable of firing a 7–to 11–kilogram (18–30 pound) shot, but this is far from certain.

30. López de Gómara 1964:23, 1965–66, 2:23.

31. Aguilar 1977:66, 1993:137; Cortés 1963:11, 1971:11; Díaz del Castillo 1908–16, 1:90–92, 1977, 1:94–96; López de Gómara 1964:26–28, 1965–66, 2:25–27; Tapia 1950:32–33, 1993:20.

32. Alonso el Sabio 1972, 2:228, 2001, 2:440; Cortés 1963:15, 1971:18; Díaz del Castillo 1908–16, 1:97–98, 1977, 1:99–100; López de Gómara 1964:28, 1965–66, 2:28.

33. Aguilar 1977:66, 1993:137; Cortés 1963:15, 1971:17; Díaz del Castillo 1908–16, 1:100–103, 1977, 1:102–104; López de Gómara 1964:30–32, 1965–66, 2:29–32; Martir de Angleria 1965, 1:416–18, 1970, 2:28–31; Tapia 1950:33–34, 1993:20–21.

34. Cortés 1963:15–16, 1971:18–20; Díaz del Castillo 1908–16, 1:106–110, 1977, 1:106–108; Gibson 1966:38–39; López de Gómara 1964:37–40, 1965–66, 2:36–39.

35. Cortés 1963:17, 1971:20; Díaz del Castillo 1908–16, 1:113–16, 1977, 1:110–12; Tapia 1950:38, 1993:23.

36. Cortés 1963:17–18, 1971:21.

37. Finer 1975:102; Salas 1950:187.

38. Cortés 1963:18, 1971:21–22; Díaz del Castillo 1908–16, 1:118–20, 153, 1977, 1:113–15, 136; López de Gómara 1964:46–47, 1965–66, 2:44–46; Tapia 1950:39, 1993:23.

39. Aguilar 1977:67, 1993:138; Cortés 1963:18–19, 1971:22–23; Díaz del Castillo 1908–16, 1:126–29, 1977, 1:119–21; López de Gómara 1964:48, 51, 1965–66, 2:47, 49; Martir de Angleria 1965, 1:421, 1970, 2:35; Oviedo y Valdés 1959, 4:9; Tapia 1950:39, 1993:23–24. See also Hassig 1998.

CHAPTER 4. THE CONQUEST OF CENTRAL MEXICO

1. Acosta 1954:238, 1970–73, 2:513; Aguilar 1977:67, 1993:138; Anales de Cuauhtitlan 1975:68; Chimalpahin 1965:121, 234; Cortés 1963:19, 1971:23; Díaz del Castillo 1908–16, 1:130–31, 136–37, 1977, 1:122, 125–26; López de Gómara 1964:54, 1965–66, 2:52–53; Tapia 1950:40, 1993:24.

2. Aguilar 1977:138, 1993:67–68; Cortés 1963:19, 1971:24; Díaz del Castillo 1908–16, 1:137–40, 1977, 1:126–27; López de Gómara 1964:56, 1965–66, 2:54; Martir de Angleria 1970, 2:38; Sahagún 1975:5–6; Tapia 1950:41, 1993:25.

3. Díaz del Castillo 1908–16, 1:141, 1977, 1:128; Muñoz Camargo 1966:174–75; Sahagún 1975:1–3, 5, 9.

4. Acosta 1954:239, 1970–73, 2:515; Díaz del Castillo 1908–16, 1:140–42, 145, 1977, 1:127–29, 131; López de Gómara 1964:57–59, 1965–66, 2:55–57; Sahagún 1975:6.

5. Acosta 1954:238, 1970–73, 2:514; Cortés 1963:28–32, 1971:40–45; Díaz del Castillo 1908–16, 1:147, 1977, 1:132; Martir de Angleria 1970, 2:45–47; Sahagún 1975:11.

6. Díaz del Castillo 1908–16, 1:142–45, 1977, 1:130–31; López de Gómara 1964:61, 1965–66, 2:58. The length of a league in early colonial Mexico is uncertain. Roland Chardon (1980a:295, 1980b:150, 1980c:465) noted that there were two types in use at that time, the statute league and the common league. Statute leagues, used for juridical matters, were approximately 4.19 kilometers in length, whereas common leagues were about 5.5 kilometers. In practice, leagues varied by terrain, being shorter uphill than downhill. What a league actually measured was travel time: five leagues was essentially shorthand for a full day's trip, regardless of the actual linear distance traversed.

7. Díaz del Castillo 1908–16, 1:150–51, 1977, 1:134–35.

8. Díaz del Castillo 1908–16, 1:151–53, 1977, 1:135; López de Gómara 1964:61, 1965–66, 2:58–59; Martir de Angleria 1965, 2:440, 1970, 2:59; Tapia 1950:42, 1993:25.

9. Alva Ixtlilxóchitl 1975–77, 2:202; Cortés 1963:20–21, 1971:25–27; Díaz del Castillo 1908–16, 1:153, 155–57, 1977, 1:136–39; López de Gómara 1964:67–68, 1965–66, 2:64–65.

10. Chaunu and Chaunu 1955–59, 7:28–31; Haring 1918:208, 227; Rees 1971:128.

11. Cortés 1963:25–27, 1971:37–38; Díaz del Castillo 1908–16, 1:158–62, 1977, 1:140–41.

12. *Crónica mexicana* 1975:413.

13. Cortés 1963:34, 1971:50; Díaz del Castillo 1908–16, 1:162–66, 1977, 1:142–45; López de Gómara 1964:62–63, 1965–66, 2:60.

14. Alva Ixtlilxóchitl 1975–77, 2:203–204; Díaz del Castillo 1908–16, 1:166–74, 1977, 1:146–51; López de Gómara 1964:69, 72–73, 76–80, 1965–66, 2:66, 69–70, 72–76; Tapia 1950:42–43, 1963:25.

15. Acuña 1982–87, 5:190.

16. Aguilar 1977:69, 1993:139; Cortés 1963:34, 1971:50; Díaz del Castillo 1908–16, 1:174–77, 1977, 1:151–53; López de Gómara 1964:81–82, 1965–66, 2:77–78.

17. Alva Ixtlilxóchitl 1975–77, 2:205; Díaz del Castillo 1908–16, 1:178–80, 182–85, 1977, 1:154–55, 157–59; López de Gómara 1964:82–83, 1965–66, 2:78–79.

18. Díaz del Castillo 1908–16, 1:186–90, 1977, 1:160–63.

19. Cortés 1963:21–22, 27–28, 1971:28, 37–46; Díaz del Castillo 1908–16, 1:192–94, 196–99, 1977, 1:164–69.

20. Aguilar 1977:68–69, 1993:138–39; Cortés 1963:34–36, 1971:51–53; Díaz del Castillo 1908–16, 1:206, 208–209, 211–15, 1977, 1:174–80; López de Gómara 1964:89–90, 1965–66, 2:85–86; Martir de Angleria 1965, 2:441–442, 1970, 2:62; Tapia 1950:43–44, 1993:25–26.

21. Díaz del Castillo 1908–16, 1:208–209, 268, 1977, 1:176–77, 216; López de Gómara 1964:91, 1965–66, 2:87; Martir de Angleria 1970, 2:61. Throughout the rest of the volume, I frequently refer to the side opposing the Aztecs as "the Spaniards" or "the Spaniards and their allies." In fact, non-Spaniards vastly outnumbered Spaniards for most of this time,. I use "Spaniards" to refer to that side because they formed a continuing presence, whereas the composition of their Indian allies varied.

22. Alva Ixtlilxóchitl 1975–77, 2:208; Díaz del Castillo 1908–16, 1:140–41, 211, 217–18, 1977, 1:128, 177, 181; López de Gómara 1964:93, 1965–66, 2:89; Martir de Angleria 1965, 2:440–41, 1970, 2:61. The Lienzo de Tlaxcala (Chavero 1964:14, 15, 17, 47) and Muñoz Camargo (1981:258v, 260, 275) depict cannons on gun carriages, but these paintings were executed decades after the conquest and probably reflect cannons of that time rather than those actually used in the conquest.

23. Díaz del Castillo 1908–16, 1:218–20, 1977, 1:181–83; López de Gómara 1964:94–95, 1965–66, 2:89–91; Martir de Angleria 1965, 2:443–44, 1970, 2:64–65; Oviedo y Valdés 1959, 4:13. See Wagner's (1944:141–44) reconstruction of the route.

24. Díaz del Castillo 1908–16, 1:221, 1977, 1:183–84.

25. Díaz del Castillo 1908–16, 1:223, 225–27, 1977, 1:185–87; López de Gómara 1964:97, 1965–66, 2:93; Martir de Angleria 1965:444–45, 1970, 2:66; Muñoz Camargo 1984:233–34; Oviedo y Valdés 1959, 4:15.

26. Aguilar 1977:70–71, 1993:139–40; Alva Ixtlilxóchitl 1975–77, 2:208; Díaz del Castillo 1908–16, 1:228–29, 1977, 1:188; López de Gómara 1964:99–101, 1965–66, 2:94–96; Martir de Angleria 1965:446–47, 1970, 2:68–69; Oviedo y Valdés 1959, 4:16; Tapia 1950:48, 1993:28–29.

27. Davis 1943:39; Díaz del Castillo 1908–16, 1:229–30, 1977, 1:188–89; Martir de Angleria 1970, 2:68–69; Rodgers 1939:340; Tarassuk and Blair 1982:49.

28. Díaz del Castillo 1908–16, 1:230, 1977, 1:188.

29. Díaz del Castillo 1908–16, 1:238, 1977, 1:194–95; Martir de Angleria 1965, 2:447, 1970, 2:69.

30. Díaz del Castillo 1908–16, 1:253–56, 1977, 1:205–207.

31. Díaz del Castillo 1908–16, 1:231–34, 1977, 1:189–92.

32. Díaz del Castillo 1908–16, 1:229–30, 235, 1977, 1:188–89, 192–93.

33. Díaz del Castillo 1908–16, 1:237–39, 1977, 1:194–96.

34. The common practice of dodging arrows was mentioned by Díaz del Castillo (1908–16, 1:43–44, 1977, 1:64) in the context of the Span-

210

iards' being confused by clouds of locusts and unable to distinguish them from arrows, so that they could not defend themselves in the usual fashion.

35. Díaz del Castillo 1908–16, 1:227–28, 230–31, 1977, 1:187, 189.

36. Díaz del Castillo 1908–16, 1:242–43, 1977, 1:198.

37. Aguilar 1977:73, 1993:141; Díaz del Castillo 1908–16, 1:244, 249, 1977, 1:199, 202–203; Tapia 1950:51, 1993:30.

38. Díaz del Castillo 1908–16, 1:242–43, 1977, 1:198.

39. Cervantes de Salazar 1914:240; Martínez Baracs and Sempat, 1994:89–90, 197–98; Muñoz Camargo 1984:38, 66, 180–81; Torquemada 1975–83, 1:275, 5:299. See also Hassig 2001.

40. Cervantes de Salazar 1914:195; Muñoz Camargo 1984:169; Torquemada 1975–83, 2:116, 127.

41. Alva Ixtlilxóchitl 1975–77, 2:211–13; Chimalpahin 1965:234; Díaz del Castillo 1908–16, 1:246–47, 1977, 1:201; López de Gómara 1964:114–16, 1965–66, 2:102–103; Tapia 1950:54–55, 1993:32.

42. Alva Ixtlilxóchitl 1975–77, 2:209; Cortés 1963:42, 1971:61; Díaz del Castillo 1908–16, 1:238–39, 247, 258–59, 1977, 1:197, 201, 209–10; López de Gómara 1964:106–107, 1965–66, 2:101–102; Martir de Angleria 1965, 2:448, 1970, 2:72–73; Oviedo y Valdés 1959, 4:18; Tapia 1950:52, 1993:31.

43. Aguilar 1977:74, 1993:142; Díaz del Castillo 1908–16, 1:261, 1977, 1:211; Muñoz Camargo 1966:185, 1984:235.

44. Díaz del Castillo 1908–16, 1:262, 265–66, 1977, 1:211–14; Muñoz Camargo 1966:187–88, 1984:236.

45. Aguilar 1977:75, 1993:142; Díaz del Castillo 1908–16, 1:264–71, 1977, 1:213–18.

46. Aguilar 1977:74–75, 1993:142; Díaz del Castillo 1908–16, 1:274, 1977, 1:218–19; López de Gómara 1964:117–18, 1965–66, 2:111; Oviedo y Valdés 1959, 4:20; Tapia 1950:53, 1993:32.

47. Díaz del Castillo 1908–16, 1:272–73, 277–79, 1977, 1:218, 221–22; López de Gómara 1964:118, 1965–66, 2:112; Muñoz Camargo 1966:191, 1984:237–38.

48. Díaz del Castillo 1908–16, 1:277–82, 1977, 1:221–25; López de Gómara 1964:121, 1965–66, 2:115.

49. Díaz del Castillo 1908–16, 1:283–85, 1977, 1:225–27; López de Gómara 1964:122–23, 1965–66, 2:115–16; Tapia 1950:55–56, 1993:33.

50. Hassig 1988:128–30, 171, 225–26, 232, 235, 256.

51. Hassig 1988:220–23.

CHAPTER 5. THE MARCH TO TENOCHTITLAN

1. Aguilar 1977:76, 1993:143; Alva Ixtlilxóchitl 1975–77, 2:214; Díaz del Castillo 1908–16, 1:290–92, 1977, 1:230–31; López de Gómara 1964:123–24, 1965–66, 2:116–17; Martir de Angleria 1965, 2:453–54, 1970, 2:78–79; Oviedo y Valdés 1959, 4:22.

2. Aguilar 1977:77, 1993:144; Alva Ixtlilxóchitl 1975–77, 2:216; Chimalpahin 1965:234; Cortés 1963:49–50, 1971:73–74; Díaz del Castillo 1908–16, 2:1–5, 7, 13, 15, 1977, 1:236–239, 242–43, 245; López de Gómara 1964:124, 126–29, 1965–66, 2:117, 119–22; Martir de Angleria 1965, 2:456–57, 1970, 2:81–82; Muñoz Camargo 1966:213, 1984:250–51; Oviedo y Valdés 1959, 4:22–23; Sahagún 1975:29, 1989:58; Tapia 1950:57–58, 60–61, 1993:33–36. See also Hassig 1998 for a discussion of La Malinche's role, or lack thereof.

3. Chimalpahin 1965:234; Cortés 1963:48–49, 1971:70–72; Díaz del Castillo 1908–16, 1:297–98, 2:10–11, 1977, 1:235, 242; Muñoz Camargo 1984:247–48; Sahagún 1975:29, 1989:57; Tapia 1950:56–57, 1993:33; Wagner 1944:175.

4. Bernard Bachrach, personal communication, 1991; Turney-High 1971:7, 1981:157–58.

5. Penitents fasted for four days. Fasts during the months of Panquetzaliztli, Huei Tozoztli, and Etzalqualiztli also lasted four days each (Durán 1967, 1:106, 108, 136, 1971:187–88, 191–93, 223–24; Sahagún 1951:27, 59, 81, 1953:106, 108, 136, 1970:26).

6. Aguilar 1977:77, 1993:144; Alva Ixtlilxóchitl 1975–77, 2:216;

Chimalpahin 1965:234; Cortés 1963:49–50, 1971:73–74; Díaz del Castillo 1908–16, 2:1–5, 7, 13, 15, 1977, 1:236–239, 242–43, 245; López de Gómara 1964:124, 126–29, 1965–66, 2:117, 119–22; Muñoz Camargo 1984:250–51; Oviedo y Valdés 1959, 4:22–23; Sahagún 1975:29, 1989:58.

7. Cervantes de Salazar 1914:254; Cortés 1963:47, 1971:69–70; Díaz del Castillo 1908–16, 1:297–98, 1977, 1:235; Leonardo de Argensola 1940:162; Muñoz Camargo 1984:167; Sahagún 1975:29, 1989:578; Torquemada 1975–83, 2:135)

8. Cortés 1963:49; Díaz del Castillo 1977, 1:243–44; Fernandez de Oviedo 1959, 4:24; López de Gómara 1965–66, 2:120. La Malinche could have mentioned it to allied Tlaxcaltecs as well, or perhaps to Totonacs who also spoke Nahuatl, but none of these could have made the leap to the Spaniards (omitting Miguel de Zaragoza, whose linguistic skills are uncertain).

9. Sahagún 1975:31, 33, 37, 1989:59–62, 64.

10. Aguilar 1977:78, 1993:145; Alva Ixtlilxóchitl 1975–77, 2:217; Chimalpahin 1965:234; Cortés 1963:51–54, 1971:76–79; Díaz del Castillo 1908–16, 2:28–31, 1977, 1:254–57; López de Gómara 1964:134–36, 1965–66, 2:126–28; Martir de Angleria 1965, 2:460–61, 1970, 2:88–89; Oviedo y Valdés 1959, 4:28–29; Sahagún 1975:37, 1989:64–65.

11. Sahagún 1975:31.

12. Acosta 1954:240, 1970–73, 2:518; Aguilar 1977:79–80, 1993:145–46; Alva Ixtlilxóchitl 1969:4–5, 1975–77, 1:451, 2:217–18; Alvarado Tezozómoc 1975b:148–49; Chimalpahin 1965:121, 235; Cortés 1963:55–58, 1971:81, 84; Díaz del Castillo 1908–16, 2:35–41, 1977, 1:259–63; Durán 1967, 2:536, 541, 1994:525, 529; López de Gómara 1964:136–39, 1965–66, 2:128–30; Martir de Angleria 1965, 2:461, 465, 1970, 2:89–90, 93–94; Muñoz Camargo 1966:215, 1984:251; Oviedo y Valdés 1959, 4:30–31; Sahagún 1975:37, 43–44, 1989:65–69; Tapia 1950:59, 1993:38.

13. Conquistador Anónimo 1941:42–48, 1993:178–81; López de

Gómara 1964:156–60, 1965–66, 2:147–51; Martir de Angleria 1965, 2:463–64, 474–75, 1970, 2:91–92, 108–109.

14. Mols 1974:41.

15. Calnek 1976:288, 1978:316; Denevan 1976b:81–82; Sanders 1970:449; Sanders, Parsons, and Santley 1979:154. But see also Hardoy (1973:154–55), who puts the population of Tenochtitlan at 300,000.

CHAPTER 6. MOTEUCZOMA'S TENOCHTITLAN

1. Acosta 1954:240, 1970–73, 2:519; Aguilar 1977:80, 1993:146; Alva Ixtlilxóchitl 1975–77, 2:218; Cortés 1963:59–60, 1971:87; Díaz del Castillo 1908–16, 2:43, 54–55, 1977, 1:264–65, 267; López de Gómara 1964:140, 1965–66, 2:131.

2. Díaz del Castillo 1908–16, 2:58, 1977, 1:269.

3. Gibson 1964:9–20.

4. Aguilar 1977:79, 1993:145; Cortés 1963:58, 1971:83–84; Díaz del Castillo 1908–16, 2:64–65, 85–86, 1977, 1:273–74, 287–88; López de Gómara 1964:152, 159, 1965–66, 2:143–44, 150; Tapia 1950:58–59, 1993:37.

5. Díaz del Castillo 1908–16, 2:85–87, 1977, 1:287–88; López de Gómara 1964:168, 1965–66, 2:159.

6. Alva Ixtlilxóchitl 1975–77, 2:218–19; Cortés 1963:60–61, 1971:87; Díaz del Castillo 1908–16, 2:87, 89–90, 1977, 1:288–91; Martir de Angleria 1965, 2:467–68, 1970, 2:97–98; Oviedo y Valdés 1959, 4:33.

7. Acosta 1954:241, 1970–73, 2:519–20; Aguilar 1977:82, 1993:148; Alva Ixtlilxóchitl 1975–77, 2:218–19; Chimalpahin 1965:235; Cortés 1963:61–63, 1971:88–91; Díaz del Castillo 1908–16, 2:87, 93–96, 1977, 1:288, 292–96; López de Gómara 1964:169–71, 1965–66, 2:159–62; Martir de Angleria 1965, 2:468–70, 1970, 2:98–100; Tapia 1950:59–61, 1993:38–39.

8. Aguilar 1977:83, 1993:149; Alva Ixtlilxóchitl 1975–77, 2:221–

23; Cortés 1963:62–63, 1971:91; Díaz del Castillo 1908–16, 2:97–98, 1977, 1:295–96; López de Gómara 1964:170, 176–77, 1965–66, 2:160–61, 166–67; Martir de Angleria 1965, 2:468–69, 1970, 2:98–99; Oviedo y Valdés 1959, 4:34–35.

9. Díaz del Castillo 1908–16, 2:98, 1977, 1:296; López de Gómara 1964:178–79, 1965–66, 2:168.

10. Cortés 1963:68, 1971:97; Díaz del Castillo 1908–16, 2:115–16, 1977, 1:308–309; López de Gómara 1964:182, 1965–66, 2:171–72; Martir de Angleria 1965, 2:471–72, 1970, 2:103; Oviedo y Valdés 1959, 4:40; Tapia 1950:68, 1993:40.

11. Díaz del Castillo 1908–16, 2:116–20, 1977, 1:309–10.

12. Chimalpahin 1965:235; Cortés 1963:68, 1971:97–98; Díaz del Castillo 1908–16, 2:121–22, 1977, 1:312–13; López de Gómara 1964:183–84, 1965–66, 2:172–73; Martir de Angleria 1965, 2:472, 1970, 2:104–105; Oviedo y Valdés 1959, 4:40–41.

13. Díaz del Castillo 1908–16, 2:125, 135, 1977, 1:315, 321; López de Gómara 1964:184–85, 1965–66, 2:173–74; Oviedo y Valdés 1959, 4:42–44.

14. Aguilar 1977:83, 1993:149; Cortés 1963:81–82, 1971:113–15; Díaz del Castillo 1908–16, 2:153–54, 157–58, 1977, 1:333, 336; López de Gómara 1964:191, 1965–66, 2:180; Martir de Angleria 1965, 2:488, 1970, 2:127; Muñoz Camargo 1966:215; Oviedo y Valdés 1959, 4:52–53; Tapia 1950:75, 1993:44.

15. Aguilar 1977:84–85, 1993:150; Cortés 1963:113–27, 1971:81–89; "Demanda" 1971, 1:437–44; Díaz del Castillo 1908–16, 2:153–220, 1977, 1:333–79; López de Gómara 1964:192–205, 1965–66, 2:181–92; Martir de Angleria 1965, 2:489–90, 1970, 2:129–31; Muñoz Camargo 1966:216, 1984:251; Oviedo y Valdés 1959, 4:52–60; Tapia 1950:76–52, 1993:45–48.

16. Aguilar 1977:85, 1993:151; Alva Ixtlilxóchitl 1975–77, 2:227; Díaz del Castillo 1908–16, 2:171, 1977, 1:346; Sahagún 1981:9–10, 66–77; Tapia 1950:75–76, 1993:45.

17. Acosta 1954:241, 1970–73, 2:520; Alva Ixtlilxóchitl 1969:7–9, 1975–77, 1:453–54, 2:228; Chimalpahin 1965:121; *Códice Aubin*

1980:85; Díaz del Castillo 1908–16, 2:219–20, 1977, 1:379; Durán 1967, 1:21–22, 2:548, 1971:77, 1994:536–537; López de Gómara 1964:207–208, 1965–66, 2:194–95; Muñoz Camargo 1966:216; Sahagún 1975:51–57, 1989:74–78.

18. Cortés 1963:89–90, 1971:128; Díaz del Castillo 1908–16, 2:219–20, 1977, 1:379.

19. Alva Ixtlilxóchitl 1975–77, 2:229; Cortés 1963:90–91, 1971:128–30; Díaz del Castillo 1908–16, 2:220–22, 1977, 1:379–81; López de Gómara 1964:206, 1965–66, 2:193; Oviedo y Valdés 1959, 4:60.

20. Aguilar 1977:88, 1993:152; Chimalpahin 1965:121; Cortés 1963:91, 1971:130; Díaz del Castillo 1908–16, 2:228–29, 1977, 1:384–85; López de Gómara 1964:211, 1965–66, 2:197; Martir de Angleria 1965, 2:491, 1970, 2:132; Sahagún 1975:59.

21. Acosta 1954:241, 1970–73, 2:521; Alva Ixtlilxóchitl 1975–77, 2:229; Alvarado Tezozómoc 1975b:149; *Códice Aubin* 1980:82, 86; Cortés 1963:93, 1971:132; Díaz del Castillo 1908–16, 2:232–38, 1977, 1:387–91; López de Gómara 1964:212, 1965–66, 2:198–99; Martir de Angleria 1965, 2:493, 1970, 2:135–36; Muñoz Camargo 1966:217, 1984:252; Oviedo y Valdés 1959, 4:62–63.

22. Aguilar 1977:88, 1993:153; Alva Ixtlilxóchitl 1969:9, 1975–77, 1:454; Chimalpahin 1965:236; Cortés 1963:93, 1971:132; Díaz del Castillo 1908–16, 2:237–38, 1977, 1:390–91; Durán 1967, 2:551, 1994:540–545; López de Gómara 1964:212, 1965–66, 2:199; Sahagún 1975:65–66, 1989:84–85.

23. Alva Ixtlilxóchitl 1975–77, 2:230; Alvarado Tezozómoc 1975b:159; Chimalpahin 1965:236; Díaz del Castillo 1908–16, 2:239, 1977, 1:391; Myers 1982:211–12, 236, 244, 284–86.

24. Acosta 1954:242, 1970–73, 2:521; Chimalpahin 1965:236; Díaz del Castillo 1908–16, 2:241–42, 1977, 1:393; López de Gómara 1964:217, 1965–66, 2:203; Martir de Angleria 1865, 2:497–98, 1970, 2:141; Muñoz Camargo 1966:218; Oviedo y Valdés 1959, 4:64–65.

25. Acosta 1954:242, 1970–73, 2:521–22; Aguilar 1977:87, 89–97, 1993:151, 153–56; Alva Ixtlilxóchitl 1975–77, 2:230; Chimalpahin

1965:122; Conway 1953:8, 17, 22, 25, 28, 30; Cortés 1963:97–98, 1971:137–38; Díaz del Castillo 1908–16, 2:242, 244–47, 249, 1977, 1:393–98; López de Gómara 1964:219–22, 1965–66, 2:205–207; Muñoz Camargo 1966:218–20, 1984:253; Oviedo y Valdés 1959, 4:65, 68.

26. Alva Ixtlilxóchitl 1975–77, 2:232; Durán 1964:304–305, 1967, 2:556; López de Gómara 1964:222–23, 1965–66, 2:208; Sahagún 1975:67–69, 1989:87–89, 91.

27. Alva Ixtlilxóchitl 1969:10, 1975–77, 1:454; P. Carrasco 1950:280; Sahagún 1975:76–77, 1989:90, 93.

28. Díaz del Castillo 1908–16, 2:250, 1977, 1:399.

29. Cortés 1963:98–100, 1971:138, 140–41; Díaz del Castillo 1908–16, 2:249, 251, 1977, 1:398–99; Muñoz Camargo 1966:225, 1984:256; Sahagún 1975:76–78, 1989:93–94.

30. Cortés 1963:100, 1971:141; Díaz del Castillo 1908–16, 2:249, 1977, 1:398.

31. Aguilar 1977:92, 1993:156; Cortés 1963:100–101, 1971:142; Díaz del Castillo 1908–16, 2:252–54, 1977, 1:400–402; Durán 1967, 2:558–560, 1994:545–547; Martir de Angleria 1965, 2:500, 1970, 2:144; Sahagún 1975:79, 1989:96–97.

Chapter 7. Flight and Recovery

1. Alva Ixtlilxóchitl 1975–77, 2:233–34; Cortés 1963:101, 1971:142–43; Díaz del Castillo 1908–16, 2:256–57, 1977, 1:403; Martir de Angleria 1965, 2:500, 1970, 2:144; Muñoz Camargo 1966:229, 1984:258.

2. Díaz del Castillo 1908–16, 2:260–62, 1977, 1:406–407; Durán 1964:306, 1967, 2:558; López de Gómara 1965–66, 2:212.

3. Chimalpahin 1965:236; Cortés 1963:101, 103, 1971:143–44; Díaz del Castillo 1908–16, 2:256–63, 1977, 1:403–407; Martir de Angleria 1965, 2:500–501, 1970, 2:145; Oviedo y Valdés 1959, 4:71.

4. Información 1870–75, 20:17, 21, 140, 145; Muñoz Camargo 1966:236, 1984:261; Sahagún 1975:80.

5. Aguilar 1977:96–97, 1993:159; Alva Ixtlilxóchitl 1969:11, 1975–77, 1:454, 2:236; Alvarado Tezozómoc 1975b:160; *Códice Aubin* 1980:86; Cook and Borah 1971:80–82; Díaz del Castillo 1908–16, 2:218–19, 273, 1977, 1:378, 414; Fenner et al. 1988:236–37; Hopkins 1983:204, 207; López de Gómara 1964:204, 1965–66, 2:191–92; Sahagún 1975:83, 1989:102.

6. Baxby 1981:16–17; Behbehani 1988:83, 89–90; Crosby 1973:35–63; Fenner et al. 1988:5, 183, 189, 195, 236; Joralemon 1982; McNeill 1977:183–88; Ricketts and Byles 1966, 1:26–28, 34–36, 39.

7. Behbehani 1988:89.

8. Cortés 1963:103, 1971:145; Díaz del Castillo 1908–16, 2:263, 1977, 1:407–408; López de Gómara 1964:231, 1965–66, 2:215–16.

9. Díaz del Castillo 1908–16, 2:259–60, 1977, 1:405.

10. Cortés 1963:103–104, 1971:144–45; Díaz del Castillo 1908–16, 2:263, 269, 1977, 1:407–408, 411–12; Oviedo y Valdés 1959, 4:74.

11. Díaz del Castillo 1908–16, 2:218–19, 273, 1977, 1:378, 414; López de Gómara 1964:238–39, 1965–66, 2:222–23; Sahagún 1989:103.

12. Aguilar 1977:94, 1993:157; Alva Ixtlilxóchitl 1975–77, 2:238; Díaz del Castillo 1908–16, 2:269–70, 1977, 1:411–12; Martir de Angleria 1965, 2:501–502, 1970, 2:146; Muñoz Camargo 1966:236, 1984:262.

13. Cortés 1963:104, 1971:146; Díaz del Castillo 1908–16, 2:270–73, 1977, 1:412–14; Oviedo y Valdés 1959, 4:75.

14. Cortés 1963:105–106, 1971:147–48; Díaz del Castillo 1908–16, 2:273, 1977, 1:414.

15. Díaz del Castillo 1908–16, 2:274–77, 1977, 1:415–17.

16. Cortés 1963:106–107, 1971:149; Díaz del Castillo 1908–16, 2:278, 1977, 1:417–18; Oviedo y Valdés 1959, 4:77.

17. Cortés 1963:107, 109–11, 1971:150–55; Díaz del Castillo 1908–16, 2:279–80, 1977, 1:418–19; Oviedo y Valdés 1959, 4:78–80; Sahagún 1989:102.

18. Díaz del Castillo 1908–16, 2:282–89, 1977, 1:420–25.

19. Alva Ixtlilxóchitl 1969:11, 1975–77, 1:454, 2:236; Alvarado

Tezozómoc 1975b:163; Chimalpahin 1965:236; *Códice Aubin* 1980:86;
Díaz del Castillo 1908–16, 2:273–74, 1977, 1:414–15; López de Gómara 1964:239, 1965–66, 2:223; Martir de Angleria 1965, 2:503–504,
1970, 2:149; Sahagún 1989:102–103.
    20. Cortés 1963:118, 1971:165; Díaz del Castillo 1908–16, 2:290,
301, 1977, 1:425, 433.

CHAPTER 8. THE RETURN TO TENOCHTITLAN

    1. Cortés 1963:112, 1971:156. Bernal Díaz del Castillo (1908–12,
2:109–10, 1977:304) wrote that during his first stay in Tenochtitlan,
Cortés built two ships, which were destroyed following Alvarado's massacre. If this were true, then the Aztecs would surely have taken the
Spaniards' maritime capabilities into account in choosing a response to
the Spanish threat, but they did not do so. This, and the fact that no other
source mentions these ships, makes me doubt the truth of this claim.
    2. Aguilar 1977:94, 1993:157; Cortés 1963:113, 116, 1971:157,
161; Díaz del Castillo 1908–16, 2:300, 302, 304, 1977, 1:432–35; Martir
de Angleria 1965, 2:504, 1970, 2:149–50; Muñoz Camargo 1966:237;
Sahagún 1989:103–104.
    3. Alva Ixtlilxóchitl 1969:11, 1975–77, 1:454–55; Cortés
1963:118–19, 1971:166; Díaz del Castillo 1908–16, 4:1, 1977, 1:436–
37; López de Gómara 1964:239, 1965–66, 2:223–24.
    4. Aguilar 1977:95, 1993:158; Alva Ixtlilxóchitl 1969:11–12,
1975–77, 1:454–55; Cortés 1963:120, 122, 1971:168–70; Díaz del Castillo 1908–16, 4:3–5, 1977, 1:437–39; Durán 1967, 2:562, 1994:550;
López de Gómara 1964:244, 1965–66, 2:228.
    5. Aguilar 1977:95, 1993:158; Alva Ixtlilxóchitl 1969:12–13,
1975–77, 1:455, 2:241–42; Alvarado Tezozómoc 1975b:149; Cortés
1963:123, 1971:172; Díaz del Castillo 1908–16, 4:7–8, 1977, 1:440–41;
López de Gómara 1964:245, 1965–66, 2:229; Oviedo y Valdés 1959,
4:89.

6. Alva Ixtlilxóchitl 1969:12–15, 1975–77, 1:455–57, 2:390–91; Díaz del Castillo 1908–16, 4:8–9, 1977, 1:441; Offner 1983:239–40.

7. Cortés 1963:123–24, 1971:173–74; Díaz del Castillo 1908–16, 4:9, 1977, 1:442; López de Gómara 1964:245, 1965–66, 2:229.

8. Alva Ixtlilxóchitl 1969:13, 1975–77, 1:456, 2:246; Cortés 1963:125–26, 1971:174–75; Díaz del Castillo 1908–16, 4:10–13, 1977, 1:442–44; López de Gómara 1964:246–47, 1965–66, 2:230; Oviedo y Valdés 1959, 4:90–91.

9. Díaz del Castillo 1908–16, 4:88–91, 1977, 1:493–95; López de Gómara 1964:246, 1965–66, 2:229. The accounts differ on the timing of this aborted insurrection (Wagner 1944:336–37) and provide no basis for determining which of the various times is likeliest. I have placed it here, after the first attack on Ixtlapalapan, as the likeliest time, following a major military setback. The other recorded times do not fall after similar incidents and thus seem less likely.

10. Alva Ixtlilxóchitl 1969:16, 1975–77, 1:458; Cortés 1963:126–28, 1971:176–78; Díaz del Castillo 1908–16, 4:14, 16–21, 40, 1977, 1:445–49, 462; López de Gómara 1964:248, 1965–66, 2:231; Oviedo y Valdés 1959, 4:91–93.

11. Díaz del Castillo 1908–16, 4:21–23, 1977, 1:449–51.

12. Alva Ixtlilxóchitl 1969:15, 1975–77, 1:457, 2:391; Cortés 1963:133, 1971:185–86; Díaz del Castillo 1908–16, 4:24, 27–28, 1977, 1:451, 453–54; Durán 1967, 2:561–62, 1994:549–550; López de Gómara 1964:249–51, 1965–66, 2:232–34; Martir de Angleria 1965, 2:521–22, 1970, 2:172–73; Muñoz Camargo 1966:237; Oviedo y Valdés 1959, 4:95–96.

13. Alva Ixtlilxóchitl 1969:15–16, 1975–77, 1:457; Cortés 1963:134, 1971:186; Díaz del Castillo 1908–16, 4:30–32, 1977, 1:455–56; López de Gómara 1964:251–52, 1965–66, 2:234–35; Oviedo y Valdés 1959, 4:98.

14. Alva Ixtlilxóchitl 1975–77, 2:247; Cortés 1963:134, 1971:187; Díaz del Castillo 1908–16, 4:32–34, 1977, 1:456–57; López de Gómara 1964:252, 1965–66, 2:235.

15. Díaz del Castillo 1908–16, 4:34, 1977, 1:458.

16. Alva Ixtlilxóchitl 1969:16, 1975–77, 1:457–58, 2:247; Cortés 1963:134–35, 1971:187; Díaz del Castillo 1908–16, 4:34–35, 1977, 1:458–59; López de Gómara 1964:252, 1965–66, 2:235; Oviedo y Valdés 1959, 4:99.

17. Alva Ixtlilxóchitl 1969:16, 1975–77, 1:458; Cortés 1963:134–36, 1971:187–88; Díaz del Castillo 1908–16, 4:35–37, 1977, 1:459–60; López de Gómara 1964:252, 1965–66, 2:235; Sahagún 1975:81.

18. Alva Ixtlilxóchitl 1969:16, 1975–77, 1:458; Cortés 1963:136, 1971:188–89; Díaz del Castillo 1908–16, 4:37–38, 1977, 1:460; Oviedo y Valdés 1959, 4:100; Sahagún 1975:81.

19. Alva Ixtlilxóchitl 1969:16–18, 1975–77, 1:458–59, 2:250; Cortés 1963:136–38, 1971:189–91; Díaz del Castillo 1908–16, 4:38–41, 44–46, 49–53, 1977, 1:460–69; López de Gómara 1964:255, 1965–66, 2:237–38.

20. Alva Ixtlilxóchitl 1969:18–19, 1975–77, 1:459–60; Cortés 1963:138–40, 142–43, 1971:191–94, 197–98; Díaz del Castillo 1908–16, 4:55–56, 58–70, 1977, 1:471–81; López de Gómara 1964:256–59, 1965–66, 2:238–41.

21. Alva Ixtlilxóchitl 1969:20, 1975–77, 1:460, 2:252; Cortés 1963:143–44, 1971:198–99; Díaz del Castillo 1908–16, 4:70–79, 1977, 1:481–87; López de Gómara 1964:259, 1965–66, 2:241–42.

22. Alva Ixtlilxóchitl 1969:20–21, 1975–77, 1:460, 2:252–54; Cortés 1963:145–47, 1971:202–204; Díaz del Castillo 1908–16, 4:81–82, 85–86, 1977, 1:488–89, 491–92; López de Gómara 1964:261, 1965–66, 2:243.

23. Cortés 1963:146, 1971:202.

Chapter 9. Conquest and Defeat

1. Aguilar 1977:95, 1993:158; Alva Ixtlilxóchitl 1969:21, 1975–77, 1:461; Cortés 1963:149, 1971:206; Gardiner 1959:125–26; López de Gómara 1964:262, 1965–66, 2:244; Martir de Angleria 1965, 2:521–22,

1970, 2:173. For a fuller consideration of these reconstructions, see Gardiner 1959:130–32.

2. Alva Ixtlilxóchitl 1969:14, 1975–77, 1:456, 2:255–56; Cortés 1963:149–50, 1971:207–208; Díaz del Castillo 1908–16, 4:91–93, 1977, 1:495–96.

3. Cortés 1963:149, 1971:206–207; Díaz del Castillo 1908–16, 4:93–94, 1977, 1:497; Gardiner 1959:125; Sahagún 1989:104.

4. Aguilar 1977:95, 1993:158; Alva Ixtlilxóchitl 1969:23, 1975–77, 1:462, 2:256; Cortés 1963:150, 1971:208; Díaz del Castillo 1908–16, 4:99–101, 1977, 2:9–10; Durán 1967, 2:563, 1994:550–551; López de Gómara 1964:263–64, 1965–66, 2:246; Oviedo y Valdés 1959, 4:115. Although Spanish accounts acknowledge a very large allied Indian force, native accounts put its number still higher. Alva Ixtlilxóchitl (1969:22–23, 1975–77, 1:461) puts it at an exaggerated 600,000 men.

5. Cervantes de Salazar 1914:654; López de Gómara 1964:266, 1965–66, 2:246; Muñoz Camargo 1984:169–170; Torquemada 1975–83, 2:271. See Hassig 2001 for an extended discussion of the killing of Xicotencatl.

6. Las Casas 1967, 2:400; Hernández 1946, 1:66; Martínez Baracs and Sempat 1994:198–99; Muñoz Camargo 1984:170, 259.

7. Cortés 1963:118, 1971:165–66; Torquemada 1975–83, 2:246–47.

8. Aguilar 1977:93–94, 1993:156–57; Durán 1967, 2:559, 1994:548; Muñoz Camargo 1966:233, 1984:170, 259; Sahagún 1989:101.

9. For a fuller discussion of Tenochtitlan's political economy, see Hassig 1985.

10. Aguilar 1977:95, 1993:158; Alva Ixtlilxóchitl 1969:26, 1975–77, 1:463, 2:258; Cortés 1963:151, 1971:209; Díaz del Castillo 1908–16, 4:103–105, 1977, 2:11–13; Sahagún 1975:82–84. See also Hassig 1981.

11. Alva Ixtlilxóchitl 1969:29, 1975–77, 1:464–65.

12. Sahagún 1975:86, 114.

13. Sahagún 1975:84, 86.

14. Alva Ixtlilxóchitl 1969:26, 1975–77, 1:463; Cortés 1963:151,

1971:210; Díaz del Castillo 1908–16, 4:105–108, 1977, 2:13–14; Sahagún 1975:84.

15. Aguilar 1977:96, 1993:159; Alva Ixtlilxóchitl 1969:26–27, 30–33, 1975–77, 1:463–64, 466, 2:257, 260; Cortés 1963:152–55, 1971:211–15; Díaz del Castillo 1908–16, 4:108–11, 1977, 2:14–16; López de Gómara 1964:266–69, 271, 1965–66, 2:248–50, 252; Oviedo y Valdés 1959, 4:118–19; Sahagún 1975:85, 87.

16. Alva Ixtlilxóchitl 1969:24, 27–28, 1975–77, 1:464–65; Díaz del Castillo 1908–16, 4:112, 1977, 2:17.

17. Alva Ixtlilxóchitl 1969:28, 1975–77, 1:465; Díaz del Castillo 1908–16, 4:112–16, 1977, 2:17; López de Gómara 1964:269, 1965–66, 2:250; Sahagún 1989:109.

18. Cortés 1963:155, 1971:215; Díaz del Castillo 1908–16, 4:117, 1977, 2:18; Sahagún 1989:110.

19. Cortés 1963:159, 1971:219–20; Díaz del Castillo 1908–16, 4:117, 1977, 2:18; Durán 1967, 2:565, 1994:552.

20. Díaz del Castillo 1908–16, 4:119–21, 133–34, 1977, 2:19–20, 28–29.

21. Díaz del Castillo 1908–16, 4:120–21, 1977, 2:20.

22. Alva Ixtlilxóchitl 1969:24, 27, 1975–77, 1:462, 464; López de Gómara 1964:280, 1965–66, 2:261.

23. Díaz del Castillo 1908–16, 4:122–24, 1977, 2:21–22; López de Gómara 1964:273, 1965–66, 2:255.

24. Díaz del Castillo 1908–16, 4:123–24, 130–32, 1977, 2:22, 26–28. Contra Gardiner (1959), who claims the pivotal role for the naval battle.

25. Cortés 1963:169–70, 1971:238; Díaz del Castillo 1908–16, 4:124, 1977, 2:22; Sahagún 1975:87.

26. Alva Ixtlilxóchitl 1969:34, 1975–77, 1:468; Sahagún 1975:95–96, 1989:115–16.

27. Díaz del Castillo 1908–16, 4:125, 1977, 2:22–23.

28. Cortés 1963:112, 1971:156.

29. Díaz del Castillo 1908–16, 4:126, 1977, 2:23–24; Sahagún 1975:98–103.

30. Díaz del Castillo 1908–16, 4:129–30, 1977, 2:25–26.

31. Aguilar 1963:159, 1977:96; Alva Ixtlilxóchitl 1969:35, 37–38, 1975–77, 1:469–70; Díaz del Castillo 1908–16, 4:132–33, 1977, 2:28; López de Gómara 1964:277, 1965–66, 2:258; Oviedo y Valdés 1959, 4:127.

32. Díaz del Castillo 1908–16, 4:135, 1977, 2:29–30.

33. Oviedo y Valdés 1959, 4:64.

34. Díaz del Castillo 1908–16, 4:135–36, 1977, 2:30.

35. Aguilar 1977:96, 1993:159; Alva Ixtlilxóchitl 1969:39–41, 1975–77, 1:472–73; Díaz del Castillo 1908–16, 4:140–41, 168, 1977, 2:33, 53; Durán 1967, 2:565–66, 1994:552–554; López de Gómara 1964:281–82, 1965–66, 2:262–63; Oviedo y Valdés 1959, 4:133; Sahagún 1975:104, 1989:121.

36. Alva Ixtlilxóchitl 1969:42, 1975–77, 1:472–73; Cortés 1963:171–72, 1971:241–42; Díaz del Castillo 1908–16, 4:141, 143–45, 149–51, 1977, 2:34–36, 39–41; López de Gómara 1964:281–82, 1965–66, 2:262–63; Oviedo y Valdés 1959, 4:133.

37. Díaz del Castillo 1908–16, 4:152–57, 1977, 2:41–45.

38. Díaz del Castillo 1908–16, 4:156–58, 160–61, 1977, 2:44–45, 47.

39. Díaz del Castillo 1908–16, 4:161, 163, 1977, 2:47–49.

40. Díaz del Castillo 1908–16, 4:163, 167–68, 1977, 2:49, 51–52.

41. Alva Ixtlilxóchitl 1969:42, 1975–77, 1:473; Cortés 1963:172, 1971:242; López de Gómara 1964:282–83, 1965–66, 2:263; Oviedo y Valdés 1959, 4:134–35.

42. Alva Ixtlilxóchitl 1969:42–43, 1975–77, 1:473–74; Cortés 1963:172–75, 1971:242–45; López de Gómara 1964:283–84, 1965–66, 2:263–65; Oviedo y Valdés 1959, 4:135–36. Díaz del Castillo's account (1908–12, 3:168–70, 1977, 2:53) reverses the sequence and the commanders of these events but otherwise largely agrees with the accounts of Cortés, López de Gómara, and Alva Ixtlilxóchitl. I have followed the last version because it was recorded shortly after the events in question, in contrast to Díaz del Castillo's gap of several decades. See also Hassig 1988:184–85, 190.

43. Alva Ixtlilxóchitl 1969:45, 1975–77, 1:475; Cortés 1963:176,

178–80, 1971:247, 250–53; Díaz del Castillo 1908–16, 4:171–72, 1977, 2:55; López de Gómara 1964:285, 293, 1965–66, 2:266; Sahagún 1975:104–105, 1989:120.

44. Aguilar 1977:96, 1993:159; Alva Ixtlilxóchitl 1969:43–44, 1975–77, 1:474; Cortés 1963:176–77, 1971:248.

45. Díaz del Castillo 1908–16, 4:172, 1977, 2:55; Sahagún 1989:112–14.

46. Sahagún 1975:105, 107–108, 1989:123–24.

47. Cortés 1963:177, 1971:249; Díaz del Castillo 1908–16, 4:172–73, 1977, 2:55–56.

48. Alva Ixtlilxóchitl 1969:46–47, 1975–77, 1:475; Cortés 1963:181–82, 1971:253–55; Díaz del Castillo 1908–16, 4:173–74, 1977, 2:56; López de Gómara 1964:285, 293, 1965–66, 2:266, 273.

49. Cortés 1963:183, 1971:256–57; Díaz del Castillo 1908–16, 4:178–79, 1977, 2:59; López de Gómara 1964:288, 1965–66, 2:268.

50. Sahagún 1975:114–16.

51. Alva Ixtlilxóchitl 1969:31–32, 1975–77, 1:466–67; Durán 1967, 2:565, 567, 1994:552–554; López de Gómara 1964:290, 1965–66, 2:270; Sahagún 1975:87–89, 116, 1989:110–12.

52. Acosta 1954:242, 1970–73, 2:523; Alva Ixtlilxóchitl 1969:48–51, 1975–77, 1:477–78; Cortés 1963:185–89, 1971:260–64; Díaz del Castillo 1908–16, 4:177, 1977, 2:58–59; Sahagún 1975:117. Sahagún (1989:131) wrote that this warrior was dressed as the god Huitzilopochtli, but this was almost surely a later rationalization of these events. His earlier version said it was Ahuitzotl's attire, and this was based on a translation of an Aztec-language account. The earlier version is the more compelling, not simply because it came from the Aztecs themselves but also because of the great detail with which the garb was described.

53. Cortés 1963:186–89, 1971:261–64.

54. Acosta 1954:242, 1970–73, 2:523; Aguilar 1977:97, 1993:160; Alva Ixtlilxóchitl 1969:52, 1975–77, 1:478–79; Cortés 1963:189, 1971:264; Díaz del Castillo 1908–16, 4:179–81, 1977, 2:60–61; López de Gómara 1964:291–92, 1965–66, 2:271–72; Oviedo y Valdés 1959, 4:151; Sahagún 1975:119–20.

55. Alva Ixtlilxóchitl 1969:52, 1975–77, 1:478–79; Chimalpahin 1965:236–37; Cortés 1965:189, 1971:265; Díaz del Castillo 1908–16, 4:183, 1977, 2:62; Muñoz Camargo 1984:213; Sahagún 1975:120, 1989:134–35.

56. Hale 1985:179–208; Hassig 1988:112.

57. Aguilar 1977:98, 1993:160; Díaz del Castillo 1908–16, 4:185, 187, 193, 1977, 2:64–65, 69; Durán 1967, 2:564, 1994;552; López de Gómara 1964:291, 293, 1965–66, 2:271–73; Sahagún 1975:85, 1989:110, 135–37.

CHAPTER 10. AFTERMATH

1. Barnadas 1984:519; Motolinía 1971:19.

CHAPTER 11. CONSEQUENCE AND CONCLUSION

1. Braden 1930:149, 170; Ennis 1977:64–65; Gibson 1964:98–135, 1966:78–79; Greenleaf 1969:7; Lea 1922:210; Schwaller 1978:5, 52–53. For an example of this syncretism a full century after the conquest, see Ruiz de Alarcón 1984.

2. Codex Osuna 1976: fol. 8–470.

3. Gibson 1964:167, 180, 1984:388–95; Wasserstrom 1983:11–21.

4. Cook and Borah 1971:9–10; Gibson 1964:448–49. I am using the estimates of Cook and Borah (1971:80–82), despite various voiced objections (e.g., Bath 1978; Zambardino 1980), because they are the most thoroughly analyzed, and I regard them as the reasonable high estimates. If these are unacceptable, then Sanders (in Denevan 1976a:291) holds what I regard as the reasonable low estimate, roughly half that of Cook and Borah. Whatever the starting figures, there is general agreement on the late-sixteenth-century numbers.

5. Lockhart and Schwartz 1983:116–17.

6. Gibson 1964:36, 1984:393–94.

7. Gibson 1964:58–97, 1966:48–67; Hassig 1985:178–79.

8. Hassig 1985:180–85.

9. Florescano 1965:571; Moreno Toscano 1965:1965:640.

10. Bejarano 1889–1916, 9:619; Cuevas 1975:249; Florescano 1965:597; García Pimentel 1897:74; Guthrie 1941:38; Hassig 1985:242–44; Lee 1947:653; Recopilación 1973: 4–10–11.

11. Bejarano 1889–1916, 1:79–80; Chevalier 1970:98; Matesanz 1965:539–43; Moreno Toscano 1965:644.

12. Hassig 1985:187–219.

13. Bakewell 1971:226, 231, 235; Borah 1951; Hassig 1985:259–261; TePaske and Klein 1981:123–29, 134.

GLOSSARY

arroba. A Spanish unit of measure, equal to approximately 11.5 kilograms (25.36 pounds).

atlatl. A spearthrower, used to throw small spears or "darts."

brigantine. A small, swift, typically square-masted ship.

cabecera. A politically dominant town governed by its own local ruler.

cacique. A Taino word meaning ruler, brought from the Indies by the Spaniards and applied to native rulers in Mexico.

calpolli. An incompletely understood Aztec organizational unit that, among other things, denoted neighborhoods or barrios.

caravel. An imprecisely defined type of seagoing sailing ship, typically carrying two masts.

culebrina. A heavy early field cannon capable of firing projectiles of up to 11 kilograms (30 pounds).

encomienda. A political grant of rights to the labor of the Indians living in a specified area.

falconet. A light cannon, typically swivel mounted on a ship's rail and, at this time, breechloading.

harquebus. A smoothbore matchlock gun similar to, but smaller than, the later musket.

harquebusier. A soldier armed with an harquebus.

hidalgo. A lesser noble, but the term was used somewhat indiscriminately during the conquest era to refer to nobles, gentlemen, or merely some degree of gentility.

league. A Spanish unit of linear measure. At least two different leagues were in use in colonial Mexico: a statute league of 4.19 kilometers (2.6 miles) and a common league of 5.5 kilometers (3.4 miles). In practice, the league often served as a vague denotation of distance; five leagues commonly referred to a day's journey, emphasizing travel time rather than actual linear distance.

macehual. A member of the indigenous commoner class, spelled *macehualli* prehispanically but *macehual* after the conquest.

macuahuitl. An Aztec wooden broadsword inset with obsidian blades.

principal. A postconquest term used to denote a member of the indigenous noble class, collapsing preconquest distinctions.

Reconquista. The reconquest of Spain from the Moors, ending in 1492 with the conquest of Granada.

requerimiento. A Spanish legal statement to be read before battle, absolving the conquistadors of responsibility. It demanded that the Indians recognize the authority of the church, pope, and king.

sujeto. A dependent community, governed from a *cabecera.*

tepoztopilli. A wooden spear inset with obsidian blades and used as a staff weapon like a halberd.

tercio. A 1536 Spanish military innovation in which soldiers were organized into 250-man companies and which emphasized the infantry.

tlameme. A human porter used to carry burdens in Mesoamerica.

tlatoani. A preconquest indigenous Mesoamerican king or ruler.

xiquipilli. A count of eight thousand; also used to refer to a basic Aztec army of eight thousand men.

xochiyaoyotl. Flower war; commonly regarded as ritual combat but actually part of an extended confrontation with powerful opponents in which they could be engaged while their attackers continued conquests elsewhere.

RECOMMENDED READING

For firsthand accounts by the Spanish conquistadors:

Cortés, Hernán. 1971. *Letters from Mexico.* Translated by Anthony Pagden. New York: Grossman Publishers.

De Fuentes, Patricia. 1993. *The Conquistadors: First-Person Accounts of the Conquest of Mexico.* Norman: University of Oklahoma Press.

Díaz del Castillo, Bernal. 1908–16. *The True History of the Conquest of New Spain.* Translated by Alfred Percival Maudslay. 5 vols. London: Hakluyt Society. (Or see any of a number of abridged versions currently available.)

For Aztec accounts of the conquest:

Lockhart, James. 1993. *We People Here: Nahuatl Accounts of the Conquest of Mexico.* Berkeley: University of California Press.

Sahagún, Bernardino de. 1975. *Florentine Codex: General History of the Things of New Spain. Book 12 – The Conquest of Mexico.* Salt Lake City: University of Utah Press.

———. 1978. *The War of Conquest: How It Was Waged Here in Mexico. The Aztecs' Own Story.* Salt Lake City: University of Utah Press.

For an account of Cortés's life:

Madariaga, Salvador de. 1969. *Hernán Cortés: Conqueror of Mexico.* Garden City, NY: Anchor Books.

For a detailed though somewhat dated analysis of the accounts of exploration and the conquest of Mexico:

Wagner, Henry R. 1942. *The Discovery of Yucatán by Francisco Hernández de Córdoba.* Berkeley, CA: Cortés Society.

———. 1942. *The Discovery of New Spain in 1518 by Juan de Grijalva.* Berkeley, CA: Cortés Society.

———. 1944. *The Rise of Fernando Cortés.* Berkeley, CA: Cortés Society.

For the Aztecs and their military situation:

Hassig, Ross. 1984. *Trade, Tribute, and Transportation: The Sixteenth-Century Political Economy of the Valley of Mexico.* Norman: University of Oklahoma Press.

———. 1988. *Aztec Warfare: Political Expansion and Imperial Control.* Norman: University of Oklahoma Press.

———. 1992. *War and Society in Ancient Mesoamerica.* Berkeley: University of California Press.

For an account of the Aztec situation after the conquest:

Gibson, Charles. 1964. *The Aztecs under Spanish Rule: A History of the Indians of the Valley of Mexico, 1519–1810.* Stanford, CA: Stanford University Press.

Lockhart, James. 1992. *The Nahuas after the Conquest: A Social and Cultural History of the Indians of Central Mexico, Sixteenth through Eighteenth Centuries.* Stanford, CA: Stanford University Press.

For the Spanish military situation:

Martínez, Rafael Bañón, and Thomas M. Barker, eds. 1988. *Armed Forces and Society in Spain Past and Present.* Boulder, CO: Social Science Monographs.

For a general overview of the European military situation:

Jones, Archer. 1987. *The Art of War in the Western World.* Urbana: University of Illinois Press.

REFERENCES

Acosta, José de. 1954. *Obras*. Madrid: Ediciones Atlas.

Acosta, Joseph de. 1970–73. *The Natural and Moral History of the Indies*. 2 vols. New York: Burt Franklin.

Acuña, René, ed. 1982–87. *Relaciones geográficas del siglo XVI*. 10 vols. Mexico City: Universidad Nacional Autónoma de México.

Aguilar, Francisco de. 1977. *Relación breve de la conquista de la Nueva España*. Mexico City: Universidad Nacional Autónoma de México.

———. 1993. "The Chronicle of Fray Francisco de Aguilar." In *The Conquistadors: First-Person Accounts of the Conquest of Mexico*, by Patricia De Fuentes, 134–64. Norman: University of Oklahoma Press.

Alonso el Sabio. 1972. *Las Siete Partidas del Rey Don Alfonso el Sabio*. 3 vols. Madrid: Ediciones Atlas.

———. 2001 *Las Siete Partidas*. 5 vols. Philadelphia: University of Pennsylvania Press.

Alva Ixtlilxóchitl, Fernando de. 1969. *Ally of Cortes: Account 13. Of the Coming of the Spaniards and the Beginning of the Evangelical Law*. Translated by Douglass K. Ballentine. El Paso: Texas Western Press.

———. 1975–77. *Obras completas*. 2 vols. Mexico City: Universidad Autónoma Nacional de México.

Alvarado Tezozómoc, Hernándo. 1975b. *Crónica mexicáyotl*. Mexico City: Universidad Nacional Autónoma de México.

"Anales de Cuauhtitlan." 1975. In *Códice de Chimalpopoca: Anales de*

Cuauhtitlan y Leyenda de los Soles, 3–68. Mexico City: Universidad Nacional Autónoma de México.

Andrews, J. Richard. 2003. *Introduction to Classical Nahuatl.* Revised edition. Norman: University of Oklahoma Press.

Arnold, J. Barto, III. 1978. "The Artifact Collection." In *The Nautical Archaeology of Padre Island: The Spanish Shipwrecks of 1554,* by J. Barto Arnold and Robert Weddle, 217–322. New York: Academic Press.

Bakewell, P. J. 1971. *Silver Mining and Society in Colonial Mexico: Zacatecas, 1546–1700.* Cambridge: Cambridge University Press.

Barnadas, Josep M. 1984. "The Catholic Church in Colonial Spanish America." In *The Cambridge History of Latin America,* vol. 1, *Colonial Latin America,* edited by Leslie Bethell, 511–40. Cambridge: Cambridge University Press.

Bath, B. H. Slicher van. 1978. "The Calculation of the Population of New Spain, Especially for the Period before 1570." *Boletín de Estudios Latinoamericanos y del Caribe* 24:67–95.

Baxby, Derrick. 1981. *Jenner's Smallpox Vaccine: The Riddle of Vaccinia Virus and Its Origin.* London: Heinemann Educational Books.

Behbehani, Abbas M. 1988. *The Smallpox Story in Words and Pictures.* Kansas City: University of Kansas Medical Center.

Bejarano, Ignacio, comp. 1889–1916. *Actas de cabildo de la Ciudad de México.* 54 vols. Mexico City.

Borah, Woodrow. 1951. "New Spain's Century of Depression." *Ibero-Americana* 35.

Boyd-Bowman, Peter. 1973. *Patterns of Spanish Emigration to the New World (1493–1580).* Buffalo: Council on International Studies, State University of New York.

Braden, Charles S. 1930. *Religious Aspects of the Conquest of Mexico.* Durham, NC: Duke University Press.

Brereton, J. M. 1976. *The Horse in War.* Newton Abbot, UK: David and Charles.

Brundage, Burr Cartwright. 1972. *A Rain of Darts: The Mexica Aztecs.* Austin: University of Texas Press.

Burne, Alfred H. 1955. *The Crecy War: A Military History of the Hundred Years War from 1337 to the Peace of Bretigny, 1360.* New York: Oxford University Press.

Calnek, Edward E. 1976. "The Internal Structure of Tenochtitlan." In *The Valley of Mexico,* edited by Eric R. Wolf, 287–302. Albuquerque: University of New Mexico Press.

———. 1978. "The Internal Structure of Cities in America: Pre-Columbian Cities. The Case of Tenochtitlan." In *Urbanization in the Americas from Its Beginnings to the Present,* edited by Richard P. Schaedel, Jorge E. Hardoy, and Nora Scott Kinzer, 315–26. The Hague: Mouton.

Carrasco, Davíd. 1982. *Quetzalcoatl and the Irony of Empire: Myths and Prophecies in the Aztec Tradition.* Chicago: University of Chicago Press.

Carrasco (Pizana), Pedro. 1950. *Los Otomíes: Cultura e historia prehispánicas de los pueblos mesoaméricanos de habla otomiana.* Mexico City: Universidad Nacional Autónoma de México.

———. 1984. "Royal Marriages in Ancient Mexico." In *Explorations in Ethnohistory: Indians of Central Mexico in the Sixteenth Century,* edited by H. R. Harvey and Hanns J. Prem, 41–81. Albuquerque: University of New Mexico Press.

Castro, Américo. 1971. *The Spaniards: An Introduction to Their History.* Berkeley: University of California Press.

Cervantes de Salazar, Francisco. 1914. *Crónica de la Nueva España.* Madrid: Hispanic Society of Madrid.

Chardon, Roland. 1980a. "The Elusive Spanish League: A Problem of Measurement in Sixteenth-Century New Spain." *Hispanic American Historical Review* 60:294–302.

———. 1980b. "The Linear League in North America." *Annals of the Association of American Geographers* 70:129–53.

———. 1980c. "A Quantitative Determination of a Second Linear League Used in New Spain." *Professional Geographer* 32:462–66.

Chaunu, Huguette, and Pierre Chaunu. 1955–59. *Séville et l'Atlantique (1504–1650).* 8 vols. Paris.

Chaunu, Pierre. 1979. *European Expansion in the Later Middle Ages.* New York: North-Holland Publishing Company.

Chavero, Alfredo. 1964. "Lienzo de Tlaxcala." *Artes de Mexico* 51–52.

Chevalier, Francois. 1970. *Land and Society in Colonial Mexico: The Great Hacienda.* Berkeley: University of California Press.

Chimalpahin Cuauhtlehuanitzin, San Antón Muñón. 1965. *Relaciones originales de Chalco Amaquemecan.* Mexico City: Universidad Nacional Autónoma de México.

Cipolla, Carlo M. 1965. *Guns, Sails, and Empires: Technological Innovation and the Early Phases of European Expansion, 1400–1700.* New York: Minerva Press.

Codex Osuna. 1976. *Pintura del Gobernador, Alcaldes y Regidores de México: "Códice Osuna."* 2 vols. Madrid: Ministerio de Educación y Ciencia Dirección General de Archivos y Bibliotecas.

Códice Aubin. 1980. Mexico City: Editorial Innovación.

Collis, Maurice. 1972. *Cortés and Montezuma.* London: Faber and Faber.

Colón, Hernando. 1984. *Vida del Almirante Cristóbal Colón.* Mexico City: Fondo de Cultura Económica.

Conquistador Anónimo. 1941. *Relación de algunas cosas de la Nueva España.* Mexico City: Editorial América.

———. 1993. "The Chronicle of the Anonymous Conquistador." In *The Conquistadors: First-Person Accounts of the Conquest of Mexico,* by Patricia De Fuentes, 165–81. Norman: University of Oklahoma Press.

Contamine, Philippe. 1984. *War in the Middle Ages.* Oxford: Basil Blackwell.

Conway, G. R. G. 1953. *La Noche Triste: Documentos. Segura de la Frontera en Nueva España, año de MDXX.* Mexico City: Antiguo Librería Robredo de José Porrúa e hijos.

Cook, Sherburne, F., and Woodrow Borah. 1971. *Essays in Population History: Mexico and the Caribbean,* vol. 1. Berkeley: University of California Press.

Cortés, Hernán. 1963. *Cartas y documentos.* Mexico City: Porrúa.

———. 1971. *Letters from Mexico.* Translated by Anthony Pagden, New York: Grossman Publishers.

Cowgill, George L. 1996. "Discussion." *Ancient Mesoamerica* 7:325–31.

Crónica mexicana. 1975. In *Crónica mexicana y Códice Ramírez,* by Hernándo Alvarado Tezozomoc, 223–701. Mexico City: Editorial Porrúa.

Crosby, Alfred W., Jr. 1973. *The Columbian Exchange: Biological and Cultural Consequences of 1492.* Westport, CT: Greenwood Press.

Cuevas, P. Mariano. 1975. *Documentos inéditos del siglo XVI para la historia de México.* Mexico City: Porrúa.

Davies, Nigel. 1974. *The Aztecs: A History.* New York: G. P. Putnam's Sons.

Davis, Tenney L. 1943. *The Chemistry of Powder and Explosives.* Los Angeles: Angriff Press.

"Demanda de Ceballos en nombre de Pánfilo de Narváez contra Hernando Cortés y sus compañeros." 1971. In *Colección de documentos para la historica de México,* by Joaquin García Icazbalceta, vol. 1, 437–44. Mexico City: Porrúa.

Denevan, William M., ed. 1976a. *The Native Population of the Americas in 1492.* Madison: University of Wisconsin Press.

———. 1976b. "Mexico: Introduction." In *The Native Population of the Americas in 1492,* edited by William M. Denevan, 77–84. Madison: University of Wisconsin Press.

Díaz, Juan. 1942. "Itinerario." In *The Discovery of New Spain in 1518 by Juan de Grijalva,* by Henry R. Wagner, 69–83. Berkeley, CA: Cortés Society.

———. 1950. "Itinerario de Juan de Grijalva." In *Crónicas de la conquista de México,* by Agustín Yáñez, 15–39. Mexico City: Ediciones de la Universidad Nacional Autónoma.

Díaz del Castillo, Bernal. 1908–16. *The True History of the Conquest of New Spain.* Translated by Alfred Percival Maudslay. 5 vols. London: Hakluyt Society.

———. 1977. *Historia verdadera de la conquista de la Nueva España.* 2 vols. Mexico City: Porrúa.

Durán, Diego. 1967. *Historia de las Indias de Nueva España e islas de la Tierra Firme.* 2 vols. Mexico City: Porrúa.

———. 1971. *Book of the Gods and Rites and the Ancient Calendar.* Translated by Fernando Horcasitas and Doris Heyden. Norman: University of Oklahoma Press.

———. 1994. *The History of the Indies of New Spain.* Translated by Doris Heyden. Norman: University of Oklahoma Press.

Elliott, J. H. 1966. *Imperial Spain, 1469–1716.* New York: Mentor Books.

———. 1984. "The Spanish Conquest and Settlement of America." In *The Cambridge History of Latin America,* vol. 1, *Colonial Latin America,* edited by Leslie Bethell, 149–206. Cambridge: Cambridge University Press.

Ennis, Arthur 1977. "The Conflict between the Regular and Secular Clergy." In *The Roman Catholic Church in Colonial Latin America,* edited by Richard E. Greenleaf, 63–72. Tempe: Arizona State University Center for Latin American Studies.

Fenner, F., D. A. Henderson, I. Arita, Z. Jezek, and I. D. Ladnyi. 1988. *Smallpox and Its Eradication.* Geneva: World Health Organization.

Finer, Samuel E. 1975. "State- and Nation-Building in Europe: The Role of the Military." In *The Formation of National States in Western Europe,* edited by Charles Tilly, 84–163. Princeton, NJ: Princeton University Press.

Florescano, Enrique. 1965. "El abasto y la legislación de granos en el siglo XVI." *Historia Mexicana* 14:567–630.

Foley, Vernard, George Palmer, and Werner Soedel. 1985. "The Crossbow." *Scientific American* 252(1):104–10.

García Pimentel, Luis. 1897. *Descripción del arzobispado de México hecha en 1570 y otros documentos.* Mexico City: José Joaquin Terrazas.

Gardiner, C. Harvey. 1959. *Naval Power in the Conquest of Mexico.* Austin: University of Texas Press.

Gheyn, Jacob de. 1986 [1607]. *The Exercise of Armes: A Seventeenth-Century Military Manual.* Edited by David J. Blackmore. London: Greenhill Books.

Gibson, Charles. 1964. *The Aztecs under Spanish Rule: A History of the*

Indians of the Valley of Mexico, 1519–1810. Stanford, CA: Stanford University Press.

———. 1966. *Spain in America.* New York: Harper Torchbooks.

———. 1975. "Writings on Colonial Mexico." *Hispanic American Historical Review* 55:287–323.

———. 1984. "Indian Societies under Spanish Rule." In *The Cambridge History of Latin America,* vol. 2, *Colonial Latin America,* edited by Leslie Bethell, 381–419. Cambridge: Cambridge University Press.

Greenleaf, Richard E. 1969. *The Mexican Inquisition of the Sixteenth Century.* Albuquerque: University of New Mexico Press.

Guthrie, Chester L. 1941. A Seventeenth-Century "Ever-Normal Granary." *Agricultural History* 15:37–43.

Hale, J. R. 1985. *War and Society in Renaissance Europe, 1450–1620.* New York: St. Martin's.

Hardoy, Jorge E. 1973. *Pre-Columbian Cities.* New York: Walker.

Haring, Clarence Henry. 1918. *Trade and Navigation between Spain and the Indies in the Time of the Hapsburgs.* Cambridge, MA: Harvard University Press.

Hassig, Ross. 1981. "The Famine of One Rabbit: Ecological Causes and Social Consequences of a Pre-Columbian Calamity." *Journal of Anthropological Research* 37:171–81.

———. 1985. *Trade, Tribute, and Transportation: The Sixteenth-Century Political Economy of the Valley of Mexico.* Norman: University of Oklahoma Press.

———. 1988. *Aztec Warfare: Imperial Expansion and Political Control.* Norman: University of Oklahoma Press.

———. 1992. *War and Society in Ancient Mesoamerica.* Berkeley: University of California Press.

———. 1998. "The Maid of the Myth: La Malinche and the History of Mexico." *Indiana Journal of Hispanic Literatures* 12:101–33.

———. 2001. "Xicotencatl: Rethinking an Indigenous Mexican Hero." *Estudios de Cultura Náhuatl* 32:29–49.

Henige, David P. 1998. *Numbers from Nowhere: The American Indian Contact Population Debate.* Norman: University of Oklahoma Press.

Hernández, Francisco. 1946. *Antigüedades de la Nueva España.* Mexico City: Pedro Robredo.

Hopkins, Donald R. 1983. *Princes and Peasants: Smallpox in History.* Chicago: University of Chicago Press.

Información. 1870–75. "Información recibida en Mexico y Puebla. El ano de 1565. A solicitud del gobernado y cabildo de naturales de Tlaxcala, sobre los servicios que prestaron los Tlaxcaltecas a Hernan Cortes en el conquista de Mexico, siendo los testigos algunas de los mismos conquistadores." In *Biblioteca histórica de la Iberia,* vol. 35, 257–501. Mexico City: I. Escalante.

Innes, Hammond. 1969. *The Conquistadors.* New York: Alfred A. Knopf.

Johnson, William Weber. 1987. *Cortés: Conquering the New World.* New York: Paragon House.

Jones, Archer. 1987. *The Art of War in the Western World.* Urbana: University of Illinois Press.

Joralemon, Donald. 1982. "New World Population and the Case of Disease." *Journal of Anthropological Research* 38:108–27.

Kirkpatrick, F. A. 1967. *The Spanish Conquistadores.* Cleveland, OH: Meridian Books.

Las Casas, Bartolomé de. 1967. *Apologética historia sumaria.* 2 vols. Mexico City: Universidad Autónoma de México.

Lea, Henry Charles. 1922. *The Inquisition in the Spanish Dependencies.* New York: Macmillan.

Lee, Raymond L. 1947. Grain Legislation in Colonial Mexico, 1575–1585. *Hispanic American Historical Review* 27:647–60.

Leonardo de Argensola, Bartolomé. 1940. *Conquista de México.* Mexico City.

Leon-Portilla, Miguel. 1966. *The Broken Spears: The Aztec Account of the Conquest of Mexico.* Boston: Beacon Press.

Lockhart, James. 1972. *The Men of Cajamarca: A Social and Biographical Study of the First Conquerors of Peru.* Austin: University of Texas Press.

———. 1993. *We People Here: Nahuatl Accounts of the Conquest of Mexico.* Berkeley: University of California Press.

Lockhart, James, and Stuart B. Schwartz. 1983. *Early Latin America: A History of Colonial Spanish America and Brazil.* New York: Cambridge University Press.

López de Gómara, Francisco. 1964. *Cortés: The Life of the Conqueror.* Translated by Lesley Byrd Simpson. Berkeley: University of California Press.

———. 1965–66. *Historia general de las Indias.* 2 vols. Barcelona: Obras Maestras.

MacKay, Angus. 1977. *Spain in the Middle Ages: From Frontier to Empire, 1000– 1500.* New York: St. Martin's.

MacLachlan, Colin M. 1988. *Spain's Empire in the New World: The Role of Ideas in Institutional and Social Change.* Berkeley: University of California Press.

MacLachlan, Colin M., and Jaime E. Rodríguez O. 1980. *The Forging of the Cosmic Race.* Berkeley: University of California Press.

Madariaga, Salvador de. 1969. *Hernán Cortés: Conqueror of Mexico.* Garden City, NY: Anchor Books.

Martínez Baracs, Andrea, and Carlos Sempat, eds. 1994. *Suma y epíloga de toda la descripción de Tlaxcala.* Mexico City: Universidad Autónoma de Tlaxcala and Centro de Investigaciónes y Estudios Superiores en Antropología Social.

Martir de Angleria, Pedro (Peter Martyr d'Anghera). 1965. *Decadas del Nuevo Mundo.* 2 vols. Mexico City: José Porrúa e Hijos.

———. 1970. *De Orbe Novo: The Eight Decades of Peter Martyr D'Anghera.* 2 vols. New York: Burt Franklin.

Matesanz, José. 1965. "Introducción de la ganadería en Nueva España 1521–1535." *Historia Mexicana* 14:533–66.

McHenry, J. Patrick. 1962. *A Short History of Mexico.* Garden City, NY: Doubleday.

McNeill, William H. 1977. *Plagues and Peoples.* Garden City, NY: Anchor Books.

Merriman, Roger Bigelow. 1962. *The Rise of the Spanish Empire in the Old World and in the New.* 4 vols. New York: Cooper Square.

Miller, Robert Ryal. 1985. *Mexico: A History.* Norman: University of Oklahoma Press.

Mols, Roger. 1974. "Population in Europe 1500–1700." In *The Fontana Economic History of Europe,* vol. 2, *The Sixteenth and Seventeenth Centuries,* edited by Carlo M. Cipolla, 15–82. Glasgow: Collins/Fontana.

Moreno Toscano, Alejandra. 1965. "Tres problemas en la geografía de maíz, 1600–1624." *Historia Mexicana* 14:631–55.

———. 1981. "El siglo de la conquista." In *Historia general de México,* vol 1, 289–370. Mexico City: Colegio de México.

Mörner, Magnus. 1976. "Spanish Migration to the New World prior to 1810: A Report on the State of Research." In *First Images of America: The Impact of the New World on the Old,* edited by Fredi Chiappelli, vol. 2, 737–782. Berkeley: University of California Press.

Motolinía [Toribio de Benavente]. 1971. *Memoriales, o Libro de las cosas de la Nueva España y de los naturales de ella.* Mexico City: Universidad Nacional Autónoma de México.

Muñoz Camargo, Diego. 1966. *Historia de Tlaxcala.* Guadalajara: Edmundo Aviña Levy.

———. 1981. *Descripción de la ciudad y provincia de Tlaxcala de las Indias y del mar océano para el buen gobierno y ennoblecimiento dellas.* Mexico City: Universidad Nacional Autónoma de México.

———. 1984. "Descripción de la ciudad y provincia de Tlaxcala." In *Relaciones geográficas del siglo XVI,* edited by René Acuña, vol. 4. Mexico City: Universidad Nacional Autónoma de México.

Myers, Henry A. 1982. *Medieval Kingship.* Chicago: Nelson-Hall.

O'Callaghan, Joseph F. 1975. *A History of Medieval Spain.* Ithaca, NY: Cornell University Press.

Offner, Jerome A. 1983. *Law and Politics in Aztec Texcoco.* Cambridge: Cambridge University Press.

Oviedo y Valdés, Gonzalo Fernández de. 1942. "Fernández de Oviedo's

Account." In *The Discovery of Yucatán by Francisco Hernández de Córdoba,* by Henry R. Wagner, 88–135. Berkeley, CA: Cortés Society.

———. 1959. *Historia general y natural de las Indias.* 5 vols. Madrid: Ediciones Atlas.

Padden, R. C. 1967. *The Hummingbird and the Hawk: Conquest and Sovereignty in the Valley of Mexico, 1503–1541.* New York: Harper Colophon Books.

Pagden, Anthony. 1990. *Spanish Imperialism and the Political Imagination: Studies in European and Spanish-American Social and Political Theory, 1513–1830.* New Haven, CT: Yale University Press.

Parkes, Henry Bamford. 1969. *A HIstory of Mexico.* Boston: Houghton Mifflin.

Parry, J. H. 1966. *The Spanish Seaborne Empire.* New York: Alfred A. Knopf.

Parry, J. H., and P. M. Sherlock. 1971. *A Short History of the West Indies.* New York: St. Martin's.

Payne-Gallwey, Ralph. 1986. *The Crossbow: Mediaeval and Modern, Military and Sporting. Its Construction, History and Management.* London: Holland Press.

Pope, Dudley. 1965. *Guns: From the Invention of Gunpowder to the Twentieth Century.* New York: Delacorte.

Pope, Saxton T. 1923. "A Study of Bows and Arrows." *University of California Publications in American Archaeology and Ethnology* 13(9):329–414.

Powers, James F. 1988. *A Society Organized for War: The Iberian Municipal Militias in the Central Middle Ages, 1000–1284.* Berkeley: University of California Press.

Quatrefages, René. 1988. "The Military System of the Spanish Hapsburgs." In *Armed Forces and Society in Spain Past and Present,* edited by Rafael Bañón Martínez and Thomas M. Barker, 1–50. Boulder, CO: Social Science Monographs.

Ramsey, John Fraser. 1973. *Spain: The Rise of the First World Power.* Tuscaloosa: University of Alabama Press.

Recopilación. 1973. *Recopilación de leyes de los reynos de las Indias.* 4 vols. Madrid: Ediciones Cultura Hispánica.

Rees, Peter William. 1971. "Route Inertia and Route Competition: An Historical Geography of Transportation between Mexico City and Vera Cruz." Ph.D. diss., University of California, Berkeley.

Ricketts, Thomas Francis, and John Beuzeville Byles. 1966. *The Diagnosis of Smallpox.* 2 vols. Washington, DC: US Department of Health, Education, and Welfare, Public Health Service [reprint of 1908 London edition].

Rodgers, William Ledyard. 1939. *Naval Warfare under Oars, Fourth to Sixteenth Centuries: A Study of Strategy, Tactics, and Ship Design.* Annapolis, MD: United States Naval Institute.

Rosenblat, Angel. 1954. *La población indígena y el mestizaje en América.* 2 vols. Buenos Aires: Editorial Nova.

———. 1976. "The Population of Hispaniola at the Time of Columbus." In *The Native Population of the Americas in 1492,* edited by William M. Denevan, 43–66. Madison: University of Wisconsin Press.

Rowdon, Maurice. 1974. *The Spanish Terror: Spanish Imperialism in the Sixteenth Century.* London: Constable.

Ruiz de Alarcón, Hernando. 1984. *Treatise on the Heathen Superstitions and Customs that Today Live among the Indians Native to This New Spain, 1629.* Translated and edited by J. Richard Andrews and Ross Hassig. Norman: University of Oklahoma Press

Sahagún, Bernardino de. 1951. *Florentine Codex: General History of the Things of New Spain. Book 2 — The Ceremonies.* Salt Lake City: University of Utah Press.

———. 1953. *Florentine Codex: General History of the Things of New Spain. Book 7 — The Sun, Moon, and Stars, and the Binding of the Years.* Salt Lake City: University of Utah Press.

———. 1970. *Florentine Codex: General History of the Things of New Spain. Book 1 — The Gods.* Salt Lake City: University of Utah Press.

———. 1975. *Florentine Codex: General History of the Things of New Spain. Book 12 — The Conquest of Mexico.* Salt Lake City: University of Utah Press.

———. 1978. *The War of Conquest: How It Was Waged Here in Mexico: The Aztecs' Own Story.* Salt Lake City: University of Utah Press.

———. 1981. *Florentine Codex: General History of the Things of New Spain. Book 2 – The Ceremonies.* Salt Lake City: University of Utah Press.

———. 1989. *Conquest of New Spain: 1585 Revision.* Salt Lake City: University of Utah Press.

Salas, Alberto Mario. 1950. *Las armas de la conquista.* Buenos Aires: Emecé Editores.

Sanders, William T. 1970. "The Population of the Teotihuacan Valley, the Basin of Mexico, and the Central Mexican Symbiotic Region in the Sixteenth Century." In *The Natural Environment, Contemporary Occupation, and Sixteenth-Century Population of the Valley: The Teotihuacan Valley Project, Final Report,* vol. 1, by William T. Sanders et al., 385–457. Occasional Papers in Anthropology, no. 3. Department of Anthropology, Pennsylvania State University.

Sanders, William T., Jeffrey R. Parsons, and Robert S. Santley. 1979. *The Basin of Mexico: Ecological Processes in the Evolution of a Civilization.* New York: Academic Press.

Sauer, Carl Ortwin. 1966. *The Early Spanish Main.* Berkeley: University of California Press.

Schwaller, John Frederick. 1978. "The Secular Clergy in Sixteenth-Century Mexico." Ph.D. diss., Indiana University.

Stone, George Cameron. 1961. *A Glossary of the Construction, Decoration, and Use of Arms and Armor in All Countries and in All Times.* New York: Jack Brussel.

Tapia, Andrés de. 1950. "Relación de Andrés de Tapia." In *Crónicas de la conquista de México,* by Agustín Yáñez, 29–82. Mexico City: Ediciones de la Universidad Nacional Autónoma.

———. 1993. "The Chronicle of Andrés de Tapia." In *The Conquistadors: First-Person Accounts of the Conquest of Mexico,* by Patricia De Fuentes, 17–48. Norman: University of Oklahoma Press.

Tarassuk, Leonid, and Claude Blair. 1982. *The Complete Encyclopedia of Arms and Weapons.* New York: Simon and Schuster.

TePaske, John J., and Herbert S. Klein. 1981. "The Seventeenth-Century Crisis in New Spain: Myth or Reality?" *Past and Present* 90:116–35.

Todorov, Tzvetan. 1984. *The Conquest of America: The Question of the Other.* New York: Harper and Row.

Torquemada, Juan de. 1975–83. *Monarquía indiana.* 7 vols. Mexico City: Universidad Nacional Autónoma de México.

Turney-High, Harry Holbert. 1971. *Primitive War: Its Practice and Concepts.* Columbia: University of South Carolina Press.

——. 1981. *The Military: The Theory of Land Warfare as Behavioral Science.* West Hanover, MA: Christopher Publishing House.

Vaillant, George C. 1966. *Aztecs of Mexico: Origin, Rise, and Fall of the Aztec Nation.* Baltimore, MD: Penguin.

Vigon, Jorge. 1947. *Historia de la artillería española,* vol. 1. Madrid: Instituto Jerónimo Zurita.

Wagner, Henry R. 1942a. *The Discovery of Yucatán by Francisco Hernández de Córdoba.* Berkeley, CA: Cortés Society.

——. 1942b. *The Discovery of New Spain in 1518 by Juan de Grijalva.* Berkeley, CA: Cortés Society.

——. 1944. *The Rise of Fernando Cortés.* Berkeley, CA: Cortés Society.

Wasserstrom, Robert. 1983. *Class and Society in Central Chiapas.* Berkeley: University of California Press.

White, Jon Manchip. 1971. *Cortés and the Downfall of the Aztec Empire.* New York: St. Martin's.

Wilson, Samuel M. 1990. *Hispaniola: Caribbean Chiefdoms in the Age of Columbus.* Tuscaloosa: University of Alabama Press.

Wolf, Eric R., ed. 1970. *Sons of the Shaking Earth.* Chicago: University of Chicago Press.

Wright, L. P. 1969. "The Military Orders in Sixteenth- and Seventeenth-Century Spanish Society: The Institutional Embodiment of a Historical Tradition." *Past and Present* 43:34–70.

Zambardino, Rudolph A. 1980. "Mexico's Population in the Sixteenth Century: Demographic Anomaly or Mathematical Illusion?" *Journal of Interdisciplinary History* 11:1–27.

INDEX